INTRODUCING
**PROTESTANT
SOCIAL ETHICS**

INTRODUCING PROTESTANT SOCIAL ETHICS

FOUNDATIONS
in Scripture, History, and Practice

BRIAN MATZ

Baker Academic
a division of Baker Publishing Group
Grand Rapids, Michigan

Published by Baker Academic
a division of Baker Publishing Group
P.O. Box 6287, Grand Rapids, MI 49516-6287
www.bakeracademic.com

Printed in the United States of America

Library of Congress Cataloging-in-Publication Data
Names: Matz, Brian J., author.
Title: Introducing Protestant social ethics : foundations in scripture, history, and practice / Brian Matz.
Description: Grand Rapids : Baker Academic, 2017. | Includes bibliographical references and index.
Identifiers: LCCN 2016045568 | ISBN 9780801049910 (pbk.)
Subjects: LCSH: Ethics in the Bible. | Christian ethics. | Christian sociology. | Protestant churches—Doctrines. | Evangelicalism.
Classification: LCC BS680.E84 M38 2017 | DDC 241/.0404—dc23
LC record available at https://lccn.loc.gov/2016045568

17 18 19 20 21 22 23   7 6 5 4 3 2 1

For "The Cent Store"

Contents

Acknowledgments

This book is the product of several years spent reflecting on and teaching principles of social ethics to students at Fontbonne University, Carroll College, Seattle University, and the Katholieke Universiteit Leuven. By no means am I finished. I got a late start, in fact. My undergraduate degree was in accounting, and the education that led me there was steeped in a worldview that gave little consideration to the questions that animate social ethics. So it is to my students, colleagues, and mentors at each of these institutions that I owe a great debt of gratitude. They have taught me far more than I once thought was needed, and they continue to remind me just how indispensable this is to our world, its people, and its cultures.

Among those many teachers and mentors is Prof. Dr. Johan Verstraeten. He was my first teacher in social ethics, and he was gracious enough to take me under his wing as a postdoc researcher at his Centrum voor Katholieke Sociale Denken / Center for Catholic Social Thought at the K. U. Leuven during 2005–9. Professor Verstraeten led me through the texts of Catholic social teaching, the extended literature of Catholic social thought, and the writings of critical thinkers such as John Rawls, Paul Ricoeur, Michael Hollenbach, and many others. Through him, I was introduced to a cadre of scholars in the field of social ethics that took me (seemingly) far outside my principal field of patristic studies. The rewards have been immensely personal as well as, I hope, beneficial to my students during the years since.

I also wish to thank colleagues and friends with whom I have shared, and occasionally debated, ideas in this book. Some of these individuals were helpful for things that they said in a conversation that seemed, even at the time, to be unrelated to this book. I thank Rev. Seth Dombach, Chris Fuller, Martha Gonzalez, Scott and Beth Haile, John Hannah, Archbishop Raymond

Hunthausen, Brenda Ihssen, Helen Rhee, Rev. John Richardson, Julie Rubio, and Jim and Krista Slagle. Thanks are also due to my research assistant, Brittany Hanewinkel, for helping prepare the index. Finally, I thank the academic institutions with which I have been affiliated: Carroll College, which blessed me with appointment to the Raymond G. Hunthausen Professor of Social Ethics; and Fontbonne University, at which I hold an endowed chair in Catholic thought. The funding from those endowed chairs provided the necessary space for writing many of the chapters of this book.

Abbreviations

Old Testament

Gen.	Genesis	Song of Sol.	Song of Solomon
Exod.	Exodus	Isa.	Isaiah
Lev.	Leviticus	Jer.	Jeremiah
Num.	Numbers	Lam.	Lamentations
Deut.	Deuteronomy	Ezek.	Ezekiel
Josh.	Joshua	Dan.	Daniel
Judg.	Judges	Hosea	Hosea
Ruth	Ruth	Joel	Joel
1–2 Sam.	1–2 Samuel	Amos	Amos
1–2 Kings	1–2 Kings	Obad.	Obadiah
1–2 Chron.	1–2 Chronicles	Jon.	Jonah
Ezra	Ezra	Mic.	Micah
Neh.	Nehemiah	Nah.	Nahum
Esther	Esther	Hab.	Habakkuk
Job	Job	Zeph.	Zephaniah
Ps. (Pss.)	Psalms	Hag.	Haggai
Prov.	Proverbs	Zech.	Zechariah
Eccles.	Ecclesiastes	Mal.	Malachi

New Testament

Matt.	Matthew	1–2 Cor.	1–2 Corinthians
Mark	Mark	Gal.	Galatians
Luke	Luke	Eph.	Ephesians
John	John	Phil.	Philippians
Acts	Acts	Col.	Colossians
Rom.	Romans	1–2 Thess.	1–2 Thessalonians

1–2 Tim.	1–2 Timothy	1–2 Pet.	1–2 Peter
Titus	Titus	1–3 John	1–3 John
Philem.	Philemon	Jude	Jude
Heb.	Hebrews	Rev.	Revelation
James	James		

General

ANF	*Ante-Nicene Fathers*
AT	author's translation
ca.	circa
cf.	*confer*, compare
chap(s).	chapter(s)
d.	died
esp.	especially
ET	English translation
et al.	*et alii*, and others
FC	Fathers of the Church
GNO	Gregorii Nysseni Opera
i.e.	*id est*, that is
LW	Luther's Works (American edition)
LXX	Septuagint (the Greek Old Testament)
NET	New English Translation
NIV	New International Version
NPNF[1]	*Nicene and Post-Nicene Fathers*, Series 1
NPNF[2]	*Nicene and Post-Nicene Fathers*, Series 2
NRSV	New Revised Standard Version
n.s.	new series
PG	Patrologia Graeca
repr.	reprint
SC	Sources chrétiennes
ST	Thomas Aquinas, *Summa Theologicae*, 61 vols. (Blackfriars edition)

Introduction

Near the end of my junior year of high school, my grandparents bought me a car. It was a used car, but only a year or so old. I had never owned anything so valuable in my life. I did what I could to protect the car from dents and scratches on the outside and from my friends' dirt-crusted shoes on the inside. One day, witnessing how neurotic I must have been about the car, my pastor and friend Dale Swanson asked me, "Whose car is it?" I told him that it was mine, of course, to which he replied, "No. The car belongs to God. And God might need to give a ride to someone with dirty shoes."

It wasn't until years later that I grew to appreciate what Dale had said. Nothing we have belongs to us. It all belongs to God. Why did God provide me a car (arguably something I did not need) when so many others have no car at all? Maybe God gave me the car so that I might use it to bless other people. Or more generally, why has God allowed things to be distributed to people unequally? Some people have more than they need; others have less than they need. Some people have the capacity to earn more income than they need; others are unable to make ends meet no matter how many hours they work. Some people are nimble with technology; others find the constant changes, software updates, and ever-new social networking tools exhausting. Some people are accepted into just about every university and hired at just about every job to which they apply; others find the education and employment landscapes impenetrable. Schools are better in some neighborhoods than in others. Churches are nicer in some neighborhoods than in others. Roads and infrastructure are better in some regions than in others. Farmers in some parts of the world are paid *not* to grow certain crops; farmers in other parts of the world struggle to get their harvest to market before it spoils. In Western cultures food banks for the hungry are regularly stocked; in other parts of the world the hungry die from malnutrition and disease.

At some point, Christians need to ask themselves what might be responsible for these disparities. Few disparities can be traced to a strong versus a lagging work ethic of individuals. Few can be traced to a society's topographic variations, climate differences, or geographic disparities. At some point, we must admit that we have built a society that produces disparity. We have done things that ensure that some will prosper at the expense of others, and we have given our tacit approval to the continuation of this disparity. If you have ever considered such disparities, you have wandered into the intellectually rich world of social ethics.

What Is (Protestant) Social Ethics?

The field of ethics may be divided into two branches. One is fundamental ethics, which studies the basic questions and terminology in the field. In fundamental ethics, one is interested in how to live the happy life—that is to say, how to live well. Understanding what does and does not contribute to living well falls within this branch of ethics. For this reason, fundamental ethicists study terms like the Greek word *eudaimonia*, which can be roughly translated as "happiness," and concepts such as "person," "virtue," "law," "justice," and "rights." Consider, for example, these questions: What constitutes personhood? What is it about persons that obliges everyone else to treat them with dignity? If persons are to be treated with dignity, then to what extent ought laws to be written to protect that dignity? To what virtues ought persons aspire in order to embrace their own dignity? These are the questions that animate fundamental ethics. It is a very exciting field, especially in our day, as technological advances in the field of artificial intelligence are quickly blurring the lines of what constitutes a person and what happiness means to beings (persons?) whose intelligence is less biologically derived.[1]

The other branch of ethics is social ethics, which is concerned with the social order. Social ethics is built on the work of fundamental ethics, particularly the terminology of "person," "justice," "law," and "ends." Thus it is helpful to think of social ethics as an application of fundamental ethics rather than something distinct from it. Social ethics is the study of what ethic is operating within a given social system. It studies the extent to which the ethic claimed by a society matches the social structures its members have built. It asks whether there might not be a universal ethic against which every society can be measured. It studies the several ways in which a society organizes itself to produce inequalities among its members, and it analyzes the mentalities of members of a society to determine to what extent they prop up or expose the inequalities.

These subjects of inquiry within social ethics do not require any particular theological lens. Nonsectarian ethicists as well as ethicists representing diverse religious traditions work in this field. The common bonds among this diverse scholarly community are the principles discussed in the third part of this book: human dignity, common good, justice, solidarity, and subsidiarity. Human dignity refers to a status held by humans entitling them to the respect of others. The common good is a measurement of the degree to which a society provides opportunities for each of its members to flourish. Justice, one of the cardinal virtues of the classical world, is the virtue of giving people their due. Solidarity refers to the unity among persons within a social organization. Subsidiarity refers to whether a society is organized in such a way that the responsibility to solve problems is taken up by those closest to, and therefore most capable of solving, the problems. Scholars from various traditions may apply slightly different meanings to these principles or use slight different terminology to describe them, but the principles have created a language by which social ethicists can speak to one another across their religious divides.

In addition to these general principles, there are two distinctly Protestant contributions to social ethics: (1) Protestantism's commitment to work from a biblically centered view of society, and (2) Protestantism's history of sustained and sophisticated analysis of the "two kingdoms" of church and state. Protestant ethicists have rightly emphasized that Scripture offers a tremendous wealth of resources for social ethics. One only has to read to the second book of the Bible, Exodus, to find God deeply enmeshed in the fine details of what is required to build a nation. God writes laws for the nation, appoints its rulers, crafts its religious system, leads its army into battle, and so on. If Exodus is not enough to prove God's interest in the work of social justice, then later books like Judges, 1 and 2 Samuel, and 1 and 2 Kings should do the trick. These texts describe how God took offense when the people insisted on a change in their leadership structure (from judges to a kingship) and turned against God repeatedly in the centuries that followed. Even in the New Testament, the Gospel of Mark reports that the very first words out of Jesus's mouth during his public ministry were, "The time is fulfilled, and the kingdom of God has come near" (Mark 1:15). Jesus was about the work of building a new *kingdom*. And while it would be a very different kind of kingdom from those described in the Old Testament, it would nevertheless be a kingdom with its own internal patterns of social life.

In addition to their emphasis on Scripture as a source and norm for social ethics, Protestant ethicists—stretching all the way back to sixteenth-century Reformers Martin Luther, John Calvin, and several among the early Anabaptist communities—have found the dynamic between God's role in building earthly kingdoms and God's role in building a divine kingdom to fit within the narrative of church and state. Some thought that meant the church was under the state, which was itself under God. Others thought the church and the state were separate spheres, equally under God. Still others argued that the two were unrelated to each other and that God works within the church and not the state. Later Protestants followed one or another of these views, and the two-kingdoms idea still animates discussions of social ethics among Protestant thinkers today.

Why This Book?

There are a number of fine books that survey the field of social ethics, discussing various thinkers and movements.[2] While this book provides a survey of the historical development of Christian social ethics, its main purpose is not to introduce readers to specific figures and schools of thought in contemporary Protestant social ethics but instead to provide students the tools they need to be able to practice social ethics for themselves. Thus, instead of surveying the contemporary field, this book discusses the language and principles of the field so that students can use them to lend their own unique voices to the enterprise.

One of my goals with this book is to highlight the distinct features of Protestant social ethics while at the same time situating Protestant social ethics within the broader history and tradition of Christian thinking on society. For Protestants, Scripture is the ultimate authority for faith, life, and doctrine, and this is no less true in the field of social ethics. Yet oftentimes books on Protestant social ethics present biblical material unsystematically or haphazardly. In contrast, this book begins with the assumption that Scripture is foundational for Protestant social ethics and therefore offers a holistic overview of the Bible with an eye to its relevance for social ethics.

Similarly, Protestant social ethics can sometimes operate in a vacuum without appreciating contributions from the broader Christian tradition, both historically and in contemporary discussions. It is my conviction, however, that doing social ethics requires an appreciation for how social ethicists today are both indebted to and different from Christians in earlier eras since every principle of social ethics emerged from a long tradition of reflection about how to follow Jesus in the world. Thus, after surveying the Bible's social teachings, this book surveys the history of Christianity's witness to social concerns and social ethics from the early church to the twentieth century.

Finally, textbooks in Protestant social ethics often treat social issues selectively or in ways that promote the political viewpoints of the author. While no book, including this one, can be completely free of biases, I have attempted in the final part of the book to provide not a series of ethical positions that students should endorse but rather a presentation of the main principles of social ethics that students can appropriate and apply in their respective lives and contexts. Protestant social ethics should be about following Jesus in this world, not about following a particular political party or economic theory. My goal is thus to provide students with the language and conceptual tools they need to follow Jesus in contemporary society.

Outline of the Book

This book is divided into three parts. Part 1 surveys the biblical literature. The five chapters in part 1 review the content of the Old and New Testaments. Chapters 1 through 3 focus on the Old Testament, divided into the books of Law (Torah; chap. 1), the writings (Ketuvim; chap. 2), and the Prophets (Nevi'im; chap. 3).[3] Chapters 4 and 5 survey the New Testament, focusing first on the life of Jesus (chap. 4) and then on the early decades of Christianity (chap. 5). Readers will soon recognize that these chapters trace one particular thread woven into the fabric of the biblical literature. The Bible presents God as on a mission to restore order out of the chaos of life in this world. That work involves creative activity, lawmaking, king making, disciplining, covenant making, and kingdom building. Restoring order out of chaos is an apt metaphor for social ethics, and we join God in this work when we apply the knowledge gained from social ethics to improving this delightful world that God has created.

Part 2 surveys the history of Christian reflection on social ethics. The five chapters included in part 2 describe the development of Christian social ethics during Late Antiquity (chap. 6), the Middle Ages (chap. 7), the Reformations era (chap. 8), and the post-Reformations, or modern, era (chap. 9). Naturally, the focus in chapters 8 and 9 is on Protestant thinkers. However, some of the most sophisticated work in Christian social ethics during the post-Reformations era has been done by Catholics, who Protestants ignore to their own academic and moral peril. For this reason, chapter 10 surveys the history of Catholic social teaching since the late nineteenth century. While not an exhaustive treatment, it provides readers with a sense of how the Catholic Church has found a way to inject its moral voice into our noisy, pluralistic world. All told, the chapters in part 2 add to the thread from part 1 (about restoring order out of chaos) another thread as they trace the development from thinking about social ethics primarily in terms of charity to thinking about it in terms of structures and justice.

Of course, part 2 by necessity is only a survey of the church's two-thousand-year history. Specialists in church history will no doubt find that the chapters do not include the ideas of one or another of their favorite individuals. Likewise, as with any survey, the material that is included no doubt glosses over matters that a more focused study would need to treat. Instructors are therefore encouraged to supplement the materials found in these chapters with resources specific to their theological or denominational traditions.

Finally, part 3 introduces readers to the language needed to reason like a social ethicist. Each of the five chapters in part 3 introduces a major principle of the discipline: human dignity (chap. 11), common good (chap. 12), justice (chap. 13), solidarity (chap. 14), and subsidiarity (chap. 15). Each term builds on the one presented before it, so it is recommended that readers work through these chapters sequentially. While other principles could have been discussed, I have chosen these principles in order to answer three questions about social ethics: Why? What? How? The questions of *why* social ethics is important and *why* students ought to be involved in this enterprise are answered with the principles of human dignity and the common good. The response to the question of *what* a society ought to do to promote the first two principles is to organize itself according to the third principle, justice. And the question of *how* a society may organize itself justly is answered by the fourth and fifth principles, solidarity and subsidiarity. A third thread of this book picked up in these chapters is the challenge of balancing many competing interests when thinking about social ethics. One way to look at the final five chapters, then, is to recognize that they answer very few of our questions. Their chief contribution to social ethics is to help ensure that students are asking the right questions. Such is the path of wisdom. It is what critical thinking is all about. The best result one can get from an education is not more information about a topic but rather a mind better equipped to understand what questions need to be asked.

A Final Thought

If readers of this book conclude after reading it that they need to take action *x* or *y* or change their views about topics *a* and *b*, then I will be delighted.

One cannot be educated about a topic without changing *something* in one's life or ideas about the world. However, I did not write this book to ensure that readers take any one action in particular. After having a mystical encounter with God, Francis of Assisi completely changed his life and started living in voluntary poverty. Hildegard of Bingen had a similar mystical experience, yet it led her not to a life of begging but to a life of research into the natural world and of writing medical books, among other things. Similarly, the experience of reading books in social ethics can lead readers in very different directions. That is perfectly natural and should be welcomed. If you begin this book as one who leans politically to the left and sense a need to shift more to the right afterward, that's great. If you begin politically to the right and move more to the left afterward, that's also great. If you decide after this that politics is hopeless, and you decide to join a commune, so be it. Just be open to what God may do to expand how you see the world and your role in it. If this book turns out to be useful in this regard, then it will have accomplished its purpose.

PART 1

Social Ethics
and Scripture

⊰ 1 ⊱

The Pentateuch

Learning Outcomes for This Chapter

» Summarize content from the Bible's first five books pertinent to the study of ethics.

» Explore three socioethical themes in this literature.

» Analyze the contribution of grace to the story of God's compassion for the created world.

The name "Pentateuch" is given to the Bible's first five books: Genesis, Exodus, Leviticus, Numbers, and Deuteronomy. They are also known as the books of Law, or Torah, and thus are designated by the *T* in "Tanakh," which is the name Jews have given to the collection of books that Christians call the "Old Testament." Whatever the name given, these books tell some of Israel's most ancient stories. They describe how the nation of Israel came to be that very nation and record the activities of Israel's founding families and their leaders.

Most casual readers of these books enjoy the stories in Genesis but, midway through their reading of Exodus, get bogged down in the details of law codes. Few make it through the laws regarding the sacrificial system outlined in Leviticus. Intrepid readers might press on to discover the story of Israel's forty years of wandering in the wilderness in Numbers. Those who make it all the way through Deuteronomy are generally confused, in the end, by the seemingly chaotic mass of laws, regulations, and practices. Rest assured, there is an order, a system, a logic (if you will) to these books and to their manner of presenting Israel's law code, and it is quite beautiful once one digs deeper to understand them.[1] Yet our purpose here is to focus instead on some key themes that emerge from across these tales of patriarchs, religious leaders, law codes, sacrifices, victories, and defeats. Our purpose is to unearth what these stories have to teach us about who God is, what God seeks from his followers, and to what type of society we ought to be contributing our energies.

Summary of the Contents of the Tanakh / Old Testament

Torah / Pentateuch	Nevi'im / Prophets	Ketuvim / Writings
Narrates stories of Israel's earliest history	Describes events occurring during the ninth to fifth centuries BC	Describes events occurring during the twelfth to sixth centuries BC
Describes the law code given to create a structure for Israelite society	God speaks to Israel through the voices of various prophets	Tells of the split of the nation into two parts: Israel (north) and Judah (south)
Recounts the lives of prominent individuals in Israel's history –Noah –Abraham –Isaac –Moses	Texts record God's judgment on Israel and on Judah for their infidelity to God and to the law code	Records activities of the kings of Israel and Judah
		Records events surrounding the exile of Israel to Assyria and of Judah to Babylon
		Includes Wisdom literature (Proverbs, Ecclesiastes)
		Includes poetry (Psalms, Song of Songs)

What does this search yield? It reveals that God takes pleasure in order. It further reveals that humans seem to take far too much pleasure in disorder, in sin. Consequently God repeatedly steps in to restore order, to heal the broken pieces of people's lives, to renew their spirits, and to give them ever-new chances in building a better future for themselves and society. The Christian tradition calls this grace. The Pentateuch reveals that God's grace even *outruns* our disordered affections. God is restoring order even when we are in the midst of bringing about disorder! This is a beautiful picture of God, of God's grace, and of the type of social justice in which everyone is invited to participate.

One further feature of the Pentateuch deserves our attention here. Repeatedly the text reveals that God takes a special interest in and has particular compassion for the struggles faced by foreigners, immigrants, or, as the text often says, by strangers. The Pentateuch puts a real face—many faces—on the myriad injustices that strangers face. In our interconnected world today, the plight of those who travel to new lands for work or other opportunities is equally pronounced. This is a socioethical problem in our day as much as it was in Israel's earliest days.

God Takes Pleasure in Order

A distinctive feature of the Pentateuch is its concern with order. The reader discovers this right away in the opening chapters of Genesis. "Now the earth was without shape and empty, and darkness was over the surface of the watery deep" (Gen. 1:2 NET). In short, matter was in a chaotic heap. No shape. Empty of meaning. Dark. An abyss. Centuries later, the Greeks understood something similar about those earliest days. Hesiod wrote in his *Theogony*, a Greek creation story, "Truly, at the first, Chaos came to be," and from chaos sprang everything that exists.[2] In Genesis, God molds this chaotic mass into something wonderful, something beautiful, something good. There is light. There is separation of land from water and of cosmic spheres from one another. Even movement is ordered. Elements within that cosmic realm evolve into patterned orbits. Rotations of planetary bodies allow for shifts between day and night, between seasons, and between temperatures. The rotations of earth subsequently foster life, and God creates myriad vegetation, fish, birds, and other animals, including especially humans. Finally, there is rest. A sufficient equilibrium has been reached that God may be said to rest at the end of his creative activity. The order resulting from the chaos is deemed not merely good, but very good.

Yet the reader of Genesis soon discovers that all is not well on the earth for long. Human activity eventually yields rejection of belief in God. Genesis 3 and 4 record stories about Adam, Eve, Cain, and Lamech, who each reject God by acting in ways that they think are better for themselves. So in Gen. 7, somewhat surprisingly, the reader discovers that God bears an equal capacity to return the ordered world back to chaos. With Noah, his family, and some animals safely ensconced on a type of boat, Gen. 7:11 tells us, "All the fountains of the great deep burst open and the floodgates of the heavens were opened" (NET). A quick check of Gen. 1:6–7 reveals that what was happening in Gen. 7:11 is a return to the original chaotic state. Those waters that once were separated reunite. Chaos is back. Thankfully, however, the chaos restored by God does not last long. Eventually, as the reader discovers, God decides to bring a new order out of this new chaos, and we find the same events in Gen. 8 as in Gen. 1. A wind from God comes to restore order (Gen. 8:1). A separation is made between the waters above and the waters below (Gen. 8:2–3). Land appears (Gen. 8:4). Vegetation eventually is revealed

The ziggurat temple at Ur (located in the province of Dhi Qar in southern Iraq).

(Gen. 8:11). Finally, the animals and humans are set free to roam about the earth (Gen. 8:15–19).

So from the very beginning of the Pentateuch the reader encounters a God capable not only of bringing order out of chaos but even of bringing chaos out of order. In either case, God is firmly in control, since even the chaos of Gen. 7 had a particular purpose. There are many similar events in the rest of the Pentateuch (e.g., the gift of manna in the Sinai wilderness is later spurned by Israel, and so God sows chaos into the community through an inordinate supply of quail; see Exod. 16 and Num. 11:31–33). Those stories introduce the reader to a faith in a God who providentially cares for a beautiful, wonderful world, and they do so even while showing that more often than not the inhabitants of that world turn away from their creator. Every new chaos is brought to some new level of order by God.

Not long after the deluge, the chaos of disbelief in the true God returned. But rather than fixing this new chaos with another re-creation event, God chose a much slower, more halting, but arguably more appreciable method. God chose to address this new chaos by building a special relationship with a family. God selects a resident of Ur (in modern-day Iraq) named Abram (later Abraham) and his wife, Sarai (later Sarah).[3] Evidence from archaeological excavations of his hometown suggests Abram began his life as a worshiper of a moon-god. However, God calls him out of that lifestyle, and a story of conversion gradually unfolds. Abraham's subsequent travels around the ancient Near East and in Egypt reveal that he alone worshiped this new God, Yahweh. His story, and the story of his descendants, then, is one in which Yahweh gradually reintroduces himself to the human race. A new day of restoring order from chaos had begun. However, this time the restoration process would take far more years than anyone could then or can now imagine.

The Pentateuch records numerous chaotic events within the story of Abraham and his descendants. Abraham, it turns out, had a propensity to lie. More than once God had to rescue Sarah and him from the frightening situations into which they had gotten themselves as a result of these lies.[4] Lying and deceit were like a twisted gene that was passed on to every one of Abraham's descendants. God repeatedly had to rescue Abraham's son Isaac and Abraham's grandsons Esau and Jacob from situations in which their deceit had gotten them into trouble. Mutual hatred and deceit landed Abraham's great-grandson Joseph into a slave's existence in Egypt, which had the unfortunate consequence of eventually landing all of Abraham's descendants into slavery in Egypt. The book of Exodus recounts how God came to their rescue more than once too.

Similarly, the story of Moses's leadership of Abraham's descendants, by then called Hebrews or Israelites, was one of halting steps forward as God restored worship of himself to the earth. God provided a miraculous escape for the Israelites from Egyptian slavery. God provided leaders to direct the map-less people from Egypt back to Abraham's former land in Palestine. God provided a law code to govern the Hebrews' social and ceremonial affairs.

Mount Sinai in the Sinai Peninsula.

When discipline was needed, God provided it. When food was needed, God provided it. When water was needed, God provided it. The stories of Exodus, Leviticus, and Numbers recount the innumerable ways in which God was restoring order out of the chaos of the Hebrews' lives.

These texts equally reveal that God was seeking a gradual restoration of knowledge of himself throughout the world. Take special note of Exod. 19. After escaping from Egypt, the Hebrews had arrived at the base of Mount Sinai, in that peninsula shared by Egypt and Israel today. Through the voice of Moses, God gave the Hebrews there the text of a law code they were to follow. The text in Exod. 19:5–6 informs us that, if the Hebrews followed this law code, they would be provided with at least three blessings: (1) they would be God's special possession; (2) they would be a kingdom of priests; and (3) they would be sacred, or set apart for a particular purpose.[5]

Note especially the second of these blessings. The Hebrews were to enjoy the blessing of being a kingdom of priests. Priests serve congregants. Priests inform congregants about God. If all the Hebrews were priests, who were their congregants? In the later books of the Old Testament, the answer becomes clear: the rest of the people in the world.

Thus Exod. 19 finally reveals to the reader what God sought from this special relationship with Abraham and his descendants all along. They were to be God's mouthpieces to the world. They were to preach to the world the beauty and the greatness both of God and of having a relationship with God. Their relationship with God was to be sufficiently winsome so that it would attract nonbelievers in God, lead them into asking questions about Yahweh, and eventually draw them out of belief in their false gods, to serve the true God. The Hebrews' story, then, is a grand narrative of God restoring order out of the chaos of people's lives in this world. The Pentateuch is a witness to those earliest days in which God gave constant attention to this restoration of order. Order seems to give God pleasure.

God's Grace Outruns Disorder

The recognition that God takes pleasure in restoring order from chaos reveals another important point. That God chooses to restore at all rather than to let chaos reign testifies to something the Christian tradition will come to call *grace*. "Grace" is an incredibly powerful word, though perhaps it loses its impact from overuse in less germane discussions. In simple terms, "grace" means God's unmerited love for us. The Latin *gratia* and the Greek *charis* suggest the wider notions of God's favor, delight, or joy. The older English word "benevolence" captures some of this too. Whatever the term, we are speaking of a decided move on God's part to show love, favor, delight, joy, and benevolence toward humans. Moreover, God is gracious toward humans despite their lack of turning to him for help. Even more to the point, the Pentateuch reveals that God's grace anticipates and *outruns* our sin and the disorder we create.

The names given to Eve in Gen. 2–3 are a great example of this. She is introduced to the reader first as "helper" (Gen. 2:18). Then she is elevated to "woman" (Gen. 2:22). Then she is called "wife" (Gen. 2:24). Finally she is called Eve, or "mother of all living" (Gen. 3:20).[6] There is yet no birth of children in the narrative, so it is surprising that she is elevated to being called the mother of all people as early as Gen. 3. Yet her participation in an act of rejecting God earlier in Gen. 3 reveals to us the meaning behind these elevations. She and Adam were supposed to be caring for the natural world as God's representatives in that world. However, due to their rejection of God's authority, she and Adam were removed from Eden. Their caretaking roles became more difficult. They needed some extra hands to share the work. How wonderful, then, to have already witnessed a transformation of Eve into being a "mother" prior to her need to be a child bearer. In other words, the choices made by Adam and Eve led to a fair amount of disorder. Yet God's grace was at work *prior* to their negative choices. God's grace anticipated the disorder they would create. God's grace was already coming to their rescue before they even knew they needed rescuing.

The flood story, mentioned above, is another good example. After the flood receded and Noah and his family exited their boat, Gen. 8:20 says Noah made a sacrifice to God. Note carefully the text of God's reply.

> And the LORD smelled the soothing aroma and said to himself, "I will never again curse the ground because of humankind, *even though the inclination of their minds is evil from childhood on*. I will never again destroy everything that lives, as I have just done. While the earth continues to exist, planting time and harvest, cold and heat, summer and winter, and day and night will not cease." (Gen. 8:21–22 NET, emphasis added)

Noah has just left his boat. No one has "sinned." No one has rejected God. In fact, Noah and his family are praising God for his grace toward them. Yet the text tells us that God is already anticipating the rejection of himself sure to come. What is more, God has decided, in advance, to show those very people grace, or favor. God has decided, in advance, not to destroy again almost everything that lives. God has decided, in advance, to let the earth and its regulated seasons exist. Grace is far outrunning anyone's sin. Grace is revealed when God tempers the impact of his justice.

Look next at Gen. 26:19–22. There is a drought, so everyone in the region of Canaan is digging wells and looking for water.[7] Isaac, Abraham's son, is doing the same, and he seems to strike water at every turn, but his neighbors dispute with him over the land in which he has dug the first two wells. Isaac knows the neighbors are just out to steal his water, but rather than engaging in a costly dispute, he moves on. On digging a third well and finding water again, his neighbors decide to leave him alone and let him have that one. But the serendipity of finding water every time he digs a well is not lost on Isaac. He says, "Now the LORD has made room for us, and we will prosper in the land" (Gen. 26:22 NET). Finding water is not due to Isaac's skill with a divining rod; Isaac knows that God provided the water. God's grace toward Isaac is obvious here, but notice what is not explicitly said in the text: God provided water not only for Isaac but also for his mean-spirited neighbors! Water is provided for everyone who needs it, including the neighbors, even before those neighbors engage in acts of aggression toward Isaac. God's grace surpassed their disordered affections for things that did not belong to them.

The calling of Moses to lead the Hebrews is an example too of grace outrunning disorder. Moses wanted nothing to do with the Egyptians—or the Hebrews, for that matter—after his flight to Midian in Exod. 2. Yet God had other plans. The hardened Moses was precisely the type of individual best suited to bearing the brunt of Pharaoh's humiliations and the Hebrews' many rejections of his leadership. God's grace in Moses's life was evident in the forty years he spent living abroad in Midian. During those years, God would provide Moses a wife (Zipporah) who would help hold him accountable to the Abrahamic covenant (cf. Exod. 4:24–26) and a father-in-law (Jethro) who would provide wise counsel at a crucial juncture in the sojourn to Mount Sinai (Exod. 18:17–27).[8] Those years would even lead to the fame of Yahweh spreading to an entirely new people group, the Midianites (Exod. 18:9–12; see also Judg. 1:16).

Likewise, the law code itself is an example of this grace. The Hebrews had yet to organize themselves into a nation or have any land they could call their own during the time period covered by the Pentateuch. Still, God antic-ipated the inevitable disarray that would come into their civic and religious affairs once they arrived in Canaan. Consequently God provided a law code—especially its sacrificial system components—to guide their behavior and the distribution of justice. Paul, in Rom. 3, remarks that this sacrificial system was actually a stopgap measure to stave off God's punishment for sin (until that punishment could fully be meted out on Jesus). Rather than punishing humans for their sin, animal substitutes could be provided. Paul says in Rom. 3:25, "God in his forbearance had passed over the sins previously committed" (NET). This is a remarkable perspective on the law code. Maintenance of the sacrificial system encouraged the Hebrews to view God as patient, forbearing, and slow to anger. Indeed, the presence of a sacrificial system within the law code is the proof of its grace-filled character.

God Loves the Marginalized

All of this talk about grace inevitably invites questions such as to whom this grace is provided, whether it is given to some necessarily, and whether others might be excluded from it. Obviously grace was not just for the Israelites. No one before the time of Jacob was, strictly speaking, an Israelite, for the name "Israelite" derives from Jacob's other name in the Pentateuch, "Israel" (cf. Gen. 32:28).[9] Adam, Eve, Enoch, Noah, Abraham, Isaac—each were recipients of God's grace, and none of them were among the group that escaped Egypt and were called by God his "special possession" (Hebrew, *segullah*; Exod. 19:5). We noted earlier too that through Jethro, Moses's father-in-law, the fame of Yahweh would spread to the Midianite people. We have even a story of God's grace being extended to a donkey![10]

Thus despite whatever puffed-up sense of pride may have entered Israelite consciousness after they were called God's "special possession," God loves and shows favor toward all people. Even more intriguing, several stories reveal how God has particular compassion for those on society's margins. In the Pentateuch, the marginalized are usually the foreigners, the "strangers" among the Israelites. One of the first traces of this special compassion of God is Gen. 12, the text that introduces God's covenant with Abram. In Gen. 12:3 the reader is told that Abram is to be blessed, and through him all the nations of the earth will be blessed. God's grace for Abram is not for his benefit alone or only for the benefit of his direct descendants; it is for the benefit of all the world's people.

Abraham later fathers a son named Ishmael through one of Sarah's servants, Hagar (Gen. 16:1–2). In time, Hagar and Sarah find it difficult to share the same household, so Hagar decides to run away. She is now an outsider, on the margins of society. Evidence of her marginalization is revealed in Gen. 16:7–8. Hagar is sitting, alone, on a deserted roadway in the empty desert. If she has resigned herself to a likely death in that lonely desert, God has other plans. In a tremendous story of rescue and compassion, God comes to Hagar's aid even before she knows she needs it. God does not wait for her to

Ibrahim Mosque in Hebron (in the West Bank of Palestine) marking Abraham's burial site.

call out for help. God does not wait to see whether she could take care of her own problems. God reaches out to Hagar. God goes to her, asks her about her needs, and meets them. This has such a tremendous impact on Hagar that she gives God a new name that the author of Genesis thought worthy to record. She calls God "the One who Sees" (Gen. 16:13; in Hebrew, *El Roi*).[11]

Consider also God's compassion for the marginalized in numerous passages of the Israelites' law code. The Ten Commandments give us several indications of this. Exhortations not to lie, steal, or commit adultery were not written to stop us from doing behavior we otherwise regularly would participate in doing. They were written to encourage us to think about the good of others as being at least as significant as the good of ourselves. Consider also the commandment about the Sabbath and the various Sabbath regulations in the law code. Recall that the Israelites had been slaves for their entire lives. They had never known a day off from work. The very idea of a Sabbath rest for Israel was a gift of God to a nation of people who had long been on society's margins.

There are also laws written specifically for the protection of the poor. One such law obliged harvesters to leave any fallen crops on the ground and not pick them up (cf. Lev. 19:10; 23:22; Deut. 24:19). That portion of the harvest was to be left for the poor, widows, and orphans to collect. Laws associated with the sacrificial system made provision for poorer Israelites to substitute cheaper animals for the more expensive ones that would otherwise have been obligatory to offer to God (e.g., Lev. 5:7, 11). Also, the tithes to be paid by Israelites were to be divided into several categories (cf. Num. 18:21–24; Deut. 14:22–29), one of which was for the maintenance of the needs of the poor (Deut. 14:28–29). There were further laws regarding the manumission of slaves, the expunging of debts at regular intervals, and the restoration of all land to its original owner every fifty years (cf. Exod. 21:2–3; Lev. 25).

In truth, the law code itself—or the very idea of a law code—existed for the protection of those on the margins. Israelites with financial and other means at their disposal to provide for themselves do not need a lot of legal protections. What they need are curtailments on their behavior to ensure that how they provide for themselves does not infringe on the ability of others to provide for themselves. People with property need to respect the boundaries of their property and the boundaries of their neighbor's property. People with greater wealth are obliged to use their greater means to alleviate the suffering of those with less. The Mosaic law code was a system that protected everyone's right to earn a living, including making provision for those who, for a variety of reasons, had less capacity to earn that living than others. As a divine gift, the law code provides extensive evidence of God's compassion for those who find themselves on society's margins. God "sees" these people. God's grace is dispensed especially for their benefit.

Summary

This chapter explored three features of the Pentateuch that impinge on our understanding of social ethics. First, God takes pleasure in bringing order out of chaos. Social ethics is about a right ordering of social structures. The experience of human sin correlates with the disordering of these social structures; consequently, we are invited to join God in seeking better-ordered, more just social structures. Second, God outruns our attempts at disorder by extending grace. We are often too quick to dismiss the difficult plights of others and reduce the social services we are willing to provide to help them because we sense that they are to blame for their own problems. This is absolutely contrary to how God treats us. The Pentateuch reveals that we worship a God who meets our needs before we even know we have them. Third, God loves the marginalized. When Jesus says that he came not for the healthy but for the sick (see Matt. 9:11–13), he is expressing a sentiment we find so beautifully expressed time and again in the Pentateuch. Everything God does is directed toward looking out for those who cannot help themselves. People with means—be they financial, educational, or social—will always find a way to have their needs met. Thus we are invited to adopt God's worldview: worry less about people with means, and worry more about people who are struggling.

Main Points of the Chapter

» God takes pleasure in order, which prompts us to seek order in social structures.

» God's grace *outruns* the disorder we have brought into our lives and into the created world, which invites us to consider others' needs, independent of whether the people are responsible for creating those needs in the first place.

» God invites us to take special care of foreigners, immigrants, and others on society's margins.

⊰ 2 ⊱

Historical, Poetical, and Wisdom Literature

Learning Outcomes for This Chapter

» Survey the historical, poetical, and Wisdom literature of the Old Testament.

» Explore the human struggle for justice and the consequences of injustice revealed in this literature.

» Analyze the contribution of God being a place of refuge for the righteous within the context of the struggle for justice.

The historical, poetical, and Wisdom literature of the Old Testament comprises books that record stories about the Israelites, or the nation of Israel, from the time of their arrival in Canaan (after their exodus from slavery in Egypt) until their various deportations to the lands of the Assyrians and, later, the Babylonians. Timewise, we are talking about a span of roughly seven hundred years, from about 1200 to 500 BC. The literature includes books such as Joshua, Ruth, 1–2 Samuel, 1–2 Kings, 1–2 Chronicles, Psalms, and Proverbs. Within the Jewish tradition, these books are grouped together and given the name Kethubim, or Ketuvim, which means "writings."

Even skimming this material—it comprises about four hundred pages in many Bibles—reveals Israel's topsy-turvy, on-again, off-again relationship with God and the difficulties its composite tribes had in getting along both with one another and with the countries around them. Since our interest in this literature is the extent to which it illuminates matters of social and ethical concern for us, the reader senses rather quickly that much of what we might stand to gain comes in the midst of these negative stories. Yet it must be remembered that it was Israelites who recorded and bothered to keep even these negative stories about themselves. They kept the stories for a reason. They kept them not merely to be a historical record of a distant people group, but to be a historical witness to this people's relationship with God. The people who wrote them, some of whom lived long after the deportation to Babylon, believed their troubles in the world had much to do with their abandonment of their relationship with God. In their own generation the writers wanted to avoid the problems that led to the deportations to Assyria and to Babylon in earlier generations. For this reason the stories tell us as much, if not more, about the character of God than they do about the Israelite people.

> *The LORD loves righteousness and justice; the earth is full of his unfailing love. (Ps. 33:5 NIV)*

Since the authors of these texts were interested, in part, to reveal the worthy character of God, our own study of the literature begins there. What do the texts have to say about God, about God's character, and about what God seeks? Second, we examine several stories about the Israelite nation in which it struggled to live out its high calling as God's chosen people. Third, and finally, we examine the role played by women and men who fought for justice in the face of opposition from others.

The Character of God

Drop into pretty much any psalm, and you will discover a song about God's character. The songwriter might be rejoicing about or lamenting something. In either case the psalm (or song) text reverberates with a vision of God as good, just, merciful, a rescuer of the oppressed, and unfailing in love. The Psalms open with an exhortation to read the book with an interest in the study of God's character and his ways. "Blessed is the one who *does not* walk in step with the wicked or stand in the way that sinners take or sit in the company of mockers, but whose delight is in the law of the LORD" (Ps. 1:1–2 NIV, emphasis added; cf. 26:1–5). The reader is encouraged to delight now in God's ways rather than in one's own ways. So what are God's ways? The rest of the Psalms works this out.

First, God's ways are good (Pss. 27:13; 31:19; 34:8). Principally this comes through in various psalms' depictions of God as providentially caring for the world and its affairs.[1] Just as a ruler who regulates the affairs of the kingdom well is considered good, so too God is presented as a good king who rules well.[2] Psalm 2 tells us that nations may conspire against God and against God's people, but God merely mocks their inflated egos and puffed-up pride (2:4; cf. 52:1–7). The right response is, "You kings, be wise. . . . Serve the LORD with fear and celebrate his rule with trembling" (2:10–11 NIV). Indeed, the goodness of God invites us to revel in God's majesty and glory. It invites praise, awe, and adoration (30:4; 31:2–3).

Second, God's ways are characterized by unfailing love for his people.[3] The Hebrew word *chesed* tries to capture this sense of unstinting, unfailing, unswerving love that is characteristic of God.[4] The psalms repeat this word frequently. *Chesed* is both a cause for joy (51:12; 68:3) and a cause for penitence (51:7–11). Since God's love is unfailing, God can be trusted to provide for his people and to lead them well (12:6; 22:23–24; 33:4). Consider Ps. 136. Praise for God's *chesed* ("His love endures forever!") occurs twenty-six times in just this one psalm! It is the refrain interspersed through the psalm's recounting of Israel's history from the dawn of creation, through its exodus from Egypt, and then to its deliverance from many enemies while returning to the promised land. Israel's restoration is due to nothing other than God's *chesed*. Indeed, God's love draws the psalm writers—and all righteous people, for that matter—into a desire for deeper intimacy with God.

Who Wrote the Psalms?

Most psalms mention the name(s) of their composer(s). In the absence of other evidence, this attribution is generally accepted.

King David is listed as the composer of most of the psalms. Other composers identified include these:

- David's son, King Solomon (Ps. 72)
- Heman the Ezrahite (Ps. 88)
- Ethan the Ezrahite (Ps. 89)
- Moses (Ps. 90)
- Asaph, a name for a temple singer (Pss. 50; 73–83)
- The "Sons of Korah" (Pss. 42; 44–49; 84–85; 87; 88, with Heman the Ezrahite)

**The Psalms
Attest
to God's
Character**

Good
Loving
Rescuer
Just
Relational

Third, another concrete expression of God's *chesed* is the proclamation of God as a rescuer, a place of refuge, and a deliverer of the oppressed.[5] Several of the psalms are classified by scholars as lament psalms.[6] The writer of the psalm is lamenting the difficulties the psalmist faces in life. More often than not, the psalmist complains to God that good people seem to suffer, while evil people seem to win and to profit. Psalm 44 is one such text; it dwells at length on the sense of being abandoned by God. It uses terms and phrases like "rejected," "humbled," "a reproach to our neighbors," "disgrace," and feeling "scorned and derided" by others. Yet lament psalms invariably end on a hopeful note. God has not abandoned the righteous, despite what those who oppose righteous people might think.[7] God wants to hear our cries for mercy, deliverance, and justice,[8] and he will provide refuge and rescue.[9] He is the epitome of a fortress, within whose walls the weary, the suffering, and the righteous find rest (28:8; 42:9; 55:22; 62:2). Sometimes God's way is to lead the righteous *through*, rather than *away from*, times of difficulty.[10] Yet once the Lord rescues, "the poor will eat and be satisfied" (22:26 NIV), and he will be experienced as a "father to the fatherless, a defender of widows" (68:5 NIV). In Ps. 72, the reader discovers that the theme of God as a rescuer and a place of refuge extends even to the work of righteous kings, whose leadership causes them to defend the afflicted, save the children of the poor, and crush oppressors.

Fourth, God's ways are just. Indeed, nearly every psalm speaks to the themes of God's justice.[11] God's way is not to take pleasure in evil (5:4). So God punishes evildoers.[12] It is true God is quick to forgive (32:1–6), but God also disciplines his own people in order that they might turn from their wicked ways (50:4–6; 60:1–3; 66:10–12).[13] Occasionally the psalm writers thank God for punishing them for their own, evil ways (e.g., 69:5–6). Yes, the psalms frequently remind us that the wheels of God's justice seem to grind rather slowly. Thankfully, however, they grind exceedingly fine.

Fifth, God is relational. Recognizing that God is *other* than us, the psalmists nevertheless encourage their readers to cultivate an intimacy, a relationship, with God and to see God as one who wants to build a relationship with them. There is joy in following the ways of the Lord (16:11; 51:12). A term typically used for a follower of God's ways is "righteous one" (Hebrew *zedek*). God seeks such people (53:2), looks out for them, and helps them.[14] Consequently, readers are exhorted to be counted among the righteous and to seek after God (34:9–10; 37:3–6; 42:1–2). Psalm writers frequently count themselves among the righteous (26:1; 30:7; 31:14; 33:20–22). Perhaps surprisingly, those who have such a relationship with God are even encouraged to challenge God and to remind God of his obligations to the righteous (30:9–10; 53:6).

The Psalms' invitation to learn about these ways of God strikes several socioethical chords. For one thing, the psalms give us historical perspective. They remind us that, while the struggle for justice may be a long one, we labor for it alongside a God whose concern for it is never failing. Also, these ways teach us to show more love for those whom God loves, to join God as a rescuer of those who are struggling on the margins of society—the poor, the widows, the orphans, the hurting, and the oppressed. As well, these ways prompt us to consider how attentive we are to ordering our own lives and our social structures toward the good that God seeks in his providential care for our world.

> *Blessed are those who have regard for the weak; the* Lord *delivers them in times of trouble.*
> *(Ps. 41:1 NIV)*

The Character of Israel

In addition to reflection on the ways and character of God, the historical books within the Old Testament's collection also recount the ups and downs of Israel's story. The narrative they tell begins with Joshua taking over leadership of the Israelites after the recent death of Moses (Deut. 34). Apparently it was not going to be an easy job. God tells Joshua to "be strong and courageous" four times in Josh. 1 alone (vv. 6, 7, 9, 18). Yet at the very same time God tells Joshua four times that by his (God's) power, not the will or strength of the Israelites, will they take ownership of Canaan (vv. 2, 3, 11, 15; see also 10:42; 11:20; 13:6; 23:10–11; Ps. 44:3). So one of the things we discover right away in this literature is that Israel's relationship with God will be marked alternatively by Israelite courage and patience while they wait on God to provide. These two things will be tested repeatedly in the books that follow.

In the book of Joshua, both tales are told. On the positive side, the Israelites will successfully wait on God to deliver Jericho into their hands. It takes seven days of seemingly irrelevant marching around the city's walls before they are called on to fight courageously against the residents of Jericho (Josh. 5–6). But not every Israelite obeys God's command to leave Jericho's spoils behind. Some are impatient for wealth; they do not wait for God to provide, and the next battle at Ai goes rather poorly (Josh. 7). This story of partial success

Remains of the ancient city of Jericho, in the Palestinian-controlled West Bank, about seven miles northwest of the Dead Sea, and about sixteen miles east of Jerusalem.

and partial failure marks the entire book of Joshua. Too often the Israelite army refuses to courageously root out all the Canaanite people. Instead, the Israelites form treaties with the locals and later end up paying the price of their reticence: constant strife with and eventual embrace of the idols of their new neighbors (Josh. 9:14; 17:12–13; 18:3; cf. Judg. 2).

The book of Judges similarly alternates between stories of the Israelites' great faith in God and their frequent abandonment of the same faith. Judges 2:10 tells us that the Israelites born after the time of Joshua "knew neither the LORD nor what he had done for Israel" (NIV). For some reason, the faith was not passed down to the children. The text even tells us that, in so short a time span as this, the Israelites had stopped worshiping Yahweh and had instead begun worshiping the gods of the Canaanite people (esp. Baal)! So much for ridding the land of bad influences. Yet every time we read a depressing story like this, the book also tells us that God chose to raise up a "judge" who would help Israel correct the error of its ways. The stories of judges like Ehud, Deborah, Gideon, Jephthah, and Samson are examples of individuals who break the repeated cycles of Israel rejecting God and turning to evil ways. Yet even some of these celebrated judges were depressing characters. Jephthah made a foolish vow that seems to suggest he would have to sacrifice his daughter (11:32–40), and Samson's illicit love life is put on extended display in the book (Judg. 16).

Even after the judges are replaced with kings, the story is not much better. Most of Israel's kings start out abysmally, and their stories end even worse. A few kings start out well—such as Saul, David, and Solomon—but, invariably, they end up either in personal moral failure, or rejecting God, or leading the country astray, or all three! David's story is particularly poignant. The reader is introduced to him as a young man of profound faith in God during a battle against Goliath and one who serves faithfully as an official in Saul's court. In the waning days of Saul's kingship, David is portrayed as trusting God while suffering as an innocent victim in Saul's ill-advised attempt to rid himself of challengers. David's eventual succession to the throne is marked by military feats that restore the glory of Israel's kingdom and by a desire to build a temple in Jerusalem to make worship of God the centerpiece of Israelite life. God even promises David an eternal kingdom as a reward for his faithfulness (2 Sam.

> *In those days Israel had no king; everyone did as they saw fit. (Judg. 17:6; 21:25 NIV)*

7). Yet none of this prevents us from seeing David behave as the genuinely human person that he is—a man capable of adultery and murder, of turning a blind eye to the sins of his children, and of being despised by his family and countrymen (2 Sam. 11–15).

The books of Samuel, Kings, and Chronicles recount repeated moral failings of both the kings and the Israelites. The lusts for power and wealth coincide with repeated displays of oppression of the marginalized. Some kings even resort to arresting and executing priests and prophets loyal to God in order to quell dissent against their disastrous reigns. Ahab and his wife, Jezebel, were especially troublesome in this regard (1 Kings 18). Their reign was so bad that even the prophet at the time, a man named Elijah, was deeply depressed. God had to give him a time-out along a river's edge in order to calm him down (1 Kings 17:1–7; 19:3–8). Throughout these years, prophets came and went. They warned of impending judgment and divine justice for the error of all of these ways, but few had more than a short-term impact. At least from a human-centered perspective, these books offer too many windows into the illicit depths to which humans are willing to go.

Still, even negative stories such as these illuminate an important socioethical lesson. Because political institutions have the power to tax and to redistribute the resources of a society, the right ordering of this power is especially critical. Yet political institutions are nothing more than a collection of human beings. Humans are prone to sin, and the combination of their illicit desires and access to power can very quickly lead to oppression of people on society's margins—its ideological margins as well as its economic and social margins. Political leaders are not immune to building a society that oppresses some in order to legitimate and to reinforce their own, or their group's, power for the future. Christians and all people of goodwill have a duty to hold all persons in political office accountable for their actions. They have a duty to stand up in protest against those in political office by pointing out injustice.

Mount Carmel in northwestern Israel, the supposed site at which Elijah carried out a contest between Yahweh and Baal.

Exhortations to Live Justly

Lest this chapter paints too unflattering a portrait of the Israelites or of humanity's penchant for sin and injustice, it is heartening to discover stories pointing in a more positive direction. One such story is that of a Moabite woman named Ruth, who decides to leave her tribe and join the Israelite community. She does so out of deep love for her Israelite mother-in-law, Naomi, who has fallen on particularly hard times. Ruth's righteous character is revealed in her willingness to love a foreign people, her openness to follow the Mosaic law in gathering fallen grain in the field, and her sole interest in providing for Naomi. Ruth's story also introduces us to Boaz, who loves God and the marginalized people that God loves, such as Ruth and Naomi. Boaz is used by God not only to provide immediate relief for these women in terms of food but also to provide long-term aid in the form of a marriage to Ruth and the fathering of a son to care for Naomi. Ruth and Naomi's story is a real delight. It reveals God's compassion for the oppressed and demonstrates his rescue of the marginalized. God provides for Ruth and Naomi in ways far beyond their expectations. The women find hope, healing, and restoration in the midst of an unjust society.

In the Ketuvim we also learn the story of Job, a righteous man who falls on especially heartbreaking, difficult times. In the span of two chapters, the reader is introduced to a man who loses not only his wealth but also nearly every member of his family. He is left only with a wife and three friends who offer little comfort. They question his faith in God through thinly veiled attacks on his moral character. Few people could weather the storm of such personal losses as Job experienced; fewer still would persist in faith after such unrelenting criticism by one's spouse and friends. Indeed, Job nearly breaks. Yet he comes through the experience with his faith intact. The closing chapters of the book invite the reader to revel in the awesome mystery that is God's providential care of the world. Job's story does not solve the problem of theodicy (God's justice in the face of evil and suffering) for its readers, but it invites the readers to accept that, somehow, even the horrific events in human history are not outside the knowledge or the control of God. While this is not intellectually satisfying, at least to people of faith it invites them to place their trust in a *who*, in a God who has experienced suffering himself and who chooses to suffer with us in the midst of difficulties, even if the *why* of those difficulties cannot be known.

Three stories, set during the late sixth and fifth centuries BC, when the Israelites were emerging from the specter of their exile in Babylon, are equally helpful. The reader of the book of Ezra discovers a man devoted to restoring worship of God in Jerusalem and its surrounding region of Judah. The text calls him "a man learned in matters concerning the commands and decrees of the LORD" (Ezra 7:11 NIV). He is mournful over the infidelity to God he finds among the Jews then living in Jerusalem, which prompts the attentive reader to recall how God had earlier punished Israel with exile for their infidelities. One of the more powerful scenes is found in Ezra 10:1, where Ezra is "praying and confessing, weeping and throwing himself down before the house of God" (NIV). Notice the very physical nature of his grief over the sins of the Israelites. The reader is invited to be as physically moved and brokenhearted over the loss of concern for God in our own day as Ezra was in his day.

Likewise, Ezra's contemporary Nehemiah is dismayed at the lack of progress the Jews in Jerusalem had made in rebuilding their city's walls. To Nehemiah, not only is the lack of a wall a danger to the Jewish population; it also indicates their lack of concern to remain faithful to God. It was also true that many of the Jews in the region were poor and had suffered tremendous financial losses. So, while serving as the appointed governor of the region, Nehemiah rebuilds the city's walls, all the while refusing to live in the opulent manner of previous governors. Nehemiah writes, "Out of reverence for God I did not act like that. Instead, I devoted myself to the work on this wall. All my men were assembled there for the work; we did not acquire any land" (Neh. 5:15–16 NIV). He even confronts the men who had earlier profited from usurious loans, reprimanding them and forcing them to return the payments to the debtors. Nehemiah's story exemplifies what servant leadership looks like. Servant leaders love the people whom God loves—in this case, the poor, the suffering, and the marginalized. In contemporary socioethical parlance, we would say Nehemiah made a "preferential option for the poor" (a phrase discussed further in chaps. 10 and 14). He easily could have taken over the land of his Jewish subjects in order to pay both for the wall's construction and for the maintenance of his own household and lifestyle. But he chose instead to love and to correct the people he was sent to serve. This meant that he worked as hard as they were asked to work in building a wall, and he took no more than he needed to make that happen.

> *Who knows but that you have come to your royal position for such a time as this? (Esther 4:14 NIV)*

Finally, Esther's story is another powerful example of the benefits of living justly. Her story upends the traditional role of a member of the Persian king's harem. After a poignant expression from her uncle of her need for courage (Esther 4:14), Esther hatches a complex plot to ensnare the king's evil advisor, Haman, and then she cashes in what little political influence she has with the king to seek Haman's removal from office. God rewards her faith and courage; the king not only grants her request while heaping on her further praise, but he also ensures that countless Israelites are spared destruction (Esth. 7–8). Sometimes justice occurs when one person steps up in courage to speak out against a sin in society.

Summary

The Pentateuch shows that God reveals goodness in the right ordering of creation and that God's grace outruns even humans' hard-charging attempts at disrupting that order. The historical books surveyed in this chapter demonstrate just how forbearing God is with people determined to disrupt the goodness and right ordering of the world. Although these books are filled with stories of Israelites, judges, and kings—and the social structures they helped to build—who abuse their power and the people under their care, the books also include stories of women and men who lived justly and are models of righteousness. These courageous women and men who stood up for justice are a leaven that can work its way throughout the dough of the wider society. The psalms suggest that the Israelite's pleas for restoration, for renewal, and for a return of justice to the earth are not ignored by God. On the contrary, God is their hope, their best place of refuge, and the one from whom they experience unfailing love.

From the perspective of social ethics, the literature surveyed in this chapter continues to challenge readers to align their interests with those of God. The stories suggest that God's interests are the needs of the righteous. While the righteous are those who seek a relationship with God, it is not as simple as their having made an intellectual assent to faith. The righteous seek a relationship with God particularly in the midst of their struggle for justice. They have either experienced injustice personally, or their hearts are broken by the injustice they witness others experiencing. Too often suffering people find their needs ignored by those with social, economic, and political power. Yet during such difficult times, the righteous turn to God as their refuge. In return they experience God's love, which encourages them to stand firm, to be courageous, and to speak up for the cause of justice in their social setting.

Main Points of the Chapter

» Being righteous, or seeking after God, is a function of being one who seeks after, pleads for, prays for, and stands up for justice.

» Justice begins when one righteous woman or man stands up—alone, if necessary—and speaks against sin in society or those who oppress others.

» The struggle for justice may be a long one, but one labors for it alongside a God whose concern for it is never failing.

3

Prophets

Learning Outcomes for This Chapter

» Identify the sins of injustice and idolatry in Israel with which the prophets were principally concerned.

» Summarize the collective view of the books of the Prophets considering Israel's past, present, and future.

» Analyze the juxtaposition of judgment and hope within each book of the Prophets.

A substantial section of the Hebrew Bible is devoted to books identified by the Jewish community as Nevi'im, the Hebrew word for "prophets." It is a collection numbering seventeen books. English Bibles start this collection with the book of Isaiah and conclude it with Malachi. Some scholars divide the prophetic books into Major and Minor Prophets, which has to do with the greater length of some compared to others (e.g., Isaiah's long length compared to the shorter length of Malachi). Also, the books span a wide chronological period in Israel's history. The prophets write about Israel's experience in the years preceding, during, and after the exiles to Assyria and to Babylon, which is a period of time spanning the eighth through fourth centuries BC. Early drafts of the books may well have been composed during those very times and by the prophets whose names are attached to the books, but it should be remembered that the books may also have been edited in later centuries and that, in some cases, the form in which we have the books today was not reached until the second century BC.[1]

The two periods of exile profoundly shape the work of the prophets. By the end of the eighth century, the northern kingdom, Israel, had been overtaken by the Assyrian Empire, and many of the Jews then living in Israel were dispersed to other lands.[2] Some of the prophets preached to the Jews in the northern kingdom before the Assyrian Empire's assault. The prophets called out Israel for its sins and warned its residents of imminent divine judgment. Other prophets preached to Israel's community in the aftermath of that exile. One of the earliest prophets, Jonah, had even preached to the Assyrian rulers themselves, nearly a century before their takeover of Israel.

The second period of exile took place in the sixth century BC. The Babylonian Empire had replaced Assyria as the dominant world power. They conquered the southern kingdom of Judah and exiled its residents nearer to the center of its empire in Mesopotamia.[3] The bulk of the prophetic literature is directed to the Jews from Judah. As with the prophets in Israel, some of these prophets lived and preached in the years leading up to the Babylonian exile, denouncing the idolatry rampant in Judah. Other prophets wrote during the time of the exile itself, and a couple wrote to the Jews from Judah in the years following their release from captivity (late sixth through fourth centuries).

Periods Concerning Which the Prophets Wrote

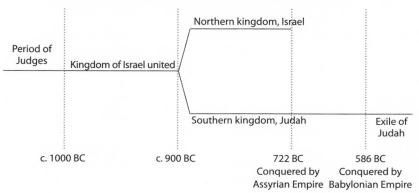

The reader of the Prophets should keep one important principle in mind. Prophetic books are far less about predictions of future events than their name implies. Instead, prophetic books are about the proclamation of God's word, God's law, and God's view of the world. While the prophets do, at times, provide insights into future events, they are far more interested in proclaiming God's judgment. They proclaim God's judgment on Israel,

Judah, and other nations for their sin, their rejection of God, their idolatry, their unjust behavior, and their lack of concern for those on society's margins. Their role as proclaimers of truth, of the law, of God's judgment, and even of God's faithfulness reveals that the prophets' real mission was to invite the Jews to seek God's forgiveness and mercy, to be reconciled with God, and to begin anew a relationship with God. For this reason we read the Prophets here with an interest in articulating what type of society God intended for Israel. This is done by identifying what they had to say about social life in Israel's past, its present, and its future. Throughout the chapter, "Israel" will be used as a reference to the Jewish community, writ large. Where particular reference to the northern kingdom called Israel is necessary, the text will indicate this.

The Prophets' View of Israel's Past

Whether or not an individual prophet wrote with the benefit of the hindsight of one or both of the two exiles (to Assyria and to Babylon), the prophets' view of Israel's past is decidedly dim. Israel had walked away from God, and the catalogs of its sins fell into two main categories: idolatry and injustice. The idolatry charge was both literal and figurative. Israel's kings and priests had produced idols made of gold, wood, or stone, and they had set up altars in honor of the gods of the people groups living within and nearby Israel's borders.[4] Figuratively, Israel had rejected Yahweh in favor of other gods. The people no longer followed the sacrificial system or any of the other rituals associated with acknowledging Yahweh's leadership of their community.

The Hebrew Prophetic Books

Proclaimed God's word to the people living in:

Israel	Judah	Other Nations	
Hosea	Isaiah	Jonah	Obadiah
Amos	Jeremiah	Nahum	(to Edom)
	Lamentations	(to Assyria)	
	Ezekiel		
	Daniel		
	Joel		
	Micah		
	Habakkuk		
	Zephaniah		
	Haggai		
	Zechariah		
	Malachi		

The sins of injustice were equally significant and numerous. The legal system was corrupt. Judges took bribes. Laws were not enforced or were enforced capriciously. The office of king was ineffectual. Centuries earlier, Samuel had warned Israel about the dangers of having a king. He predicted that the kings would take advantage of the people to secure for themselves wealth, power, and privilege. Yet the people dismissed Samuel's warnings, only to find out too late that the kings were even worse than he predicted. Israel's kings stole land, taxed mercilessly, maintained plural marriages, and led the nation into wars it could not win. Besides all of this, there were the countless social injustices: loaning money at interest, stealing from the poor, temple prostitution, rejection of prophets, and persecution of the righteous. All things considered, the destruction of Israel and its exiles to Assyria and Babylon came almost as a relief to the prophets. The torrent of sin eventually came to a just end.

Several key texts from the Prophets stand out in regard to Israel's sins of idolatry and injustice. One is the book of Lamentations. The author of the text is unknown. Some speculate that it was Jeremiah, since the book is a lament over the destruction of the southern kingdom of Judah at the hands of the Babylonians. The author asks his readers,

> Is it nothing to you, all you who pass by?
>   Look and see
> if there is any sorrow like my sorrow,
>   which was brought upon me,
> which the LORD inflicted
>   on the day of his fierce anger. (Lam. 1:12)

The destruction of Jerusalem was immense. Who, the author wonders, could possibly see the city and not wonder what the residents of that former city had done to deserve such complete destruction? Moreover, while it was true that Babylon carried out the destruction, the verse tells the reader that the destruction was really the work of God. Lamentations 2:1–8 offers vivid descriptions of this destruction: "He has bent his bow like an enemy" (2:4); "he has destroyed his tabernacle" (2:6); and "The Lord has scorned his altar" (2:7). Why did God do these things? It was because of the complete and thorough sin and corruption of the people of Israel. Several passages list these sins, including most notably Lam. 3:34–39 and 4:3–5. Israel mistreated their prisoners. They denied people their basic human rights. They deprived people of justice. They became heartless toward the cries of those who suffered. Income inequality was great, and food was not distributed equitably to all who had need.

In another key text, the prophet Amos speaks equally about these same concerns, writing about the people in Israel,

> They sell the righteous for silver,
>   and the needy for a pair of sandals—
> they who trample the head of the poor into the dust of the earth,
>   and push the afflicted out of the way;
> father and son go in to the same girl,
>   so that my holy name is profaned;
> they lay themselves down beside every altar
>   on garments taken in pledge;
> and in the house of their God they drink
>   wine bought with fines they imposed. (Amos 2:6–8)

If that is not enough, 2 Kings 17:16–27 adds the practices of magic, sorcery, and child sacrifice to the list of Israel's sins.

Little wonder that God was exasperated with Israel. What was supposed to be a model state of what it is like to live under God's reign and to proclaim God's love to the world had become a nation filled with people consumed by greed, grabbing whatever wealth they could get their hands on, even if that meant destroying the lives of the young, the weak, and the defenseless in the process. Yet books like Lamentations and Amos only begin to tell this story. Another key text is Ezekiel, likely composed by the prophet of that name. Ezekiel went to Babylon to explain to the Jews living there why God had allowed them to go into captivity in the first place. The book's forty-eight chapters deride Israel for its love of idols.[5] Living among the Canaanite peoples, Israel had grown to love the worship practices of their Canaanite neighbors. So they syncretized their own worship of Yahweh with the worship of the Canaanite peoples' gods. The people of Israel fervently worshiped gods made of wood, stone, and precious metals. They loved setting up poles in their town squares devoted to the goddess Ashtoreth. Consider what Ezekiel writes:

> Thus says the Lord GOD: This is Jerusalem; I have set her in the center of the nations, with countries all around her. But she has rebelled against my ordinances and my statutes, becoming more wicked than the nations and the countries all around her, rejecting my ordinances and not following my statutes. . . . Therefore, as I live, says the Lord GOD, surely, because you have defiled my sanctuary with all your detestable things and with all your abominations—therefore I will cut you down; my eye will not spare, and I will have no pity. (Ezek. 5:5–6, 11)

The obelisk, right, records affairs during the reign of the Assyrian King Shalmaneser III. The topmost section of the obelisk, shown in greater detail above, records the surrender of King Jehu to Shalmaneser. (Assyrian Hall of the British Museum)

This could not be less depressing to read than it was for Ezekiel to write. What is more, Ezekiel did more than just write about this—he also had to live it. Ezekiel 4:4–8 recounts that Ezekiel was told by God to lie down along a road for 390 days on his left side and then forty more days on his right side. Each of the 390 days symbolized a year of time in which God had put up with the northern kingdom of Israel's sins of injustice and idolatry. Each of the forty days symbolized the number of additional years God had to put up with southern kingdom of Judah's sins of injustice and idolatry. Israel and Judah's pursuit of wealth, pleasure, and power led to their increasing comfort with the practices of injustice. Their pursuit of living like the Canaanites around them, rather than being uniquely identified as God's treasured possession, led to their increasing comfort with the practices of idolatry. It sickened Ezekiel and the other prophets.

A fourth text to consider is Hosea. Like Ezekiel, Hosea was a prophet who had to reenact the experience of Israel's sins. God told Hosea to give his children names that reflected his relationship with Israel. Hosea named one of his children *Lo-ammi*, which means "Not my people"; he named another child *Lo-ruhamah*, which means "Not pitied"; and he named a third child *Jezreel*, which means "God sows," a sign that God was sowing (and would soon reap) punishment for the injustices created by Jehu, the king at that time. More astounding than these names for the children is that Hosea fathered them through a woman named Gomer, who was a local prostitute![6] God had ordered Hosea to take a prostitute for a wife as a symbol of how Israel had forsaken its first love, God, and had instead prostituted itself before the nations of the world. If that were not already enough, Gomer ran out on Hosea more than once to return to her prostitution lifestyle, and each time God told Hosea to find her and to redeem her. This act of redemption was meant to symbolize that God had repeatedly come to Israel's rescue, but it was to no avail. Israel had moved so far away from any love for God that even God's attempts at redemption were unwelcome.

Having said these things, it is not the case that the prophets write only about these depressing scenes in the history of Israel. They also recall God's past favor toward Israel, reminding Israel of how God delivered them from their enemies in previous generations. For example, the prophets recall God's deliverance of Israel from slavery in Egypt. They remember that God delivered the nation from their enemies among the Philistines, Moabites, Ammonites, and certain Canaanite groups. They remind Israel of God's forbearance with them during previous times of injustice and idolatry. According to the prophets, God's past faithfulness ought to spur the present generation to repent of their sin and to turn back to God. God's past faithfulness is proof to those in exile that he will continue to be faithful and that one day he will restore the ruined fortunes of Israel.

Isaiah 51 illustrates this more positive feature of prophetic proclamations regarding Israel's past. Recalling the deliverance from Egypt, Isaiah writes,

> Awake, awake, put on strength,
>   O arm of the LORD!
> Awake, as in days of old,
>   the generations of long ago!
> Was it not you who cut [Egypt] in pieces,
>   who pierced the dragon?

> Was it not you who dried up the sea,
> the waters of the great deep;
> who made the depths of the sea a way
> for the redeemed to cross over?
> So the ransomed of the LORD shall return,
> and come to Zion with singing. (Isa. 51:9–11)

God's faithfulness to Israel has not ended simply because Israel is now in exile. God's unfailing love persists. This is why Isaiah can ask God to waken, to restore the fortunes of Israel. This is why Isaiah can say to the Jewish people that one day,

> though your sins are like scarlet,
> they shall be like snow;
> though they are red like crimson,
> they shall become like wool.
> If you are willing and obedient,
> you shall eat the good of the land. (Isa. 1:18–19)

Something similar is found in Jer. 18:7–8: "At one moment I may declare concerning a nation or a kingdom that I will pluck up and break down and destroy it, but if that nation, concerning which I have spoken, turns from its evil, I will change my mind about the disaster that I intended to bring on it."[7] There is hopefulness in these texts. They reveal God's unremitting grace. God's work to restore order out of the chaos the Israelites have made of their lives remains pertinent.

The Prophets' View of Israel's Present

Prophets who wrote about Israel's present situation, whether before, during, or after an exile, alternatively express sadness over the current situation and encouragement for Israel to return to God so that it may enjoy a better future. Ezekiel found that the Jews living in exile had changed little about their view of God since being taken captive to Babylon (cf. Ezek. 8:9–14:23). Their exile had not (yet) produced the intended effect of calling them to repentance for their idolatry, so Ezekiel was sent to proclaim God's word to the people. Isaiah also laments that Israel continued to be unaware of just how destructive sin and injustice can be within a community. He writes,

> The earth dries up and withers,
> the world languishes and withers;
> the heavens languish together with the earth.

> The earth lies polluted
>   under its inhabitants;
> for they have transgressed laws,
>   violated the statutes,
>   broken the everlasting covenant.
> Therefore a curse devours the earth,
>   and its inhabitants suffer for their guilt;
> therefore the inhabitants of the earth dwindled,
>   and few people are left. (Isa. 24:4–6)

The people in Judah were so oblivious to the gravity of their injustices that they did not recognize the curse, the imminent destruction, encircling them. Indeed, as Isaiah writes in 32:9–15, the destruction was little more than one year away.

Amos found the same thing to be true a couple of centuries earlier, in the northern kingdom of Israel. The people were so oblivious to their own sins that Amos felt it necessary to begin his message with proclamations of God's judgment on all the nations around them (cf. 1:3–2:5).[8] Hearing that God was upset with Damascus, Gaza, Tyre, Edom, Ammon, Moab, and even Judah would have caused his audience in Israel to perk up. News of God's anger at Israel's enemies, including Israel's own kinfolk south of them in Judah, would have been welcome news. But Amos does that only to soften up his audience. His real message is God's judgment on Israel. He knew they would not listen to him unless he got their attention in this way first.

The prophets did not speak into a world that was interested in what they had to say. This makes sense. If everything is going well, there should be no need for a prophet. Yet things were rarely going well. So some of the prophets weep or otherwise lament over what they see in the Jewish communities of their day (cf. Mic. 1:8; Hab. 1:2). When the people did not listen, at least one prophet, Micah, turned to proclaim God's word to the mountains and other features of the natural landscape (Mic. 6:1–2). Through the voices of the prophets, God repeatedly offers forgiveness and mercy, but these entreaties are largely ignored (Isa. 42; 44:1–5; 55).

Still, at least two prophets were able to inspire behavioral changes in Israel and Judah. The prophets Jonah and Zephaniah experienced some notable success. Jonah was sent to Assyria to call the Assyrians to repentance in order that they might avoid an impending judgment from God. Much to Jonah's frustration, they apparently did just that. The Assyrians engaged in a lengthy period of penance and repented of their idolatrous ways. Jonah was so upset over God's grace and mercy toward the Assyrians that he spent days pouting about it outside the Assyrian capital, Nineveh.[9] Zephaniah, a great-great-grandson of King Hezekiah (of Judah), proclaimed a call to repentance in Judah in order to avoid destruction. Soon thereafter, the young king Josiah took charge of Judah. He quickly moved to tear down his father's and his grandfather's altars dedicated to false gods, and he ended reprehensible worship practices such as prostitution and child sacrifices. Josiah also reinstated celebration of the religious festivals proscribed in the Torah, and he restored the use of the temple to worship of Yahweh (2 Kings 22–23). Yet in the case of both Jonah and Zephaniah, their "successes" were short-lived. Assyria continued to exist long enough to later destroy Jonah's own people in the northern kingdom of Israel. King Josiah's reforms staved off God's judgment for only a short period. The people in Judah were eventually rounded up by the Babylonians, which Zephaniah initially predicted (Zeph. 1).

The Prophets' View of Israel's Future

In contrast to the prophets' dim view of Israel's past and present, their view of Israel's future is largely positive. They look ahead and see several reasons for measured optimism. One of those reasons is the restoration of Jerusalem and a return of Jews from their exile to their homeland. The book of Isaiah addresses this at length in several passages (cf. chaps. 25–27; 44–45; 52; 54). At one point the prophet urges,

> Awake, awake,
>   put on your strength, O Zion!
> Put on your beautiful garments,
>   O Jerusalem, the holy city;
> for the uncircumcised and the unclean
> shall enter you no more. Shake yourself from the dust, rise up,
>   O captive Jerusalem;
> loose the bonds from your neck,
>   O captive daughter Zion! (Isa. 52:1–2)

The text also records the sense of relief that will come over the people when this happens:

> Then the Lord GOD will wipe away the tears from all faces,
>   and the disgrace of his people he will take away from all the earth,
>   for the LORD has spoken. (Isa. 25:8)

The author of Lamentations is equally encouraged by the future restoration when he writes,

> The steadfast love of the LORD never ceases,
>   his mercies never come to an end. . . .
> For the LORD will not
>   reject forever.
> Although he causes grief, he will have compassion
>   according to the abundance of his steadfast love. (Lam. 3:22, 31–32)

More vividly, Ezekiel crafts his message of restoration around the fascinating image of a valley of dry bones brought back to life.

> Then he said to me, "Mortal, these bones are the whole house of Israel. They say, 'Our bones are dried up, and our hope is lost; we are cut off completely.' Therefore prophesy, and say to them, Thus says the LORD God: I am going to open your graves, and bring you up from your graves, O my people; and I will bring you back to the land of Israel. And you shall know that I am the LORD, when I open your graves, and bring you up from your graves, O my people. I will put my spirit within you, and you shall live, and I will place you on your own soil; then you shall know that I, the LORD, have spoken and will act, says the LORD." (Ezek. 37:11–14)

Despite the devastation wrought on the kingdoms of Israel and Judah by foreign nations, the prophets anticipate that God will restore the fortunes of his people. They will not remain in exile forever. The God known to the prophets restores order from the chaos of life in exile.

With the restoration of the Jewish homeland, the prophets also looked ahead and saw that God would establish a new covenant with his people.[10] The exile of

Inspired by the resurrection image of Ezek. 37, the Capela dos Ossos (Chapel of Bones) in Évora, Portugal, is one of many churches around the world that prominently display "dry bones."

Judah to Babylon concluded the long but troubled history of this independent Jewish state. It was supposed to have been governed by a law code given to the Israelites through Moses when they left Egypt, but that law code no longer resonated with the experience of life in exile. There was no society to organize in the way the legal code envisioned. There was no land to manage in accordance with the legal codes. There was no temple to maintain the sacrificial system. So prophets like Jeremiah proclaimed that a day would come in which that older code would no longer govern the people's relationship with God. A new covenant would be established between God and his people. Jeremiah writes,

> The days are surely coming, says the LORD, when I will make a new covenant with the house of Israel and the house of Judah. It will not be like the covenant that I made with their ancestors when I took them by the hand to bring them out of the land of Egypt—a covenant that they broke, though I was their husband, says the LORD. But this is the covenant that I will make with the house of Israel after those days, says the LORD: I will put my law within them, and I will write it on their hearts; and I will be their God, and they shall be my people. (Jer. 31:31–33)

Notice that the promised new covenant will not be like the covenant made with those who came out of Egypt. That former covenant was not broken by God when he allowed the Jews to be swept off into exile; it was broken by the Israelites countless times in the centuries leading up to their exile. That God is willing to start over—and not only that, but to start over with a covenant that engraves itself on the conscience of each person—attests to God's unfailing love for his people.

Connected to the establishment of a new covenant, some of the prophets also foresaw the work of an "anointed one," a Messiah.[11] This Messiah would form the people into a new nation and thereby reunite the people with God. Isaiah's prediction of a young woman who will give birth to a son (Isa. 7:14) is later tied to the story of Jesus in Matthew's Gospel (Matt. 1:23). Isaiah 9 proclaims the eventual arrival of someone from Galilee who will bring light to the darkness, who will be called by the people "Wonderful Counselor, Mighty God, Everlasting Father, Prince of Peace" (v. 6). Isaiah also says this person will restore the kingdom and the throne of David and will restore peace to the world. Likewise, the prophet Micah foresees a person born in Bethlehem who will rule over Israel. Micah writes,

> And he shall stand and feed his flock in the strength of the LORD,
>   in the majesty of the name of the LORD his God.

> And they shall live secure, for now he shall be great
>   to the ends of the earth;
> and he shall be the one of peace. (Mic. 5:4–5)

Finally, this anticipation of a Messiah who would restore the kingdom and with that also restore the people's relationship with God corresponds to several prophets' expectation of a "kingdom of righteousness" to be established on the earth (cf. Isa. 32; Ezek. 37–48; Dan. 9:24). While the details of so much of this remained murky to the prophets and their audiences alike, it was nevertheless clear that the God of refuge and hope was planning the rescue of Israel even before the Israelites knew they needed to be rescued.

Thus the language in the Prophets about the restoration of Jerusalem, the establishment of a new covenant, the emergence of a Messiah, and the anticipation of a new creation combine to instruct readers about the person and the character of God. The God known to the Hebrew prophets wants to restore order out of the chaos in Israel. The prophets proclaim a God who hears his people's cries, who reaches out to them in compassion, who offers them an olive branch of mercy and peace, and who invites them back into a relationship with him. The prophets testify to a God of limitless grace, and that grace always seeks to restore order to the lives of people and of nations.

Summary

Idolatry and injustice were rampant in the divided kingdoms of Israel and Judah. God spoke through prophets throughout these centuries to warn the people to turn from their sinful ways. Only after repeated rejections of God and of the proclamations of God's words by the prophets did God allow Israel, and then Judah, to be taken captive by enemy nations. Yet the exiles of Israel and Judah were not the end of the story. In every case, the prophets looked ahead to a day when God would restore the fortunes of his people. God was going to restore order out of the chaos that Israel and Judah had made of the lives of their people. God's love, mercy, and compassion remained unfailing. Still, the prophets remind Christian social ethicists today that God treats the sin of injustice more seriously than we tend to treat it. The plight of the poor and those suffering on the margins of society was so important to God that he was willing to humiliate an entire nation (his treasured possession) to reveal it. Working for justice, then, is caring about the people whom God cares about. And, just like the prophets did, hope must be maintained even in the midst of this difficult work.

Main Points of the Chapter

» An alarming number of Israelites practiced social *injustice* by going out of their way to harm the poor and those on the margins of society.

» This injustice, combined with idolatry, marked the communities of Israel despite God's repeated attempts to reach out to the people through the prophets.

» No amount of prior acts of injustice can remove one from God's love. The opportunity for repentance is always available.

» Work for justice must be marked by a hopeful expectation that God will eventually restore order.

4

Jesus in the New Testament

Learning Outcomes for This Chapter

» Summarize features of Jesus's life that reveal how he modeled love for the people and the things that God loves.

» Explore how Jesus challenged the sinful and repressive social structures of his day.

» Evaluate ways in which Jesus's followers may respond to his challenge to selflessly love whom God loves and to disrupt the privileges of those in power.

Naturally, the Christian tradition has been most profoundly shaped by the life, the stories, and the redemptive work of Jesus. This is no less true for the field of social ethics than it is for systematic, biblical, and historical theology. Every aspect of Jesus's life—his birth, childhood, years of itinerant ministry, death, and resurrection—deepens our insights into the dignity of persons, the common good, justice, solidarity, subsidiarity, and other socioethical themes. Jesus invited his followers to think in entirely new ways about how they may relate to God, how they ought to live in harmony with others, and how social structures may be reconfigured in order to facilitate the furtherance of both.

Most scholars agree that Jesus was born sometime during the year 4 or 5 BC. His death and subsequent resurrection occurred around AD 30.[1] He spent nearly all of those thirty-four or thirty-five years within a few miles' radius of the Sea of Galilee, which was in a small, poor, and insignificant region of the Roman

Empire known as Galilee. He was born during the time of the Caesars and their appointed rulers in each province. Jesus's life overlapped the rule of Herod the Great and then Herod's four sons, including especially Herod Antipas, tetrarch of Galilee (west of that sea) and Perea (east of the Jordan River), and Herod Philip, tetrarch of Batanea and other districts northeast of the Sea of Galilee. Ostensibly, the Herodians were Jewish rulers over a predominantly Jewish people. Yet they were thoroughly corrupt, and so were the various religious officials they appointed to assist them in controlling the populations of Judea and Galilee.[2] Amid this corruption, sometime around AD 27, Jesus left his work in carpentry and began an itinerant ministry of teaching, healing, and redemption. It should not be surprising that his ministry included sustained attacks on the political and economic status quo of that region.

The poor and oppressed residents of Judea and Galilee were receptive to the voices of various people who came along inciting revolt, preaching nationalism, or otherwise challenging the sinful economic and political structures. Initially Jesus was viewed in the same way as those other "messiahs."[3] Yet when asked by his followers whether revolt, militarism, or nationalism was his plan, he outright rejected those ideas. Jesus offered his followers an entirely different way to relate to the world around them. His was a radical path: his followers would be asked to make incredible sacrifices for the sake of an admittedly slower but perhaps surer and more thorough transformation of the world and its affairs. Jesus's path was to love whom God loved and to challenge what God despised.

Some Perspective about Jesus

The principal New Testament texts for a study of Jesus's life are known as Gospels, or "good news" texts. There are four Gospels in the New Testament, identified by the names of their reputed authors, which are Matthew, Mark, Luke, and John.[4] Each of them was written decades after Jesus's own lifetime. The earliest, Mark's Gospel, dates to the 50s AD; John's Gospel, the latest, dates to the 90s AD. This means that, even though the Gospels appear first in the New Testament collection of books, they actually were written much later than most of the other literature in the New Testament.[5] This is significant, since it means that Paul, for example, who wrote many of the other New Testament texts and whose conversion took place in the mid-30s AD (i.e., only a few years after Jesus's lifetime), is a witness to the profound impact that the stories about Jesus's life were having even before those stories were ever written down.

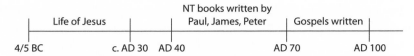

In the New Testament, the Gospels appear first, yet they are among the last books to be written. Thus much of what the earliest Christian community understood and believed about the person and work of Jesus may be gleaned from other New Testament writings.

There are at least two important consequences of this. First, of course, is that some of what Christians want to glean from Jesus's life for how to love whom God loves and how to challenge what God despises can be found in the experiences of Jesus's followers in the decades between the time of his life and the time when the Gospels were composed. Second, and arguably more important, is that in those other texts—particularly Paul's letters to Philippi (Phil. 2:1–11) and to Colossae (Col. 1:1–20)—Christian readers are taught that Jesus was not only a human person, but that he was also God. As later productions, then, the New Testament Gospels have been and continue to be read by Christians as testimonies to God taking on human flesh. Because of his human nature, Jesus knew what it meant to eat, sleep, weep, poop (yes, even this), and die. Because of his divine nature, Jesus could forgive people of their sins, heal diseases, tame the natural elements, multiply food, and resurrect people from the dead.

The humanity and the divinity so united in Jesus that what we witness in the stories about his life are the stories of God incarnate, a God-Man, if you will, whose humanity has been divinized. To wit, what Jesus offers his followers is the opportunity for the same thing to happen to them. The Christian life of faith facilitates the indwelling of God's Spirit, which produces in Jesus's followers something that Paul in Romans calls "Christlikeness." In other words, if Jesus could divinize his humanity, then surely he can divinize the humanity of others who are similarly indwelled by God. There is a difference, of course, in that Jesus's divinity was natural to him. He was God by nature. Jesus's followers' experience of divinity is, as Paul says in Eph. 1:5 and Rom. 8:14–17, by adoption.

Recognizing these things, the following survey of what may be gleaned from Jesus's life for our understanding of social ethics emerges from witnessing not just how a human person named Jesus lived but also how God chose to live among us. That is to say, when we see how Jesus loves, we are witnessing how God loves. When we see Jesus weeping with those mourning the death of a friend, we witness God expressing his deep sadness at the pain so many people in this world experience. And when we see Jesus reproving hypocritical leaders and opposing the repressive political and economic structures of his day, we witness God expressing his disdain for these same things. In short, the Gospels tell us far more than they let on, because Christians read them with the insight gained from other New Testament literature.

There is one further matter to keep in mind. The Gospels overlook the vast majority of Jesus's life. From his childhood there is mention of a visit of wise men to see him while he is still an infant (Matt. 2:1–12). We are told of his flight to Egypt as a toddler (Matt. 2:13–18). We are told he grew up in Nazareth and that he visited Jerusalem on a regular basis for festivals (Matt. 2:23; Luke 2:41). Luke's Gospel records a story of how Jesus, at age twelve during one of the Jerusalem visits, did not travel home with his family but stayed behind in Jerusalem to talk with the religious leaders in the temple (Luke 2:42–52). Finally, we are told that his earthly father Joseph worked as a carpenter (Greek *tektōn*; Matt. 13:55), and it is reasonable to conclude that Jesus grew up learning this trade as well. Yet outside these bits of information we know little else. More than a few Christian texts of the second and later centuries sought to fill in the gaps with imagined stories and events. Some are quite entertaining (such as the *Infancy Gospel of Thomas*), but they offer little helpful insight. Instead, the New Testament writers considered Jesus's three years of public ministry, the last three years of his earthly life, to be the most worthy of publication. Even more to the point, the writers devoted greatest attention to just the final few weeks of Jesus's life. Stories about Jesus's three years of public ministry set the stage for his final weeks. So we must be content to restrict our gleaning mostly to the field of material about Jesus's later years rather than the whole of his life. Still, as generations of later Christians have shown, there is profit enough in this material to move forward.

Loving Those Whom God Loves

In recounting Jesus's life, the Gospels reveal much about how one might love those who are loved by God. Even before Jesus was conceived in Mary's womb, we are confronted with the testimony of Mary to the remarkable things her future son will teach us. Luke 1 records a song composed by Mary at that time.[6] Drawing on the prophets, Mary exclaims,

> His mercy is for those who fear
>   him from generation to generation.
> He has shown strength with his arm;
>   he has scattered the proud in the thoughts of their hearts.

He has brought down the powerful from their thrones,
    and lifted up the lowly;
he has filled the hungry with good things,
    and sent the rich away empty.
He has helped his servant Israel,
    in remembrance of his mercy. (Luke 1:50–54)

Beware to those with power and wealth who use their resources to oppress others. Mary says Jesus is coming to bring such people down. Justice is about to be restored to the earth. God's mercy is coming to the righteous. God's love for the lowly and the hungry is about to be more fully expressed. In these few lines Mary provides a nice summary of what is found throughout the Gospel stories.

Indeed, the birth of Jesus provides further insight into what it means to love what God loves. Details of the birth narrative are well-known. Mary gave birth to Jesus in Bethlehem with the aid of her husband, Joseph. Presumably some animals were there. Shepherds visited the baby soon after his birth. Wise men arrived some time later. All of this is dutifully recorded in Matthew and Luke's Gospels. What is left unstated in the Gospels is the significance of God having been born in the first place. Imagine God in the form of a zygote!

Church of the Nativity in Bethlehem, which was built over the supposed grotto in which Jesus was born.

Imagine God taking on human shape in Mary's womb. Genesis 1 affirms the dignity of human beings by stating that they are made in God's likeness, but now we have living proof of God's great love, compassion, and mercy toward the human species. God himself chose to become human. There is something deeply moving about entering into a relationship with a God who understands what it means to struggle through childhood, to confront family conflict, to practice a trade, to make and to lose friends, to suffer persecution, and to experience death. Yet even if we have none of these other stories about Jesus's life, we have enough proof of our inherent dignity before God simply in the knowledge that God chose to be born a human too.[7]

Next, Jesus's later, public ministry offers us numerous opportunities to discover how one might love those whom God loves. Recall from chapter 1 that God brings order out of chaos and that this ordering of the world's affairs is called "good." The heavens are good. The earth is good. Plants are good. Animals are good. Humans are good. All creation is "very good." Yet Jesus met many people whose experience of life in this world is *not good*. Such difficulty is not what God intended. Humans are supposed to revel in the goodness of this world, but many have found life here too difficult, too painful, too stressful, and just not good. If left too long in this spiral of hopelessness, they will come to reject that a God even exists—certainly not a good God.

These were the people whom Jesus sought out. These are the people whom God still seeks out. Consider a few examples. In John 4, while traveling northward from Judea to his home region of Galilee, Jesus goes through the region of Samaria. The travel makes him thirsty. He stops by a well, and it just so happens that a woman, whose experience of life in this world has been not good, comes to the well at the same time. Speaking in a gentle yet corrective way, Jesus invites her to experience a different type of life in this world. Not only does he invite her to walk away from her destructive cycles of adultery; he also invites her to establish a relationship with God. He tells her that God is worshiped not solely in Jerusalem, which is far from her land, but that God is near to every person and may be worshiped in one's heart—in spirit and in truth. Even people who have long engaged in activities unbecoming to their divine, image-bearing design can experience the joy of a relationship with God.

Jesus loves spending time with people like this woman. While walking through the town of Jericho, he seeks out the town's tax collector, Zacchaeus (Luke 19:1–10). Zacchaeus needs to climb a sycamore tree to peer over the crowd and see Jesus, but the Gospel narrative tells us that Jesus stops at the tree to be sure to meet him (Luke 19:5). Jesus wants to spend his day and to have a meal with this much-hated man. Zacchaeus is hated because he represents everything sinful about the extortionate practices of Roman-era tax

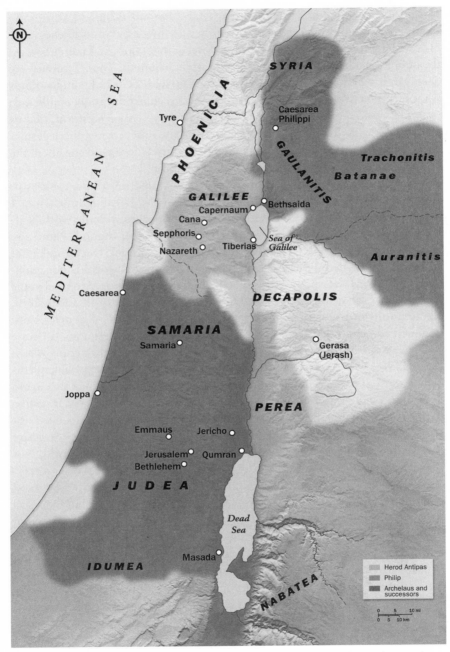

Map of the region in which Jesus traveled during his ministry years. It also marks off the regions overseen by Herod the Great and then by his sons.

collectors.[8] He has grown rich from these practices, but, as often the case, the riches have left him friendless and with a bankrupt soul. One can imagine the town gossip all afternoon as people learn with whom Jesus has chosen to spend his day. Yet the very fact that this by-then widely regarded rabbi would deign to enter Zacchaeus's house leads Zacchaeus to propose an immediate renouncement of his wicked ways. Friendless Zacchaeus has a friend in God. Zacchaeus will not be the same again. Jesus tells the gathered crowd, "Today salvation has come to this house" (Luke 19:9). What a change in fortunes for Zacchaeus, and all because God seeks him out.

Jesus's selection of twelve men to be his close disciples also reflects his pattern of seeking out those whose experience of life in this world had been not good. One disciple was a tax collector like Zacchaeus. Most of the rest were fishermen, a trade that provided little more than a subsistence income.[9] For reasons unknown to everyone, Jesus plucked these men out of their difficult lives, and he offered them new hope in God and in what God intended to do in this world. He then turned over to these rough-hewn men the task of transforming an entire planet with the knowledge of God's deep love and compassion for the human race. Jesus's actions confirm that instilling new and vibrant life in people stuck in dead-end lives is precisely what God enjoys doing.

Something similar happened when a woman allegedly caught in an adulterous act was brought before Jesus for condemnation (John 7:53–8:11).[10] Her accusers were ready to stone her, but again, doing things the way no one else would expect, Jesus never directly answered them. Instead, he bent down to the ground to write something in the dust. Then he invited anyone who is sinless to throw the first stone, and he again bent to write with his finger. Remarkable! What Jesus wrote has been the subject of much speculation.[11] It seems

Voted "Least Likely to Succeed"?

Perhaps some graduating seniors at American high schools still participate in a voting process at the end of their school year. They vote to determine which one of their fellow seniors is most likely to succeed, or most likely to become rich, or most likely to cure cancer, and so on. Can you imagine such a graduating class voting one of their fellow students *least* likely to succeed? The type of people Jesus sought were those who would have won such an unfortunate award. It is shocking when one stops to consider just how much trust Jesus placed in his motley crew of disciples and other followers to carry forward his mission. They were, indeed, a most unlikely bunch.

that individuals bend to the ground amid a raucous crowd only when they want to get away from the noise of the crowd for some perspective. Perhaps Jesus was wondering just how many people in the temple court besides this woman really were deserving of death by stoning: based on their sin-filled lives, every one of them; based on the mercy of God that Jesus had come to reveal, none of them. Once the area cleared of all accusers, Jesus simply turned to the woman and offered words of incredible hope, forgiveness, and redemption: "Neither do I condemn you." Then, so that she might enjoy a better relationship with God in the future, he continued, "Go your way, and from now on do not sin again" (John 8:11).

One could continue with more stories, including not a few of Jesus's parables, in which Jesus's invitation for us to love the people whom God loves continues to beckon. We could examine Jesus's encounter with the gentile woman who begs to have her daughter healed (Matt. 15:21–28), or any of the several healing stories told in the Gospels (cf. Mark 5; 7:31–37; 8:22–26; 9:14–29; 10:46–52). We could consider the love repaid to the woman who anointed Jesus with perfume in the days leading up to his crucifixion (Matt. 26:6–13). We could study Jesus's forgiveness of Peter for having denied him three times during the trial (Luke 22:54–62; cf. John 21:15–19). These and other accounts would merely continue to confirm for us that God desperately loves those who have fallen to the margins of society, those who are struggling, those whose experience of life in this world has been not good. To follow the way of Jesus is to love such as these.

Challenging What God Despises

Jesus's story is not all about acts of love, mercy, and compassion. Such acts are balanced with sustained attacks on the hypocrisy of the religious leaders. The leaders are identified in the Gospels by the titles Pharisees, Sadducees, and scribes.[12] When some Pharisees accuse Jesus of being demon possessed after he exorcises a man, Jesus responds, "Then the kingdom of God has already overtaken you" (Matt. 12:28 NET). Once Jesus calls the religious leaders "whitewashed tombs" (Matt. 23:27), and he refers to them as a "brood of vipers" destined for hell (Matt. 23:33). Clearly Jesus had not read books about how to win friends and influence people. Moreover, by critiquing the leaders, Jesus is also challenging the repressive religious, political, and economic social structures they maintained to hold back the common people.

Jesus's problems with the religious leaders were extensive. First, they oppressed God's people with far more laws than God had intended. On the

Who Were the Religious Leaders Jesus Opposed?

Pharisees A political-religious group that included teachers of the "oral law"; worked to maintain the synagogue communities; participated in the Jewish ruling council known as the Sanhedrin

Sadducees A political-religious group that included most of the priests and those of the ruling class; worked to maintain the temple and its cult; participated in the Sanhedrin

Scribes Committed to preserving the Torah in written form and teaching it to others; generally were members of the Pharisee group, but distinct from them professionally

one hand, the religious leaders believed that one reason Israel had suffered so much in its past was its infidelity to the Mosaic law code. To prevent future disaster, the religious leaders reasoned that additional laws should be crafted: if followed, they would ensure that no one came close to breaking any of the laws contained in the Mosaic law code. So they developed a tradition of oral law that surrounded and protected the Mosaic law code. One has to give these religious leaders credit for wanting to protect Israel's fidelity to God. Unfortunately, on the other hand, they turned an already burdensome Mosaic law code (with its more than 600 laws) into something far more burdensome (the oral law may have included as many as 2,000 additional regulations). Who would love a God who seemed to oblige obedience to so many rules, regulations, and policies? Who would love a God who could easily find so much fault in every person? According to Jesus, no one would love that kind of God.

So what did Jesus do? He dismantled the entire system. He replaced it with two things that were far more manageable and, for that matter, far more attractive to people. First, Jesus reduced the entire legal code to just two laws: love God, and love your neighbor as yourself. This sums up the entire Law and the Prophets, according to Jesus (Matt. 22:37–40). With this simple statement, Jesus dispensed with the entire legal system propped up by the religious leaders. Gone were the thousands of laws. Gone was the need for religious leaders to police obedience to those laws. Gone was the sense of depression among fallible people who knew they could never measure up. Welcomed in was a renewed joy of being in relationship with God.

In addition to dramatically reducing the number of legal burdens, Jesus did something else that was critically important. He taught people that following God's laws was less about external behavior and more about the motives and the condition of one's heart. Jesus taught this new principle in his Sermon on the Mount (Matt. 5–7; Luke 6). Consider the following words of Jesus:

> You have heard that it was said to those of ancient times, "You shall not murder"; and "whoever murders shall be liable to judgment." But I say to you that if you are angry with a brother or sister, you will be liable to judgment. . . .

> You have heard that it was said, "You shall not commit adultery." But I say to you that everyone who looks at a woman with lust has already committed adultery with her in his heart. . . .

> It was also said, "Whoever divorces his wife, let him give her a certificate of divorce." But I say to you that anyone who divorces his wife, except on the ground of unchastity, causes her to commit adultery; and whoever marries a divorced woman commits adultery.

> Again, you have heard that it was said to those of ancient times, "You shall not swear falsely, but carry out the vows you have made to the Lord." But I say to you, Do not swear at all, either by heaven, for it is the throne of God, or by the earth, for it is his footstool, or by Jerusalem, for it is the city of the great King. . . .

> You have heard that it was said, "An eye for an eye and a tooth for a tooth." But I say to you, Do not resist an evildoer. But if anyone strikes you on the right cheek, turn the other also. . . . (Matt. 5:21–42)

Notice the repeated refrain, "You have heard . . . But I say . . ." Jesus has flipped on its head the old way of thinking about how a relationship with God works. Jesus had a different attitude in mind when it came to living righteously before God. You follow the law against murder simply by refraining from harboring anger toward other people. You follow the law against adultery by refraining from lustful thoughts. You follow the law against not fulfilling one's vows by simply not swearing at all. So, to Jesus, life is not about following the letter of the many laws but about living according to the spirit of those laws. Refraining from anger, from lust, and from swearing is about setting one's heart in the right place—toward loving God and toward loving one's neighbor. In so doing, obedience to the law code takes care of itself.

Another area in which the religious leaders oppressed the common people was in the money exchanging and animal selling they did in the temple courts

Temple coin, front and back, from the Roman era.

during festival seasons. This was particularly insidious behavior since it preyed on the poorest and most vulnerable members of the Jewish community. One aspect of the celebration of religious festivals was giving an offering to God at the temple or sacrificing an animal. The religious leaders would sell the appropriate animal to festivalgoers who did not bring one with them, or for those who did bring their own animal, the leaders would inspect the animal to determine if it was appropriate. Too often, it seemed, festivalgoers were told that their animal was defective and that they needed to buy one of the animals for sale in the temple courts. Invariably this need to purchase a "better" animal proved to be more expensive to festivalgoers than the cost of bringing their own animal.

And there is more. In addition to obliging festivalgoers to buy an "approved" animal from the temple courts, the religious leaders obliged them to purchase the animals with a temple currency different from their regular, everyday Roman currency. Fortunately, those religious leaders were also running a money-exchange desk to facilitate this transaction. Unfortunately, since they were the sole distributors of temple currency, they had little incentive to maintain reasonable exchange rates. Indeed, the whole festival system was ripe for corruption.

What made this scene doubly tragic was that the festivals were established to remind the Jewish community of God's favor toward them. They were either a reminder of some historical event in which God had rescued them or a celebration of God's provision during a harvest season. So the festivalgoer was supposed to find the festivals to be joyful events. Yet it would have been rather hard to find joy in a festival when one was worried about breaking one of the thousands of laws, or not having just the right animal, or not having enough money to buy that right animal, or not having the right kind of money in the first place. Worship of God had become more burdensome than joyful. So Jesus showed his followers that God despised such practices. Jesus walked into the temple courts during one of those festivals and turned over the tables of the money changers. He took a whip and drove out the "approved" animals from their pens. He declared that the religious leaders had turned God's house into a den of thieves (Matt. 21:13; Mark 11:17; Luke 19:46). What a sight that must have been.

Principal Jewish Festivals

Time of Year	Feast	Scripture Reference(s)
March/April	Passover/Feast of Unleavened Bread	Exod. 12:3–20
May/June	Pentecost	Exod. 23:16; 34:22
September/ October	Rosh Hashanah Day of Atonement Feast of Tabernacles/Feast of Booths	Num. 29:11 Lev. 23:26–31 Lev. 23:34
November/ December	Hanukkah/Feast of Lights	1 Macc. 4
February/March	Purim	Esther 9

A third problem Jesus had with the religious leaders was their flat-out hypocrisy. It was bad enough that they oppressed others with their laws and oppressed festivalgoers (esp. poor folks) with their extortionate monetary practices. Even worse was that they also did not live what they preached. Consider this critique by Jesus:

> Then Jesus said to the crowds and to his disciples, "The scribes and the Pharisees sit on Moses' seat; therefore, do whatever they teach you and follow it; but do not do as they do, for they do not practice what they teach. They tie up heavy burdens, hard to bear, and lay them on the shoulders of others; but they themselves are unwilling to lift a finger to move them. They do all their deeds to be seen by others; for they make their phylacteries broad and their fringes long. They love to have the place of honor at banquets and the best seats in the synagogues, and to be greeted with respect in the marketplaces, and to have people call them rabbi. . . . All who exalt themselves will be humbled, and all who humble themselves will be exalted.
>
> "But woe to you, scribes and Pharisees, hypocrites! For you lock people out of the kingdom of heaven. For you do not go in yourselves, and when others are going in, you stop them. Woe to you, scribes and Pharisees, hypocrites! For you cross sea and land to make a single convert, and you make the new convert twice as much a child of hell as yourselves." (Matt. 23:1–7, 12–15)

This is just the start. In the next several verses of this passage, Jesus calls the religious leaders hypocrites, fools, or blind guides at least ten more times. These leaders held themselves up as examples of following God's law, but their hearts were far from God and from caring about what God loves. They were destroying people's love for God. They had to be opposed, so Jesus modeled for his followers how to oppose such people.

Kingdom of God

Loving what God loves and despising what God despises are connected to Jesus's remarkable teaching on another subject. The first words out of Jesus's mouth in Mark's Gospel are "The time is fulfilled, and the kingdom of God has come near; repent, and believe in the good news" (1:15). Mark's Gospel is here picking up on language suggested to David in 2 Sam. 7. David was told that a day would eventually come when an eternal kingdom of perpetual peace would be established, and on the throne of that kingdom would sit one of David's descendants. This is why Matt. 1 connects Jesus's family tree to the line of David. The "kingdom of God" language in the Gospels also picks up on messianic expectations in the prophets (discussed in chap. 3). The people of God need healing. They need a protector. This is why the book of Hebrews draws connections between Jesus and the Old Testament offices of priest and king. This new kingdom has come, demonstrably if not yet fully, in the life, ministry, and work of Jesus.

Just how Jesus proclaims his own role in the establishment of this kingdom is what is most striking of all. Recall that Jesus made a point of connecting with people whose experience of life in this world was not good. They need healing. They need to feel protected. They need a king, a benefactor who will take care of them. Thus the experience of God's grace, mercy, and compassion for the lowly, the hungry, the poor, and the outcast is constitutive of this kingdom of God. When Jesus decried injustice, he was, bit by bit, proclaiming a kingdom of justice. Every time Jesus healed a child, man, or woman, he revealed the kingdom of God to be a place free from suffering. Every time Jesus drove out a demon, he revealed the kingdom to be a place free from deception. Every time Jesus forgave people their sins, he revealed the kingdom to be a place of peace with God. When Jesus raised someone from the dead, and when he rose from the dead himself, he revealed the kingdom to be a place of eternal life.

Consider Jesus's encounter with the centurion (Matt. 8:5–13). Here is a Roman military official, a gentile, who comes to Jesus and asks for his servant to be healed of a disease. Jesus told the centurion he would visit the sick servant at his bedside, but the centurion stopped him and declared his belief that Jesus could heal the servant merely with a word. Matthew writes that "Jesus was astonished" (8:10 AT). Imagine! God incarnate was astonished. Consider the type of faith the centurion must have had in the power and authority of Jesus. With nothing more than a word, Jesus could heal people he did not even see or touch. This is the type of king who reigns over the kingdom of God. The centurion was in awe of this power. Jesus was in shock that someone outside the Jewish community could see it. Moreover, Jesus tells the crowd witnessing the event that the centurion's belief is proof that the kingdom of God is open to people from every corner of the world. "Many will come from the east and the west, and will take their places at the feast with Abraham, Isaac and Jacob in the kingdom of heaven," Jesus tells them (Matt. 8:11 NIV). The kingdom of God is big enough to include everyone who wants to be there.

Yet Jesus did not only express the kingdom of God in the tangible ways of healing, exorcising, forgiving, and raising people from the dead; he also took advantage of several occasions to speak about the kingdom of God. He told a series of parables about it in Matt. 13 and 25. These parables suggest that the kingdom is a mystery being revealed only to those who are faithful (Matt. 13:1–23). The kingdom helps to distinguish those who are faithful from those who are unfaithful to God (Matt. 13:24–30). The kingdom is something that slowly, gradually builds until—finally!—it consumes the entire world (i.e., like yeast in dough; Matt. 13:31–33). The kingdom is something for which all people ought to be making themselves ready by remaining faithful to God (Matt. 25:1–13).

If the reader of Matthew had still not yet grasped the point of these stories and parables, a rather fine point on the kingdom is provided in Matt. 25:31–46. Jesus informs his followers that their behavior toward people with needs initiates one or another of two eternal consequences: eternal life or eternal death. The way that leads to eternal life includes compassion-filled action to alleviate the suffering of the poor, the hungry, the naked, and the imprisoned. Why? Because it is in the lives of such people that we see both the suffering of Jesus and the cause of justice for which he suffered.

Summary

In Jesus's story, we discover the priorities of social ethics. First, social ethics requires us to love human life itself. God so loved what he had created that he took on, of all things, human flesh. The incarnation itself is a testament to God's special love and care for humans. This is why the first principle in social ethics is human dignity, a topic to which we will return in chapter 11. Second, social ethics prompts Christians to cultivate a love for those whom God specially loves. Because the creation, so very much loved by God, was declared to be "good," Jesus went out of his way to touch the lives of women and men whose experience of life in this world had been not good. Christians are invited to follow Jesus's example and to give deference to the needs of those on society's margins before addressing the concerns of those with economic and political power. Third, social ethics trains Christians to challenge the things that God despises. Such things include the people and the structures that oppress the needy and trap the poor in a perpetual state of poverty. They also encompass people and structures that make worship of God intolerable by their legalism or by the hypocrisy of their adherents. In addressing these priorities, social ethics becomes a framework by which Christians can measure their participation in the work of the kingdom of God.

Main Points of the Chapter

» Jesus modeled for his followers the need to maintain a special care and compassion for people who have found life in this world to be particularly hard or difficult.

» Jesus modeled opposition to people who oppress the poor and who make loving God undesirable.

» Jesus's proclamation of the kingdom of God and his work in bringing that kingdom to earth reveal what a socially just world can be.

⟨ 5 ⟩

The Early Decades of Christianity

Learning Outcomes for This Chapter

» Summarize socioethical themes in the literature of the New Testament focused on events after the life of Jesus.

» Analyze the impact of Jesus's life on early Christian attitudes toward the suffering of those on society's margins.

» Evaluate the usefulness of this literature in light of its striking cultural setting compared to our own societies and cultures.

Readers of the New Testament may be justly surprised at how quickly the nascent Christian community spread across an empire through its transportation and cultural networks. That spread involved crossing language barriers (from Aramaic to Greek to Latin, etc.), ethnic lines (from Jew to gentile), and religious identities (from Judaism to many Roman state and mystery cults). Moreover, within another century the Christian community crossed still more lines when it spread to Mesopotamian peoples, to those living in the further reaches of North Africa, and to northern Europe. And within a century after that, it had spread to the Caucasus, the British Isles, and perhaps even as far south in Africa as Ethiopia.[1] This expansion was due to the willingness of Christian missionaries to travel in foreign lands, to learn new languages, to translate the story of Jesus into meaningful symbols in new cultures, and to either co-opt or to dismantle the symbols and festivals of the older religious ideas in those areas. The seeds for this movement were planted in stories recounted in the New Testament book of Acts, Paul's Letters (and the related Pauline literature), and texts by other Christian leaders such as Peter, James, and John, nearly all of which were composed during the middle part of the first century AD.

A New Social Order

Social ethics concerns itself with the structures in society and the manner in which they promote or discourage human dignity, the common good, justice, and the like. Social ethicists speak of social sin and sinful structures when they refer to societies organized to discourage these things. The New Testament does not easily fit into this same way of speaking. This is because the New Testament does not challenge many of the underlying social structures that led to oppression, grinding poverty, and early death for many in the lower classes of Roman society. The New Testament writers do not speak in ways similar to social ethicists today about matters such as the Roman Empire's unjust tax system, its practice of slavery, its bent toward misogyny, or its unequal treatment of citizens and noncitizens in the courts. One can find evidence in the New Testament of tacit acceptance of these realities, even while reframing in more healthy terms some of these social institutions (Eph. 5:22–6:4), including even the slave–master relationship (cf. Eph. 6:5–9; Philemon). So one should not read the New Testament looking for evidence of what exactly characterizes a just society. Instead, one should read the New Testament with an interest in what the early Christian community was teaching about the world, about social life, and about its place within these things.

One of the big, overarching principles taught in the New Testament is the idea that Christians are living in a world that is, in literal and figurative ways, passing away. A new order was established by Jesus, a kingdom of God, in which Christians are called to participate. Paul writes in his second letter to the Christians living in Corinth,

> For the love of Christ urges us on, because we are convinced that one has died for all; therefore all have died. And he died for all, so that *those who live might live no longer for themselves, but for him* who died and was raised for them. From now on, therefore, we *regard no one from a human point of view*; even though we once knew Christ from a human point of view, we know him no longer in that way. So if anyone is in Christ, there is a new creation: *everything old has passed away; see, everything has become new!* All this is from God, who reconciled us to himself through Christ, and has given us the ministry of

reconciliation; that is, in Christ God was reconciling the world to himself, not counting their trespasses against them, and entrusting the message of reconciliation to us. So we are ambassadors for Christ, since *God is making his appeal through us*; we entreat you on behalf of Christ, be reconciled to God. (2 Cor. 5:14–20, emphasis added)

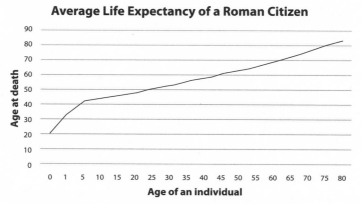

Average Life Expectancy of a Roman Citizen

Difficulty of life during the Roman Empire is partly measured by the average life expectancy of an individual. Infant mortality rates were high (ca. 35 percent of infants born did not survive to age one). But, if you lived until age ten, you had a good chance of living until your mid-forties. Data from T. G. Parkin, *Demography and Roman Society* (Baltimore: Johns Hopkins University Press, 1992), 144.

A new order to the world had come, and it is one in which Christians live not for themselves, but for the sake of sharing the message of Jesus. Christians are not to look at people with human eyes, but with the eyes of a compassionate and merciful God. Why is this important? Because, most shocking of all, God had decided to make his appeal to the world through the followers of Jesus. Yes, the ragtag collection of people who had chosen to follow Jesus were to be God's spokespeople. Despite their many inadequacies, they had been assigned the role of speaking for God on this earth.[2] One wonders whether anything was more surprising to Paul's readers than this.

The idea of a transitioning world continues in other texts. Paul says to his Roman readers that they ought not to mold themselves to the ways of this world (Rom. 12:1–2). Instead, they ought to prepare themselves for a new way of life by renewing their minds and by sacrificing their lives—that is, their worldly minded hopes and dreams and their aspirations for wealth, power, and comfort—to God. The book of Hebrews contrasts the world pre- and post-Jesus's life as the shadow and the actuality, respectively, of the good things to come (Heb. 10:1; see also 7:18). "Christ came as a high priest of the good things that have come" (Heb. 9:11). A couple of passages in the New Testament employ a form of the Greek word *apokatastasis*, which means "restoration" (Matt. 17:11, which is reminiscent of the LXX of Mal. 4:6; Acts 3:21).[3] The contexts in which the word is found suggest that a time is coming when all that exists will be restored to God. This is the fulfillment of the work being done in this new order of the world. Gradually God is restoring all creation back to himself in the building of this new kingdom. The followers of Jesus are invited—perhaps "obliged" is a better term—to participate in this work.

The World in Transition

Scripture	Pre-Jesus	Post-Jesus
Jer. 31:31–34	Life under Mosaic law code	Law is written on one's heart; everyone will know the Lord
Acts 3:17–21	Sinning out of ignorance	Repentance and refreshment; restoration of all things by God
Rom. 12:1–2	Conformed to the world	Transformed by the renewing of one's mind
Gal. 2:15–20	Struggle for justification under Mosaic law code	Justification by faith in Christ
Eph. 4:22–23	Old self / corrupted and deluded by lusts	New self / righteous and holy
Heb. 10:1	The world is a shadow of truth	The fullness of truth is revealed

Christian social ethics incorporates a theology of hope. This hope is based, in part, on biblical texts that speak to an experience of life in a world that is in transition between what Jesus came to do (establish God's kingdom) and the eventual completion of that work. As these select passages attest, this transition is experienced at both the individual and the global level.

Another set of passages in the New Testament witnesses to a social world in transition when it speaks of the relationship between the Jewish and Christian communities. Even though Jesus and all of his earliest disciples were members of the Jewish community, already in Acts 10 readers discover that the composition of the new Christian community is about to change. Peter is invited to the home of a Roman official named Cornelius. It turns out that God has been at work in Cornelius's life previously, and now he is ready to learn about the person and work of Jesus. Peter too needs some work. He was unprepared for the concept that being a follower of Jesus could be open to non-Jews. Peter adjusts, but that is not easy.[4]

A few years later, when Paul encounters much success converting non-Jews to the way of Jesus throughout Asia Minor and southeastern Europe, Peter and other disciples of Jesus take issue with Paul's more libertarian attitudes toward fidelity to the practices of the Abrahamic and Mosaic covenants. Surprising for its candor about the situation in early Christianity, Paul says in Gal. 2:11 that he had to confront Peter and to publicly correct him for refusing to dine with some non-Jewish converts. It is probable that the statement in 2 Pet. 3:16, claiming that some of Paul's teaching is "hard to understand," refers to the struggle Peter was having over this new world God was creating.[5]

Yet Paul felt justified in challenging Peter and other disciples because he had earlier been given support for his position at a gathering of Christian leaders in Jerusalem. Acts 15 records the story of this meeting and its results. Some of Jesus's disciples wanted the non-Jewish converts to be circumcised and to follow other Jewish practices. Paul said that was wrong. In a decision with remarkably far-reaching consequences, the leaders agreed that the converts did not need to follow the Mosaic law code, or be circumcised, or anything else to Judaize them. They were asked only to "abstain from what has been sacrificed to idols and from blood and from what is strangled and from fornication. If you keep yourselves from these, you will do well" (Acts 15:29).[6] The Christian community was now prepared to spread into nearly any culture imaginable. The message of Jesus, the way of Jesus, transcends the religious world of Judaism. It is what the Abrahamic and Mosaic covenants had envisioned all along (as discussed in chap. 1).

Not content merely to invite non-Jews into the Christian faith, Paul goes several steps further in his Letter to the Romans. In Rom. 9 he argues that being a physical descendent of Abraham means little; far more important is being a spiritual descendent of Abraham, which means being a follower of Abraham's deep faith in God. This is open to Jews and non-Jews alike. In Rom.

The New Testament Writer Paul

✓ Originally Saul, a well-educated member of the Pharisee group.
✓ Early critic of the Christian community; sought to arrest its members.
✓ Converted to Christian faith after a miraculous encounter with Jesus while journeying to Damascus.
✓ Led the Christian community in its transformation into becoming a group welcoming people from outside the Jewish faith.
✓ Articulated Christian ideas about salvation by grace.

11 he describes the Christian community as a plant whose seed and visible frame, intimately connected to the Jewish tradition, have been transformed by multiple engraftings of non-Jews. Then in Rom. 14 Paul dispenses with any remaining notion of the Christian religion as tied to any legalistic practices of Judaism when he writes that a relationship with God has no connection to what one eats, what one drinks, or when one worships. Finally, in Rom. 15, Paul quotes from several passages in Hebrew prophetic writings that testify to God as having always sought the inclusion of non-Jews into the community of the faithful. In sum, the crafting of a Christian community from multiple cultural streams with few rules for the faithful reveals just how wide and deep is God's love for those who have yet to "taste and see that the LORD is good" (Ps. 34:8), and that God harbors great compassion, love, and mercy for them. A new social order is on display.[7]

Finally, of course, Revelation provides the greatest amount of New Testament material regarding the new kingdom being built by God. Though drenched in symbolism, the book nevertheless leaves the reader with the unmistakable impression that this world will one day pass away. It will be replaced by a world in which an entirely new set of rules operates, including God returning to be among us and the end of death, crying, and pain.

> Then I saw a new heaven and a new earth; for the first heaven and the first earth had passed away, and the sea was no more. And I saw the holy city, the new Jerusalem, coming down out of heaven from God, prepared as a bride adorned for her husband. And I heard a loud voice from the throne saying,
>
> > "See, the home of God is among mortals.
> > He will dwell with them;
> > they will be his peoples,
> > and God himself will be with them;
> > he will wipe every tear from their eyes.
> > Death will be no more;
> > mourning and crying and pain will be no more,
> > for the first things have passed away."
>
> And the one who was seated on the throne said, "See, I am making all things new." Also he said, "Write this, for these words are trustworthy and true." (Rev. 21:1–5)

The Christian tradition teaches its followers that their feet are planted in two worlds: the present world, in which they physically dwell, and the world to come, in which they are already beginning to participate. However, the texts are equally clear that one's feet need not be planted with equal firmness in both. The present world ought to be held loosely; it is passing away, as are the many things within it that people love and pursue. The new social order that God is building, the kingdom of God, invites men and women instead to love the people whom God loves. How Christian men and women organize social life in this world tutors those who are not yet following God in what God's kingdom will one day more fully be.

God Dwelling with His People

Gen. 3:8	Jer. 31:34	John 1:14	Rev. 21:3
They heard the sound of the LORD God walking in the garden at the time of the evening breeze.	They shall all know me, from the least of them to the greatest, says the LORD.	And the Word became flesh and lived among us.	See, the home of God is among mortals. He will dwell with them; they will be his peoples, and God himself will be with them.

The presence of God among his people is one mark of the kingdom of God. Christian social ethics sees Christians as the embodiment of God's presence in the world today while we await the world described in Revelation.

A New Community for a New Social Order

The previous section focused on the big picture of what the New Testament has to say regarding the transitions taking place in the world and its social order as a consequence of Jesus's life and the work of his followers. This section examines the place of *koinōnia* (Greek), or fellowship, within this transition.[8] Koinonia (English) is the defining principle of this

---

Koinonia

In the New Testament, *koinōnia* (with its cognates) means "fellowship," "participation," or even "a [financial] collection" (as indicated in italics):

> They devoted themselves to the apostles' teaching and *fellowship*. (Acts 2:42)

> We know that as you *share* in our sufferings, so also you *share* in our consolation. (2 Cor. 1:7)

> After you had been enlightened, you endured a hard struggle with sufferings, sometimes being publicly exposed to abuse and persecution, and sometimes being *partners* with those so treated. (Heb. 10:32–33)

new community. Its koinonia is a microcosm of the new order of things, the new kingdom, which God is building. Two features of early Christian fellowship are important for thinking about social ethics. One is their fellowship around a common mission. The other is their fellowship around shared financial burdens.

If they did not realize it while he was alive, once he was gone Jesus's followers quickly recognized that his compassion for those on society's margins also applied to them. They were the oppressed minority within society, the marginalized. The larger Jewish community was not readily open to their beliefs. If they did not find a way soon to channel their newfound hope into a more organized community, the whole movement would seem destined to be a footnote in first-century history. Thankfully, Jesus's promise to send his Spirit to lead and to guide the community came true (cf. John 16:13; Acts 2:1–4). Within days of Jesus's departure, Acts 2 records the story of the Spirit inspiring the early Christians to leave their fear-filled huddle and to preach their beliefs about Jesus boldly. That day the followers of Jesus stood up for what they knew to be true about Jesus and about the good news of hope, joy, and salvation he had brought. Furthermore, the Spirit continued to inspire many more such acts of courage and power, all of which combined to give the early Christian movement the strength it needed to continue.

Those involved in the movement had to appreciate how difficult it was going to be to accomplish the mission they had been given by Jesus. He told them that, while going about the world, they were to preach, to make disciples, to baptize converts, and to teach them to obey his commands (Matt. 28:19–20). This commission seems to be simple enough: many of Jesus's followers were willing to face courageously some very dangerous circumstances to bring Jesus's message to the far reaches of the known world. Indeed, tradition reports that several early Christians met a tragic fate at the hands of civil authorities.[9] Yet what held the group together? What was common about the preaching and disciple making going on in places as distant from one another as North Africa and Persia? In other words, what maintained fellowship between Christians living in distant places and likely never knowing that each other existed?

Paul's teaching in Eph. 4 provides some insight. He writes, "There is one body and one Spirit, just as you were called to the one hope of your calling, one Lord, one faith, one baptism, one God and Father of all, who is above all and through all and in all" (Eph. 4:4–6). Christian fellowship was built across the geographical and chronological divides by a shared commitment to these things. It did not matter what gender you were, what language you spoke, how you dressed, what you ate, or whether you were a slave or a freeborn person.

Christianity Embraced Diversity

Paul laid the groundwork for a diverse community of faith when he taught, "There is no longer Jew or Greek, there is no longer slave or free, there is no longer male and female; for all of you are one in Christ Jesus" (Gal. 3:28).

Christianity offered its quickly diversifying community something greater than themselves to which they could belong.

Moreover, the community recognized that God had uniquely gifted every person with a capacity to contribute to its mission and its *koinōnia*. Not every contributor to the Christian mission needed to be traveling and preaching. Indeed, passages such as Rom. 12; 1 Cor. 12; and Eph. 4 each list various types of charisms, or spiritual gifts. In terms of social ethics, these passages reinforce some of the themes to which we will turn in part 3 of the book. First, human dignity is enhanced by the cultivation of responsibility, and these texts reveal that every person not only has the capacity but also the responsibility to participate in the mission of the community. Second, charism lists teach the principle of solidarity. Proclamation of the gospel is a product of every part of the "body," the Christian fellowship, working together. Third, the lists of charisms highlight the principle of subsidiarity: they remind Christians of their responsibility to do the work they are capable of doing and not expect others to do it for them.

The practice of communion also helped to build cohesive community among followers of Jesus spread throughout the Roman Empire and neighboring countries. Celebrating the same meal in the same way every week, and knowing that fellow believers in disparate regions of the world were doing the same thing, helped to meld the Christian community together. In addition, the second-century text known as the *Didache* reveals that Christians developed standardized prayers to be said before, during, and after the communion meal. This enhanced the awareness of early Christians that they shared this meal with people they would likely never meet but with whom they nevertheless had a common bond of faith. Not surprisingly, Paul, in 1 Cor. 11, called this meal a Eucharist, a meal of thanksgiving. It both encouraged reconciliation among fellow believers in the same community and strengthened the solidarity of Christians across the regions.

Thus one of the features of Christian koinonia was its shared commitment to a mission. This mission was held together by a few principles of faith, by each member's commitment to employing their unique and divine gifts, and by regular participation in a common meal. A second feature of Christian koinonia was its economic fellowship. One of the first things we are told about the new Christian community is that members recognized how they were not merely socially, culturally, and religiously marginalized; they were also predominantly cast from the same economically marginalized class. In other words, most of the early Christians were poor. Their strength would be in numbers, and we learn in the later part of Acts 2 that their growing strength lent itself to a unique openness to share their limited resources with one another:

> All who believed were together and had all things in common; they would sell their possessions and goods and distribute the proceeds to all, as any had need. Day by day, as they spent much time together in the temple, they broke bread at home and ate their food with glad and generous hearts, praising God and having the goodwill of all the people. And day by day the Lord added to their number those who were being saved. (Acts 2:44–47)

The early Christians shared their meager wealth with any in their community who had need. During the late nineteenth and early twentieth centuries, academics spilled much ink over whether this story was evidence of Christian support for communistic forms of social organization.[10] If it was a story about this, we have little evidence in the remaining books of the New Testament that the community maintained it for very long. However, such a debate misses the point of the story. The Acts 2 community was responding to the needs on the ground. No one was obliged to participate, but the community greatly appreciated those who felt moved by God's Spirit to share their excess with others who had less.

Summary

The readiness of early Christian leaders to engage their world with a faith in the life-transforming person of Jesus already speaks to several socioethical themes, including especially the dignity of every person. The content of the New Testament literature that the early leaders left behind adds additional insight into how early Christians viewed the world in which they lived—its political, economic, and social structures—and what it meant for them to be followers of Jesus, who was with them in spirit but no longer physically present. Combined, this material exhorts New Testament readers today to continue the same passion for transforming societies and social structures with the love God has for every person and, indeed, for every part of God's creation.

Main Points of the Chapter

» The temporary nature of this world heightened the earliest Christians' sense of responsibility for representing God well to others.

» Once non-Jews had joined, the Christian community broke down further barriers by embracing forms of ministry that crossed boundaries of language, race, ethnicity, social class, and gender.

» Early Christian *koinōnia* was marked by a shared sense of responsibility for the success of the community and the financial well-being of each member of the community.

Part 1 Summary

The Bible invites us into a relationship with God. This relationship ought to transform the way we view the world and the way we behave within the world. One of the things we discover in the process of reading Scripture is God's love for restoring order out of chaos. God transformed the chaos of the natural realm by giving it a structure, making it beautiful, assigning it a purpose, and assigning to its individual parts a natural end. God restored order from the chaos of individuals' lives as a result of their sin. That came by way of miraculous provisions of food or water, rescue from slavery, discipline when appropriate, sacrificial practices by which sins could be atoned, new leadership for the community, and even taking on human flesh and experiencing the world along with us. This work of restoring order where it does not exist is also our calling. We are invited to join God in this life-affirming work.

Scripture further reveals God's unfailing love for those on the margins of society—the poor, the sick, the suffering, the foreigner, the stranger, the widow, the orphan, and so on. These are individuals whose lives are in chaos, and God's desire to restore them is particularly pronounced in the Scriptures. Consequently Scripture invites its readers to love these people whom God specially loves. To do so likely will require changes in our attitudes toward people on the margins. It will require changes in the way we think about their needs. It will require changes in our advocacy for them too, and in our politics, our voting, our buying habits, our understanding of taxes, our career choices, the way we organize our daily activities, and our willingness to organize political, social, and economic life to be better oriented toward meeting the needs of the marginalized before meeting the needs of those with power.

The student interested in social ethics may quickly find all of this overwhelming. In a sense, it is overwhelming. Many of us have lived long in a culture designed to meet the needs of a majority of persons, a culture that accepts, as a fact of life, that there will be those left out of society's benefits. In such a society, the existence of marginalized people is tolerated because the system works well enough for "most" people. But if you have read this far in the book, you know that this is not at all acceptable to God. The Scriptures reveal a God who disrupts our notions of comfort and who seeks to meet the needs of the marginalized *before* meeting the needs of the "most," or majority. A society that tolerates the existence of marginalized people is not one in which Christians ought to be participating—at least not without doing what we can to disrupt the privileges of those in power.

This last sense ought to help the student interested in social ethics find this to be not so overwhelming after all. More will be said about this in the third part of the book, but the socioethically minded person contributes toward building a more ethical society, one act, one thought, one vote, one advocacy, and one buying decision at a time. We may not advocate for the marginalized or seek to disrupt social structures the best way every time. We may fail more often than we succeed. Yet, as we saw in the previous chapters, Scripture takes a long view of social change, and we are invited to adopt a similarly long perspective about the work of restoration, concerning which God never tires.

Finally, at this point the reader may be struck by how little was said in the preceding chapters about riches and poverty in the Bible. This is because the Bible neither univocally condemns wealth nor univocally praises poverty. Biblical wisdom regarding wealth and poverty may be found in Prov. 30:8, which says, "Give me neither poverty nor riches; feed me with the food that I need." Furthermore, Jesus does not condemn wealth. He praises those who share their excess wealth with the poor, the hungry, the naked, the oppressed, and so on. Moreover, Jesus and his disciples are among those poor people who are tremendously helped by the generosity of wealthier people when those wealthier people provided them meals, lodging, and money during the years of Jesus's itinerant public ministry. Even at Jesus's death, a wealthy disciple donated his private burial tomb for Jesus's body. Instead of focusing on the reality of wealth and poverty in our world, these chapters have sought to understand such realities with the lens of the character and work of God, which is how the prophets and Jesus saw them.

We noted in the introduction that Protestant social ethics takes Scripture as its foundation, and we have therefore devoted part 1 to understanding the Bible's social teachings. At the same time, it would be a mistake to think that Protestant social ethics is strickly a matter of going back to the Bible to see what it says about particular social issues. Rather, as we will see in part 2, Protestant social ethics developed out of a long history of Christian reflection on social issues. Students interested in social ethics would do well to understand that history, to which we now turn.

Social Ethics
in Christian History

⟨ 6 ⟩

Late Antiquity

Learning Outcomes for This Chapter

» Summarize key developments in the history of Christianity in Late Antiquity.

» Explain Christians' theoretical understanding of wealth and its acquisition in Late Antiquity.

» Analyze the connection between critiques of wealth and the Christians' concern to build structures for social welfare.

Christians and Christian churches have been invested in social justice work since the religion's earliest days. Paul took up a collection for the poor in Jerusalem during his missionary journeys. Documents from the second century attest to Christians' interest in not only continuing such collections but also in using the funds to provide for the needs of those who were not even Christian. Churches would even collect money to pay for the burial expenses of non-Christians whose families were too poor to pay those expenses themselves. This commitment to caring for the real, physical needs of others was recognized as a constitutive expression of gospel proclamation, and in later centuries this commitment expanded into new areas (e.g., health care and education).

This chapter surveys the expansion of Christians' understanding of social ethics during the historical period known as Late Antiquity. It is a period that spans the second through sixth centuries of our era. Within that time frame, this chapter surveys the socioethical ideas of Christians living in as disparate places as the Middle East, the Caucasus, North Africa, the European continent, and the British Isles. Despite the many geographical and political differences across these regions, the dozens of languages spoken by Christians in these areas, the diverse leadership structures under which the Christians lived and worshiped, and the many generations of Christians who lived during this massive span of time—there are a surprising number of convergences in the work of Christians on behalf of social justice. Here we consider Christians' commitment both to providing immediate, charitable relief and to facilitating structural changes in social conditions by their engagement in social welfare programs, health care, education, and politics.

Brief Historical Review

During Late Antiquity, Christians largely lived in the Mediterranean region and witnessed the decline of the Roman Empire. During these centuries there was a small but growing community of Christians in the Middle East within a resurgent Persian Empire under the Sassanid dynasty, and nascent Christian communities could also be found in the British Isles and the Caucasus region. Still, the majority of Christians during this time lived within the bounds of the Roman Empire. Yet the vast size of the Roman Empire meant that even the Christians within it represented a large amount of diversity in terms of language, religious climate, economic status, educational attainment, and even theological ideas.

The great diversity within the Christian community during these centuries meant that any developments emerging during this period were the product of numerous discussions and multiple gatherings of church leaders, representing the considered opinions of many generations of Christians about how to interpret Scripture. Chief among these developments are three things. One is Christianity's formation of a canon of sacred texts, which would become its New Testament.[1] Although the Gospels of Matthew, Mark, Luke, and John found a receptive audience by the middle of the second century, other books took time to gain acceptance. This is because, quite literally, dozens of books identified as Gospels or as letters from one Christian leader or another also circulated during this time, and the community needed centuries to determine which ones deserved to be retained, which were best left for personal devotion, and which were best discarded as unworthy of further attention.[2]

During this period a second development was the formation of an administrative structure to govern the churches. The house-church model of the first century proved unwieldy with the numerical growth in the Christian community and the need for greater dialogue among its members to deal with scriptural and disciplinary problems. The Christians settled on a system of dividing up the empire along the same administrative lines as the political powers had done. Individual regions of the Roman Empire became dioceses of the Christian church, and one or more bishops were appointed over each. Assisting those bishops would be pastors of local churches. The position of deacon continued (from its first mention in Acts 6) as an assistant to pastors and bishops, though its precise role varied over time and in different regions. This somewhat more hierarchical system served the church well in helping it to build networks of greater solidarity among Christians between cities, across regions, and around the empire.[3]

The third development during this period was in doctrine. In part an outgrowth of the changes in the church's administrative structure, Christian theologians had greater opportunities to dialogue about the religion's understanding of God and of the person and work of Jesus. These discussions and debates spanned almost the entirety of this period, and they resulted in development of the doctrines of the Trinity and of Jesus possessing two

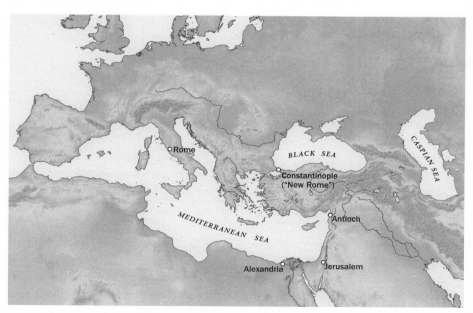

Christianity's increasing ability to administer its affairs, which the creation of dioceses and the appointment of bishops helped it to do, meant that it could better mobilize its limited resources for social improvements.

natures. The Nicene Creed, originally composed in AD 325 and modified at a meeting in 381, records Christians' view that the one divine nature is present in three persons. In 451, at a meeting in the city of Chalcedon, Christian leaders gathered to sort out several decades' worth of debate regarding the person of Jesus. There they stated that Jesus possessed two natures—one human and one divine—and that those natures were united within the one person of Jesus. In the years that followed, Christians seemed happy to continue to promote these two doctrines. Still today they form the core of Christian doctrine.[4]

Although the period of Late Antiquity closes with the decline of the last vestiges of the Roman Empire at the end of the sixth century, keep in mind that Christianity's reflection on what constitutes Scripture, what constitutes proper administration of the church's affairs, and what constitutes right doctrine each had an impact on the development of Christianity's social ethics during this and later periods. Being attentive to social structures is intimately linked with what one senses is the proper response to the person and message of Jesus as found in books of Scripture. Being able to change those social structures was very much a function of the church's effective ability to harness its limited resources. Those resources contributed to a vibrant practice of preaching about the needs of others. They also contributed to the construction of facilities and institutions that would alleviate the suffering of the needy.

Councils of Nicaea (325) and Constantinople (381)	Council of Chalcedon (451)
Doctrine of the Trinity	*Doctrine of Christology*
"*We believe in one God, the Father* Almighty, creator of all things visible and invisible;	"We all with one accord teach men to acknowledge one and the same Son, our Lord Jesus Christ, at once *complete in Godhead and complete in humanity*, truly God and
And in one Lord Jesus Christ . . . of one being/essence as the Father, . . .	truly man consisting also of a reasonable soul and body; of *one substance with the Father* as regards his Godhead, and at the same
And in the Holy Spirit, the Lord, the Giver of Life . . ."	time of *one substance with us* as regards his humanity . . ."

Practicing the Preaching of Charity

Indeed, as a consequence of its interest in addressing social needs, several features of Christianity's social ethics emerged during Late Antiquity. The first and most important feature was its commitment to charity. Social ethicists tend to think about charity very differently from how they think about justice

---

Tertullian (flourished ca. 200)

Very little is known about Tertullian's life except that he was a church father who lived in Carthage (North Africa). He wrote several important texts. One was his *Apology*, which defended Christianity from its would-be critics. He also wrote one of the earliest texts about God as a Trinity of three persons who share one substance. He was married to a Christian woman, to whom he also wrote at least two significant texts on marriage (*To His Wife* and *Monogamy*). Later in life he joined a sectarian Christian movement known as Montanism. For this reason, he was not considered a "saint" by later Christian leaders.

---

work, a topic to which we will return in chapters 9 and 13, but the distinction was less clear in Christianity's earliest days. In the second and third centuries Christian charity was already a socially disrupting force. It marked Christians as a certain type of group within the wider Roman society. As Christians grew more confident in their charity and expressed it more publicly, they naturally found themselves building social structures that offered justice for those on society's margins.

One of the earliest instances of Christian charity was when it set aside some of the money collected from regular offerings for the needs of the poor. Among our earliest testimonies to this are the writings of Justin Martyr and Tertullian. Both authors wrote texts with the title *Apology*, which had nothing to do with apologizing, but which meant they had written a defense (an apology) for the Christian faith to respond to critics in the wider society. One reason Christians should not be criticized by those in the secular society, according to Justin and Tertullian, is the Christians' commitment to care for the poor. Justin's text says money collected in offerings from the church's members helped to support orphans, widows, the sick, and any person who found themselves in need.[5] Tertullian's *Apology* adds further details while framing that specific form of charity within the religion's love for our shared humanity.

> Though we have our treasure chest, it is not made up of purchase-money, as of a religion that has its price. On the monthly day, if he likes, each puts in a small donation; but only if it be his pleasure, and only if he be able: for there is no compulsion; all is voluntary. These gifts are, as it were, piety's deposit fund. For they are not taken thence and spent on feasts, and drinking bouts, and eating houses, but to support and bury poor people, to supply the wants of boys and girls destitute of means and parents, and of old persons confined

now to the house; such, too, as have suffered shipwreck; and if there happen to be any in the mines, or banished to the islands, or shut up in the prisons, for nothing but their fidelity to the cause of God's Church, they become the nurslings of their confession.[6]

The very fact that Christians care for the financial needs of their fellow Christian and non-Christian citizens alike is a testimony to their respect for the common human nature that binds together all persons. Unfortunately, according to Tertullian, one is too often hard-pressed to find such a sense of shared respect and camaraderie in secular society.

The fourth and fifth centuries were a remarkable period of growth in Christian charity. Much of that growth was shaped by Christian preaching that sought to educate Christians about the real needs of those on society's margins. One good example is the preaching of John Chrysostom.[7] Hundreds of his sermons have survived to the present day, and several dozen of them incorporate themes consonant with a concern for a more economically just society. Consider, for example, one homily in which Chrysostom talks both about the breadth of poverty in Roman society and also about the insufficient concern of the wealthy for the needs of the poor.

> For I am now ashamed of speaking of almsgiving [here addressing the "wealthy" in his audience], because, having often spoken on this subject, I have effected nothing worth the exhortation. For some increase indeed has there been, but not so much as I wished. For I see you sowing, but not with a liberal hand. Wherefore I fear too lest you also "reap sparingly." To prove that we do sow sparingly, let us inquire, if it seem good, which are more numerous in the city, poor or rich? And how many are they, who are neither poor nor rich, but have a middle place? A tenth part is of rich, and a tenth of the poor that have nothing at all, and the rest of the middle sort. Let us distribute then amongst the poor the whole multitude of the city, and you will see the disgrace and how great it is. For the very rich indeed are but few, but those that come next to them are many; again, the poor are much fewer than these. Nevertheless, although there are so many that are able to feed the hungry, many go to sleep in their hunger, not because those that have are not able with ease to aid them, but because of their great barbarity and inhumanity.[8]

Chrysostom reveals a couple of important things in this quote. One is that he roughly divides society into three economic classes: upper, middle, and lower. Although recent scholarship on Roman society has revealed a far more complicated economic stratification than this, Chrysostom's point is that everyone who has more than they need at any one moment in time—the

John Chrysostom (347–407)

John Chrysostom was a priest in Antioch before being appointed bishop of the imperial capital, Constantinople. In Antioch he preached a series of sermons to plead for the emperor's mercy while quelling a riot that had, among other things, caused the defacement of sculptures of the emperor's image. In Antioch and in Constantinople, he preached several sermons on compassion for the poor. During the early 400s, his several critiques of the empress Eudoxia for her profligate displays of power led to his being exiled from the bishop's office more than once. His moniker, Chrysostom, means "golden-mouthed." This name was given to him for his beautifully crafted rhetoric and speech.

upper and middle classes—is obliged to share that excess with those in the lowest strata, the desperately poor who have been reduced to begging for their subsistence.[9] This means even those who consider themselves to be poor are not off the hook when it comes to sharing their food, supplies, and housing with the desperately poor. There is always *something* that can be shared with the one who has nothing. Second, the suffering of those in the lowest strata is due to one thing only: the barbarity and inhumanity of those in the middle and upper classes. Along with many of his fellow Christian leaders in Late Antiquity, Chrysostom shares the concern to see economic redistribution not in terms of a need for economic equality but in terms of a need to appreciate the equal dignity of every person. It is this higher calling, if you will, that compels Christians to seek justice for the oppressed, not just charity.

Another example of how preaching shaped the expansion of social justice work is the ministry of Basil of Caesarea, a Christian leader in the Roman Empire's region known as Cappadocia (in modern-day Turkey).[10] A handful of his sermons on topics related to social ethics have survived to our own day. One of those is *Homilies* 8, written in response to the devastation that had come in the wake of a recent famine. Taking a cue from the prophet Amos, Basil argues that the problems associated with the famine will not abate until the people turn from their materialistic ways, from their callous disregard for the needs of others, and from their mistreatment of the poor. He invites his readers to become like the Ninevites in Jonah's story—repenting of their sins, fasting, assuming postures of penitence. Rich and poor alike are in need of forgiveness from God. Yet Basil laments that too few Christians join him in prayer for the healing of the land. So he tries a new tactic in this sermon. He

Roman Law on the Church and Social Work

By the mid-fourth century, imperial legislation had drawn the Christian bishops and their clergy into a more organized system of relief for the poor. This law prevented wealthy Christians from avoiding "compulsory public services" (i.e., taxes and other duties) by joining the clergy. Thus the wealth of citizens was to be for the benefit of the state; the wealth of churches was to be for the benefit of the poor.

appeals to their sense of pity on the suffering poor. He gives a long, physical description of a person dying from starvation.

> Famine is a slow evil, always approaching, always holding off like a beast in its den. The heat of the body cools. The form shrivels. Little by little strength diminishes. Flesh stretches across the bones like a spider web. The skin loses its bloom, as the rosy appearance fades and blood melts away. Nor is the skin white, but rather it withers into black while the livid body, suffering pitifully, manifests a dark and pale mottling. The knees no longer support the body but drag themselves by force, the voice is powerless, the eyes are sunken as if in a casket, like dried-up nuts in their shells; the empty belly collapses, conforming itself to the shape of the backbone without any natural elasticity of the bowels. The person who rushes by such a body, how greatly worthy is he of chastisement? . . . Should he not be reckoned with the savagery of the beasts, accursed and [murderous]?[11]

These changes to the starving person's body multiply the pains from hunger and the mental anguish at finding neither food nor a person who will share their food. Readers today can still sense Basil pleading with his readers to reconsider their need to love the poor better than they do.

Building Social Structures

As a consequence of confronting the desperate plight of the poor, Basil was able to direct the resources of his Cappadocian diocese toward building social structures that would help such people. He enlisted the aid of his friend and fellow Cappadocian preacher Gregory of Nazianzus to travel about the region and to preach about the devastation left in poverty's wake.[12] Basil's brother, Gregory of Nyssa, also later joined the effort.[13] The combined efforts of these and other Christian leaders contributed to the construction and later

The rocky hills in the region of Cappadocia, the home of Basil of Caesarea and the other Cappadocian fathers, proved useful for locating churches during the Byzantine period.

maintenance of a Christian-run hospital complex in the regional capital city of Caesarea. It was perhaps one of the first such institutions of its kind in human history, practically a city unto itself of buildings that would provide a place for the desperately poor to come for aid and, where necessary, to die with a sense of dignity.[14] Basil named it *Basileia*, which was a play both on his own name and on the Greek word for "kingdom." He and other Christian leaders in Late Antiquity were channeling the financial resources of Christian churches into building the kingdom of God. Preachers like Basil knew that to care for the needs of the poor was a constitutive expression of their commitment to preaching what Jesus also preached—the arrival of God's kingdom to this earth.

Basil was not alone among Christian bishops and pastors in doing this. Other Christian leaders in the fourth and fifth centuries built their own hospital-like structures. Also, structures were built to collect donated food and clothing in order to distribute them freely to those who had need.[15] Christians built inns to accommodate pilgrims visiting sacred sites—something sorely needed, since inns were hardly known for their safety in Roman times. Christian educators recruited local pupils for new schools, and translators worked to make the Scriptures available to people who could not read Greek

Basil of Caesarea (330–71)

Basil was the Christian leader of the region known as Cappadocia (in the central part of modern-day Turkey) during the third quarter of the fourth century. Together with his equally famous brother, Gregory of Nyssa, and friend Gregory of Nazianzus, Basil wrote important works on the doctrine of God, including especially works that articulated Christianity's trinitarian understanding of God. Besides this, he wrote extensively about ascetic life, and he even wrote a "rule" to guide those who chose the ascetic life. His preaching duties led him to craft important commentaries and sermons on many books of the Bible. He also wrote at least three vivid sermons on the suffering of the poor (*Homilies* 6–8), which helped to spark construction of the Basileia.

or who found the Old Latin translations problematic.[16] Each of these things was helped in no small measure by the increase in the number of people joining Christianity and the comparatively greater wealth of these converts compared to those of earlier centuries. Political changes in the empire during the fourth century, which made joining the church and supporting its work more fashionable, also helped.

One of the keys to understanding why Christians were so successful in channeling their wealth into the building of social services for those on society's margins is the teaching on wealth found in early Christian writings. One of the most important contributors to this discussion in the Christian community was a homily by Clement, the bishop in Alexandria, from the middle of the third century. His homily *Who Is the Rich Man That Will Be Saved?* (Latin: *Quis dives salvetur*), or *Salvation of the Rich*, is an interpretation of Jesus's words to the rich man in Mark 10:21, "Go, sell what you own, and give the money to the poor." Clement argues if one were to follow this command of Jesus literally, then one would be violating Jesus's commands in other passages, such as Matt. 25, that direct people to feed the hungry, clothe the naked, and so on. That is to say, if you obey Mark 10 and give everything away, then you necessarily violate Matt. 25 by not being able to share. The solution, according to Clement, is to admit that Jesus did not mean for his followers to take his words in Mark 10 literally. The command "Go, sell what you own, and give the money to the poor" is to be interpreted as "banish from [one's] soul notions about wealth."[17] In other words, Jesus meant for his followers to stop loving money, in order that they may be able cheerfully to part with it for the sake of helping those with needs. This may be called a detachment view of wealth. Christians may have wealth and have access to wealth, but they are to be emotionally detached from that wealth. The assumption, then, is that the more emotionally detached from wealth one becomes, the more generous one will be in sharing that wealth with others.

This detachment idea found in Clement's homily became the dominant teaching among Christians, and it continues today to resonate in the Christian church. Yet today, as also in Late Antiquity, some Christian writers have felt that wealth is more problematic than Clement made it out to be. Those writers have recognized that the prevalence of wealth among a few is precisely the cause of the lack of wealth among so many. An unknown author wrote in the early fifth century a text titled *On Riches*.[18] It castigates the wealthy for hoarding scarce resources. It argues that there are poor people *because* there are rich people. The author argues that wealth, per se, is neutral, or not sinful, but that the acquisition of it is through sin. Either way, one should steer clear of wealth. Moreover, the author criticizes an argument apparently made by some who are supportive of the acquisition of wealth: since the Old Testament says that God made some people quite wealthy (e.g., Abraham and David), riches are justified in that they may be a gift from God. However, according to the author of *On Riches*, the Christian's allegiance is to the teachings of Christ, especially where those teachings transcend Old Testament accounts. Very little of the ways that men like Abraham or David lived is validated by Christ (such as Abraham sleeping with Hagar, or David's adultery with Bathsheba).

After recounting these things about the preaching of John and of Basil and about the various teachings on wealth, we should admit that one feature absent in their (and other early Christian leaders') writings is a call for

---

Early Christian Reflection on "The Rich Young Man" (Matt. 19; Mark 10; Luke 18)

What then was it which persuaded [the rich young man] to flight, and made him depart from the Master, from the entreaty, the hope, the life, previously pursued with ardour?—"Sell thy possessions." And what is this? He does not, as some conceive off-hand, bid him throw away the substance he possessed, and abandon his property; but bids him banish from his soul his notions about wealth, his excitement and morbid feeling about it, the anxieties, which are the thorns of existence, which choke the seed of life.

—Clement of Alexandria
Salvation of the Rich 11

structural changes in the organization of society itself. These writers knew that corrupt officials, oppressive tax policies, inadequate government services, an overstretched military, declining infrastructure (such as roads), and a seeming incapacity on the part of the imperial government to respond to natural disasters—all contributed substantially to about 80 percent of the population living at or just below a subsistence level of income, and roughly 15 percent of the population living sufficiently below that level as to be reduced to begging desperately for their and their family's survival. Yet, remarkably from our twenty-first-century perspective, none of the early Christian writers make anything more than a passing comment about these contributing factors. They do not call for social action intended to right these wrongs. They do not call for an overthrow of the imperial regime. Instead, what we conclude about Christian social ethics in Late Antiquity is that they satisfied themselves with the role of building a social welfare system and safety net that would catch those who fell through the many cracks in the imperial system; they never made a point of trying to fix the cracks that caused those problems in the first place. This is why it may be said that early Christian charity eventually led Christians into socially transforming justice work, but it would be many centuries until Christians recognized that their commitment to justice needed to go even further than building safety nets.

Summary

The first six centuries of Christianity's history witnessed tremendous change and more than a few significant contributions to our understanding of Christianity's social ethics. Thankfully, Jesus's special concern to reach out in compassion to those suffering on society's margins was not lost on his later disciples. Christians in Late Antiquity found ever-new ways to integrate themselves into the messiness of the world's affairs. It began with Christians agreeing to share their meager resources with those even poorer than themselves, including their fellow citizens who were not even followers of Jesus. It continued with Christians' interest in building a social safety net with funds and buildings designed to help the sick, house the homeless, clothe the naked, and feed the hungry. Indeed, Protestant social ethics is absolutely indebted to the literally hundreds of years of painstaking and caring labor by dozens of generations of Christians. They were building and maintaining a platform from which the Christian church could have the moral authority to address the diverse societies in our world and to call those societies to account when they do not adequately demonstrate compassion for those suffering on the margins.

Main Points of the Chapter

» The formalization of Christianity's administrative structure (bishops, priests, dioceses, etc.), combined with its developing interest in doctrine (Trinity, Christology), encouraged Christians to strengthen their social and economic ties to one another.

» The growing social and economic ties made the sharing of resources across regions possible and even desirable.

» Resource sharing made it possible for Christians to provide charitable relief to the poor, including non-Christians.

» During the fourth and fifth centuries, Christians shifted their resources into the construction of formal structures of social welfare, such as hospitals, schools, and *diakonia* (collection centers for food and goods that could be distributed to the poor).

✥ 7 ✥

Middle Ages

Learning Outcomes for This Chapter

» Summarize elements of Christianity's history during the Middle Ages that contributed to its formation of social ethics.

» Evaluate the merits of Christianity's engagement with the state during the Middle Ages.

» Identify the contribution of Thomas Aquinas to Christianity's development of its social ethics.

This chapter continues the survey of Christians' understanding of its social ethics during the historical period known as the Middle Ages. This period spans the seventh through fifteenth centuries of our era. Within that time frame, this chapter surveys the socioethical ideas of Christians living on the European continent and the British Isles. During this time, Christianity also expanded into cultures as far away as China and Southeast Asia, deep into western Asia, and the lands of the Russian people, and it was making inroads down the eastern coast of Africa. Yet the developments taking place in Europe had the more profound impact on Protestant social ethics in later centuries, and so it is best to restrict our study of this period to that region. Principal features of this historical period are the development of universities, the advent of several monastic orders that took particular interest in the needs of the poor, and fundamental shifts in the role of the church in society.

Brief Historical Review

The Middle Ages was by no means a monolithic story of one political or one religious power center. Politically speaking, the Middle Ages opens in the sixth century with much of southern, central, and western Europe under the authority of very different people groups. What was once a unified Roman Empire had been carved up into territories controlled by groups such as the Goths, the Visigoths, the Lombards, the Merovingians, and others. During the seventh and eighth centuries, the Merovingians, from their political base in western Europe (roughly located where France is today), consolidated power over much of the region. During the late eighth century, the Merovingian dynasty faded and was replaced by the Carolingian dynasty. The Carolingian emperors—especially Charles the Great, or Charlemagne—expanded the empire's size to include most of western and central and even some parts of eastern Europe. Attacks from the Vikings and the Danes in the late ninth century chipped away at much of the territory, and this led to a decline in the power of the Carolingians. In the tenth century the Carolingians were replaced in central Europe by a new dynasty of rulers known as the Ottonians, named after their first ruler, Otto the Great. The Ottonian Empire held sway over much of western and central Europe until the rise of independent nations—such as those of the French, the Spanish, the Italians, the Dutch, and the Germans—at the end of the Middle Ages.[1]

Germanic Peoples

Merovingian Dynasty	Carolingian Dynasty	Ottonian Empire	Formation of independent nations
6th–7th Centuries	8th–9th Centuries	10th–13th Centuries	14th–15th Centuries

This general timeline outlines the significant geopolitical shifts in Europe during the Middle Ages. Christianity's role in the formation of European culture could not help but be inextricably linked with the work of these different political powers.

Throughout these centuries, culturally speaking, Europe remained a very diverse place. Distinct languages of the people were preserved even when Latin was used as the language of the courts and the churches. Taxation policies, coinage, trade routes, and education opportunities rarely were fixed across the region. During the early part of the Middle Ages, there were dukes and lords, peasants and serfs, but during the later Middle Ages new classes of people emerged, such as those with degrees from the new universities, craftspeople who formed themselves into guilds, and merchants and explorers whose world extended far beyond the confines of Europe. During the later centuries of

Baptism of Clovis (December 25, 496)

The baptism of the Merovingian ruler Clovis marked a new beginning for church-state relations in the aftermath of the collapse of the Roman Empire. Not only did this provide Christians a platform from which to address the political sphere; it also enabled orthodox Christianity to establish a new foothold in western Europe. This was particularly helpful in order to combat the widespread Arian heresy among the Germanic tribal groups.

this period, new religious communities were formed for men and women that opened unique "career" paths for those willing to make vows of poverty and of chastity. And these more sophisticated classes of the population increasingly sought life in cities. In the later part of the Middle Ages, a significant percentage of the population abandoned rural areas and headed to the urban areas, the new centers of culture and power.[2]

There were equally dramatic shifts in Europe's religious landscape during this time period. In the sixth century, Christianity was in shambles, picking up the pieces of a destroyed Roman culture and trying to fashion something new. By the mid-ninth century, Christianity began to find its footing as it overhauled its monastic communities, standardized its religious services, created education systems for its aspiring clergy, and began to embed itself more deeply into the fabric of political society.[3] A rapid expansion of Christianity's influence took place during the twelfth through fourteenth centuries, as it began systematically to build university systems of education throughout the European continent and in England. Christians built schools of law, medicine, theology, literature, and the full range of the liberal arts. Christianity's creation of this widely regarded education system ensured it would have a long reach into the political sphere too, as future kings, rulers, and civil servants would all pass through its doors.[4] Looking beyond the Middle Ages, it is ironic that Christianity's gift of education to Western culture would become the breeding ground from which would emerge those who upended the Christian religion that they knew—be it the likes of Martin Luther, John Calvin, and other Protestants in their turn against Roman Catholicism, or Immanuel Kant, René Descartes, and other Enlightenment-oriented thinkers in their turn against religious mentalities, generally.

In sum, Europe was a frequently changing place during the Middle Ages. Very little was stable in terms of its politics, its cultures, its Christian communi-

Coronation of Charlemagne (December 25, 800)

The Carolingian emperor Charlemagne (742–814), who had ruled much of western and central Europe from his capital in Aachen, eventually turned to aid the Christian churches in his regions and to help the bishop of Rome to secure the borders of his papal state in central Italy. Pope Leo III acknowledged Charlemagne's support of the church by arranging to crown him "Holy Roman Emperor," but in the ceremony Charlemagne seized the crown and put it on himself. The title implied a rebirth of that earlier empire and the political unity and power of all the peoples of Europe once part of it.

Charlemagne apparently took his responsibility to protect and to help the church seriously. He instituted broad reforms of Benedictine monasticism, founded and financially supported new monasteries and churches, helped to standardize Christian worship services across the empire, and took a personal interest in revisions to the Latin translation of the Bible known as the Vulgate.

ties, or even its pursuit of an educated culture. It was not an easy time to live and die: wars, massive plagues, conditions of oppression, and subsistence-level economic life were the reality for too many. Yet a very rich array of cultures developed during these centuries, and scholars today know that there is much still to discover about those cultures in texts yet to be studied and material culture yet to be examined or even unearthed.

Reforming Western Society

In terms of Christianity's social ethics during the Middle Ages, one can infer at least three significant features from what has been said above. First, Christianity self-consciously and consistently expanded its commitment to building social structures. Under this category, one can classify Christian contributions to education, to health care, to an ordered religious life, and to facilitating stable political regimes. That Christianity committed its resources to education and to health care should not be surprising, since these were prominent features of Christianity in Late Antiquity as well. Yet what was different in the Middle Ages was the support of the state for the church's initiatives. Monasteries received imperial charters and land grants during the Carolingian era, and in return they were to provide the empire with young men who were sufficiently educated and literate to serve as civil servants or to work as priests and thereby to extend that education to the laypeople attending worship services on Sundays. Hospitals too received state support, and some Christian men and women grew increasingly sophisticated in their understanding of surgical procedures and in the use of herbs for medicinal use. Each of these contributed to a better-functioning society.[5]

A second feature of Christianity's social ethics during the Middle Ages was a more structured church organization. The building of a more ordered religious life grew, in part, out of a concern that the diverse cultures of Europe might easily be lost to Christianity, or at least misled about its precepts, if there was not a more uniform understanding of its belief in Jesus as Savior, its Scripture books, its doctrines, and its eschatological hope. Thus the Middle Ages witnessed a remarkable expansion in the administration of Christian churches. There were systems for educating priests and systems for selecting bishops to administer dioceses. Christian leaders met regularly to discuss such wide-ranging issues as theological differences, the proper location for constructing a new church building, and the war plans of the current emperor. How Sunday services were conducted was regularized by copying and distributing to local priests standardized prayers, lectionaries, and even prewritten sermons. Arguably, any one of these structural improvements in the organization of Christianity considered in isolation would not be a meaningful socioethical contribution. Yet when one considers that Christianity was largely responsible for the conveyance of a system of values, ethics, and virtues to European societies throughout the Middle Ages, the combination of these structural changes is rather immense. The standardization and the repeatability of the Christian experience and Christian ministry is what ensured the continuance of this contribution to the building of a just European society over hundreds of years.[6]

Third, Christianity was involved in the state as part of its social ethics. Attention to education and health care alongside the increased ordering of the religious sphere corresponded to Christianity's facilitation of stable political regimes. From the baptism of the Merovingian ruler Clovis in the late fifth century, to the reserving of the pope's right to choose and crown emperors beginning in the ninth century, to the twelfth-century declaration that even political powers are subject to the authority of the spiritual powers, particularly the bishop in Rome—Christianity embedded itself in the maintenance of the political sphere. To be sure, this was almost always a messy business. Most political rulers paid only enough religious obeisance to maintain the support of the bishop in Rome. Most rarely had the high ideals of serving God. Few lived morally upright lives. And most political rulers thought nothing of undermining the authority of Christian bishops if

---

Church over the State in the 1200s

The princes should recognize as they do (and have in our presence)
that the right and authority of examining the person elected king and
of promoting him to the imperial office pertains to us, since we anoint,
consecrate and crown him. It is regularly and generally observed that
the person who places his hands upon a candidate may examine him.
Then if the princes would elect a sacrilegious, excommunicated, tyrannical, fatuous, and heretical, even a pagan, person not in discord but
unanimously, ought we anoint, consecrate and crown a man of this
sort? Of course not.

—Pope Innocent III
Venerabilem (March 26, 1202)

---

they felt that would further their own political cause. Christian leaders could
be equally conniving and morally dubious. Yet the embedding of Christian
leaders into the political processes had the benefit of ensuring the proclamation of Christian values—if only in name or in idealized form—among
European peoples. In other words, even when Christian leaders supported
bad emperors, it was at least clear to most people, or would be clear soon
enough, what the problems with the emperor were. The cardinal virtues,
which Christianity promoted, were a well-known yardstick by which every
person could be measured.[7]

Justice and the Natural Law Tradition

Christianity's construction of schools, churches, and hospitals and its contribution to the political sphere increased its sensitivity to the physical needs
of the European peoples. This helped to foster an increasing sophistication
about what a just society is or can be. Such increasing sophistication led to the
promotion of a consistent set of values and virtues, including especially the
promotion of the concepts of natural law and justice in the Middle Ages. One
of the more important Christian writers on the topics of justice and natural
law was Thomas Aquinas, a member of the Dominican religious order and
an itinerant professor during the thirteenth century.

In his work *Summa Theologicae* (*ST*), Thomas began his consideration
of justice by separating it from the other virtues (courage, temperance, and
prudence) as the one virtue directed toward relationship with others. Justice
"denotes a kind of equality" (*ST* II-II.57.1), and it requires that we render

---

Thomas Aquinas (1225–74)

Born into an aristocratic family in Italy, Thomas was educated by the Benedictines at Monte Cassino, starting at age five. He joined the Dominicans by the time he was eighteen. He studied at the universities in Paris and Cologne. At age thirty-two, he began as a professor at the university in Paris. He later founded a school in Naples for the Dominicans.

Thomas was as prolific in recording as he was brilliant in his ability to digest vast amounts of data from works by earlier philosophers and theologians. His argument that language functions by way of analogy (*analogia entis*) would animate debate for the next three centuries over how one might be able to talk about God. He is perhaps best known for his arguments, or proofs, demonstrating the reasonableness of belief in the existence of God (in his *Summa contra Gentiles* 1.9–14).

---

to others what is due to them (*ST* II-II.58.1). The idea that a just individual renders to others or that a just society renders to its individual members what is due to them invites the question *how* such rendering may be done. Thomas proposes at least four ways of talking about the mechanics of justice. He says we practice a "legal justice" when we live in conformity with the law and so build up the common good (*ST* II-II.58.5). We practice "particular justice" when we rightly treat individual persons around us (*ST* II-II.58.7). Since there may be more than one way of rightly treating the individuals with whom we come into contact, Thomas subdivides particular justice into two further categories.

One way we treat others rightly is by being fair in our dealings with them. This is called "commutative justice" (*ST* II-II.61.1). One example is the practices of buying and selling. Sellers behave justly when they price their products fairly. Buyers behave justly when they pay a fair price to the seller. Another way we treat others rightly is by distributing society's benefits and burdens in accordance with each person's position. This is called "distributive justice" (*ST* II-II.61.1). Thomas writes regarding this, "In distributive justice the mean is observed, not according to equality between thing and thing, but according to proportion between things and persons: in such a way that even as one person surpasses another, so that which is given to one person surpasses that which is allotted to another." In other words, whereas commutative justice is concerned about fairness in terms of equality, distributive justice accepts inequality as potentially still fair if that inequality is based on the different status of individuals within a community or the different contributions of individuals to the community.[8] For example, in the United States, the president is given a private plane, a private helicopter, a private fleet of vehicles, a free home to live in, dozens of staff assistants, and countless gifts and perks. If viewed from the perspective of the president being a person like any other person, then these privileges are an unequal distribution of society's resources; however, considering the duties of the presidential office for the good of American society, American citizens have accepted that this unequal distribution of resources is nevertheless fair and just.

Justice in Thomas Aquinas's *Summa Theologicae*

If these concepts of justice seem to readers to be self-evident or otherwise obvious, that is not without good reason. It is because of something else that the Christian church helped to convey during the Middle Ages: the idea that there exists a "natural law." Laws help us to distinguish between the good things we ought to do and the bad things we ought not to do. Laws are the result of a process by which individuals reason together regarding what is good and what is not; thus laws originate with human reason. Christians further believe that human reason originates with God and that it is the means by which humans express the *imago Dei* within themselves. For this reason, natural law reflects something of God, God's "law," or an eternal law, which orders all creation toward a good end. Thomas writes, "Wherefore, since all things subject to Divine providence are ruled and measured by the eternal law, . . . it is evident that all things partake somewhat of the eternal law, insofar as, namely, from its being imprinted on them, they derive their respective inclinations to their proper acts and ends . . . and this participation of the eternal law in the rational creature is called the natural law" (*ST* I.II.91.2). In other words, the natural law is something innate that allows persons to know how to behave well in order to reach their proper end, which is happiness in the presence of God.[9]

The impact of this idea is transformational for Western society. It means that, since individuals are bearers of the image of God, they have the capacity to reason. If they reason well, they will develop a sense of what is right and

Natural Law

The faculty of a person's reason that allows one to know how to behave well in a given circumstance. Within the Christian tradition, "to
behave well" is to order one's actions toward their proper end, which
is happiness in the presence of God.

wrong; that is to say, they will more capably understand what is the natural
law. And to the extent they appreciate natural law, they will behave justly.
So what is required is training in right reason, which partly explains why
Christians (and others of goodwill) had such a strong commitment to build
institutions that educate well, to strengthen families to raise their children
well, to promote virtue, and to encourage habits of just behavior.

"Alternative Culture" Movements

Sometimes building social institutions is not enough to address social and
structural sins. The institutions may not be sufficiently able to overcome the
desire of some to concentrate wealth and power in the hands of themselves
and others in their social class. Thus during the Middle Ages some Christians developed alternative-culture movements specifically intended to refute
those enthralled with power within society, politics, the economy, and even
the church. Here one thinks especially of the religious orders, especially the
mendicant orders such as the Franciscans and Dominicans, and the cloistered
orders such as the Carmelites.

During the early thirteenth century, two men living in different parts of
Europe and independent of each other gathered together a group of men
(and eventually women) willing to follow their example of living as wandering preachers and teachers and begging both for their own needs and for the
needs of the poor. These men, Dominic of Osma and Francis of Assisi, whose
followers became known respectively as Dominicans and Franciscans, taught
a renewed commitment to "evangelical poverty," or the poverty evidenced
by Jesus in the Gospels.[10] The early Dominicans and Franciscans believed
that too many people had too great a love for wealth and for power. By their
example of living as poor people who were also pious, they sought to initiate
conversations among Christians about just how much people really trusted
God to meet their needs, how much wealth was enough, and how much
compassion people had for the poor. Both groups also sought to reform the

The Mendicant Orders

The word "mendicant" means begging. Thus the mendicant orders, or mendicant religious groups, were formed within the Middle Ages and begged both for their own living and also to raise money to help the poor, the sick, and the oppressed.

The two principal mendicant orders were the Franciscans, founded by Francis of Assisi, and the Dominicans, founded by Dominic of Osma. Both groups were organized in the early 1200s, and they received approval from the bishop of Rome to carry out their unusual spiritual life. It was unusual not only because they begged for money but also because they felt that begging, or living like a poor person, was the nearest imitation of the life led by Jesus. Those who witnessed their way of following Jesus could not help but draw a contrast, generally positive, between their lifestyle of poverty and the more affluent lifestyle maintained by clergy and by monks in the Benedictine order.

By the end of the 1200s, though, there were debates within the mendicant orders as to just how much poverty a member of the group really needed to experience. The Franciscans and Dominicans who worked as professors at universities or who served as priests felt that they needed access to more resources than a strict lifestyle of poverty might otherwise allow. Divergent views about what constituted a lifestyle of poverty led to the formation of different branches of the mendicant orders in the fourteenth and later centuries.

church along these same lines by training members of their communities to join the priesthood or to serve as professors at universities. By embedding themselves within the structures of the church, they ensured the continuity of their message long after the deaths of their founders.

Similarly, Teresa of Ávila, who lived in the sixteenth century, led a reform and a renewal of the Carmelite communities in southwestern Europe.[11] Although educated and living for a time at a Dominican convent, in that community she found too great a laxity in piety and spiritual commitment. She thought things would be better in a Carmelite community nearby, but there too she found too much love for the world and its affairs among her fellow nuns. So when given the opportunity to lead the Carmelite community, she closed the convent to the outside world. She obliged those who wished to remain with her to become *discalced*, shoeless, which meant they agreed to close themselves into the convent. They would no longer need shoes since they agreed never again to venture outside the walls of the convent. Teresa's actions inspired many other men and women to become shoeless as well, and she spent most of the later years of her life working to reform existing or open new Carmelite communities.[12] Behind their walls were men or women willing to sacrifice the pursuits available in the world for a life of complete devotion to God, by living more simply. They were a constant witness against the vanities of wealth and worldliness to those outside the walls. They invited those outside to ask themselves what excuse they had for continuing to revel in such profligate luxuries.

Summary

Jesus's compassion for those on the margins of society led, during Late Antiquity, to the systematic organization of the Christian community's resources to alleviate suffering where it could. During the Middle Ages, this commitment expanded even further into the construction of schools (and later universities) to train people in the arts of medicine, law, and theology so they might not only expand the reach of the ministry but also discover better ways to provide that care. Also, the standardization of Christian worship helped to create social bonds across Europe's diverse peoples while ensuring the propagation of Christianity's values across the ages. Even Christianity's reach into politics, while especially messy, helped to strengthen social life by offering a vision of justice and of a just ruler. Combined, the Middle Ages produced a social ethic in which construction of a Christian society was seen as a surer way to the common good than charity-based ministries alone. Theologians and philosophers like Thomas Aquinas helped the church to navigate the theoretical waters needed to build this society. The Protestant Reformers, to be discussed in the next chapter, could not help but inherit some of this vision for a society in which the church and the state would work together for the common good.

Main Points of the Chapter

» During the Middle Ages, Christianity's investment in cultural institutions, such as education and politics, was a constitutive expression of its gospel witness.

» Thomas Aquinas's four-part framework for talking about justice initiated a revival in Christian thinking about the roles of church and state.

» The natural law tradition can be the basis for dialogue between Christian social ethics and the social ethics practiced by other religious and even secular traditions.

» The mendicant religious orders, among others, helped Christians to see that sometimes the best way to challenge the status quo of an unjust society is to live differently in the face of that society.

⟨ 8 ⟩

Reformations Era

Learning Outcomes for This Chapter

» Identify discontinuities between the social ethics of the Middle Ages and those of the Reformations era.

» Compare and contrast views of church-state relations among the various Protestant Reformers.

» Explain how Protestant theologies of God and of sin influenced the Protestant Reformers' ideas about the state.

During Late Antiquity and the Middle Ages, Christian social ethics developed out of two converging forces. One was Jesus's life of compassion for those on society's margins, which Christians recognized as their duty to continue. The other was Christians' increasing participation in political life over these centuries, which encouraged them to consider how a society might best be structured for the common good. These forces continued in the Reformations period. Yet this period, traditionally spanning only the sixteenth century but here including the seventeenth, was shaped by at least one new force that would affect Christian social ethics. This was the collapse of Catholic Christianity in many parts of Europe. Those who were once protesters on the outside of the Catholic community soon found themselves at the center of a new type of Christian community in much of Europe. The Protestants now had to offer the types of principled instructions regarding social life that had previously

Key Dates for the Reformations

1517	Luther posts his Ninety-Five Theses; start of German Reformation
1519	Ulrich Zwingli takes over as pastor in Zurich
1520	Pope excommunicates Luther with the document *Exsurge Domine*
1525	Anabaptist reforms begin in Switzerland
1526–29	"Lutheran" church is formed throughout Germany
1530s	Reformation spreads into Spain
1534	Ignatius Loyola founds Society of Jesus
1534	Henry VIII breaks Church of England from Roman papacy
1536	John Calvin begins Reformation in Geneva
1545	Council of Trent begins meeting
1558	Elizabeth I: Church of England officially becomes Protestant
1560s	Reformation spreads into Netherlands
1580s	Reformation spreads into Scandinavia

been supplied by Catholic intellectuals. It seemed possible that some new directions in social ethics might emerge.

Brief Historical Review

We call this period "Reformations," rather than simply "Reformation," for the simple reason that there were multiple reforms developing in Europe simultaneously during this time period. There were, of course, reform movements within Christianity in the centuries before this too, such as the rise of mendicant religious groups discussed in the previous chapter. There were also reform-minded monastic communities such as the Benedictine community at Cluny, by church leaders such as Jan Hus, and by educators like Desiderius Erasmus. Yet during the sixteenth and seventeenth centuries several reform movements coalesced around various key figures, and those movements created structures that had a lasting influence not only on Europe but also on the many parts of the world to which Europeans would spread during the eighteenth and later centuries. These reform movements included Lutheranism (inspired by Martin Luther) in Germany and the Scandinavian countries; Calvinism (inspired by John Calvin) in Geneva, parts of France, Scotland,

and the Netherlands; Anglicanism (led first by Thomas Cranmer, then by Queen Elizabeth I) in the British Isles; and several communities of Anabaptist Reformers in and around Zurich, southern Germany, and the Netherlands (inspired by Ulrich Zwingli, led by Menno Simons and many others). Reform movements even broke out within the reform movements, as we see in the development of "free Lutherans" within Lutheranism, a separation between Genevan and Dutch Calvinists, and the creation of communities of Baptists, Puritans, and Methodists out of the Anglican movement.[1]

During this period the Roman Catholic Church responded to these many Protestant reform movements with attempts at reforms of their own. One was the Council of Trent, which met for nearly two decades (1545–63) to discuss and to implement reforms of its clergy, its education, and its theological and philosophical commitments (esp. the doctrine of justification).[2] Another reform was the emergence of the Jesuit religious order. Jesuits sought to address deficiencies in the education system that had led too many Europeans to be swayed by Protestant mentalities. Jesuits typically led the intellectual charge against Protestant theologians in the education centers of Europe. Also, due to their commitment to mission work beyond Europe, the Jesuits helped the Roman Catholic Church look to Africa, Asia, and the Americas for the rebuilding of its community.[3]

The Council of Trent met in Santa Maria Maggiore church in Trent, Italy, in 1545–63.

Catholic Counter-Reformation

✓ Formation of the Society of Jesus
✓ Council of Trent (1546–63)
 • Addressed moral failings of the clergy
 • Renewed focus on clergy training
 • Instituted moral and educational reforms of the laity
 • Encouraged missionary activity
 • Called for an end to disobedience to the papacy
 • Called for an end to superstitious practices by laity

Carter Lindberg, in his excellent study of the Reformations era, concluded that the relative success or failure of the several reform movements corresponded to their capacity to harness the "crisis of values" that had emerged in late medieval society.[4] He argued that the church of the late medieval period proved incapable of guaranteeing the "symbols of [eternal] security." The Avignon papacy period exposed the church's internal divisions, which in turn spawned anticlericalism throughout Europe.[5] Then approaches to solve the problems—such as an attempt by those attending the Council of Constance in 1415 to make councils, not the pope, the locus of authority—too often failed to take hold.[6] To make matters worse, during the Renaissance era (the fourteenth and fifteenth centuries), papal investments in the arts and in building projects masked increasing frustration among the laity over the exorbitant taxes and the selling of indulgences required to pay for these expenses.

At the start of the sixteenth century, too much of the church's authority in matters related to symbols of security rested on a teetering house of cards. Yet it would take several cultural winds to bring that house down. During the late Middle Ages, one such wind was the rise of a monetary-based economy, in which individuals with skills in various crafts and trades could earn a living apart from farming. Guilds had formed to protect regional patrimonies in crafts such as goldsmithing and the manufacturing of goods as diverse as lace, chocolate, textiles, wine, and cheese, among many others.[7] This naturally led to increased urbanization because urban centers provided greater access to markets, particularly to traveling merchants and to the more distant markets they represented. These urban centers also attracted educational enterprises. Any prince or king with an urban center worth its medieval salt made sure that his city built its own university. The universities helped to attract even more urban investment, such as the development of the printing press and

Invention of the Printing Press

Earlier efforts at reform within the Roman Catholic Church, such as those by Jan Hus and John Wycliffe, would perhaps have met with greater success had they had the benefit of the printing press. Introduced into Europe by Johannes Gutenberg sometime during the 1440s, it was put to great use by Martin Luther and other Protestant Reformers. Scholars believe that perhaps as many as two thousand different printings of Luther's works (usually 1,000 copies in each printing), generally in the form of pamphlets, were made during just the first decade of the German Reformation.

the work of professional printers, besides the education they provided in the liberal arts, theology, law, and medicine. Moreover, the nearer one's location to a university, the greater the likelihood of exposure to the theological ideas of the day.

This seems rather well and good. Yet urbanization had at least one significant downside during the period leading up to and during the Reformations era. The maintenance of trade networks combined with poor sanitation policies meant that diseases from outside the community could enter and then spread quickly among the population. The black (bubonic) plague of the fourteenth century was so devastating—it wiped out 30–60 percent of Europe's population—because it had infested so many urban centers.[8] Thus although cities were centers of economic and intellectual activity, they were also ever-present reminders of the fragility of life. In addition, urban centers provided places to escape from the traditional mores of agrarian society. They fomented mentalities of independence, which proved helpful to Protestant Reformers offering new kinds of religious affiliations.

The sixteenth and seventeenth centuries were marked by a continuation of this expansion and growth. The monetary economy increased. Urbanization increased. Trade routes lengthened. A near-global trading and shipping industry was built. European countries established colonial outposts on nearly every continent. More universities were built. The invention of the printing press transformed the ability of intellectuals to spread their ideas. Book publishing increased exponentially. And new discoveries were made regularly. The so-called scientific revolution began during the seventeenth century. That was when Galileo (1564–1642) recorded his discoveries about the cosmic realm. It was when Isaac Newton published *Principia* (1687), which outlined his understanding of the laws of motion. Those living in the seventeenth century also witnessed the birth of the intellectual movement called the Enlightenment. Philosophers and political theorists proposed entirely new ways of thinking about the world, about humanity's place within that world, and about the role of the state in the lives of individuals. At the same time, the era witnessed a tremendous penchant for internecine wars among Europeans. The Spanish and the Dutch fought each other in 1568–1648. The Spanish and French fought each other in 1635–59, and the Germans fought each other during the Thirty Years' War in 1618–48.

In the final analysis, the sixteenth and seventeenth centuries witnessed rapid shifts in Europe's cultural and social landscapes. The decentralized Protestant communities of Europe proved more nimble than the Roman Catholic Church at picking up the pieces of that shifting landscape. Consequently they proved to be more capable of offering meaningful "symbols of security." The remainder of this chapter summarizes some of the ways in which Protestants who thought about society and social ethics responded to the new landscape they had helped to create.

The Two Kingdoms

The single most significant contribution to Christian social ethics during this period was the Protestant idea of two kingdoms. Whereas Christians in the Middle Ages had sought to build a Christian society by greater cohesion between church and state, including even, at times, seeing the church as over the state, the Protestants argued that a Christian society would emerge only with greater separation between these two "kingdoms." Yet different Protestant leaders had different ideas about how this should be done. Martin Luther shifted duties once managed by the church to the state, and he was content to allow the state some control over the administration of church affairs. John Calvin more strictly separated the work of the church from that of the state, but he taught that God was sovereign over both kingdoms. For this reason, it was imperative that Christians become involved in the state to ensure that it remained faithful to God's ultimate headship. According to the Radical Reformers, such as those among the various Anabaptist communities in eastern Switzerland and southern Germany, the two kingdoms were so distinct that they were to have nothing to do with each other.

Martin Luther

To understand Martin Luther's two-kingdom concept, one needs to recall his theology of justification by grace. Prior to and in the years immediately following his posting of the Ninety-Five Theses on the Wittenberg church door, Luther had been teaching at the University of Wittenberg on the New Testament book of Romans and on Pauline theology in general. While teaching, Luther came to the conviction that humans are declared justified by God through nothing more than God giving, or imputing, grace to a person to respond in faith to the person and work of Jesus.[9] This was perceived to be in contrast to church teaching going back to the writings of Peter Lombard (his *Books of Sentences*)[10] and others within the universities and churches who taught that grace was infused into an individual over time by virtue of their participation in the sacraments, which were deemed to be meritorious works. But to Luther, salvation was completely a work of God in the life of a person and not a consequence of their particular actions within the church. In short, the church needed to be a place of greater freedom in order for people to cultivate a love for God motivated by the experience of God's grace in their lives.

Martin Luther (1483–1546)

✓ Joined the Augustinian Order in 1505.
✓ Studied at the new University of Wittenberg during 1508–12 and joined its faculty soon thereafter.
✓ Protested the Roman Catholic Church's promise of remission of sin for the price of an indulgence with the posting of Ninety-Five Theses in 1517.
✓ Excommunicated from the Roman Catholic Church in 1520; the Lutheran Church was formed in the years immediately following.
✓ Widely known for his teaching that salvation comes by grace rather than by meritorious works.
✓ Married a former nun, Katharina von Bora, in 1525, with whom he had six children.

Prompted by these ideas to consider the role of the church in an individual's life, Luther also took the opportunity to rethink the role of the other kingdom, the state. Insight into Luther's thinking in this regard can be gleaned from a number of texts. Considered here are just two of them. The first is his *To the Christian Nobility of the German Nation* (1520). It is, first, a critique of the Roman Catholic Church for insulating itself from political and lay oversight, including especially its claiming the right to appoint rulers of the state. Luther argues that bishops have no more right than anyone else—based on the concept of a priesthood of all believers—to appoint someone to a political office. "There is no true, basic difference between laymen, princes and bishops, between religious and secular, except for the sake of office and work, but not for the sake of status."[11] Second, the text states that each kingdom has its own separate duties.

> Therefore, just as those who are now called "spiritual" . . . are charged with the administration of the Word of God and the sacraments, which is their work and office, so it is with the temporal authorities. They bear the sword and rod in their hand to punish the wicked and protect the good. . . . Further, everyone must benefit and serve every other by means of his own work or office.[12]

Here the church has no role in punishing the wicked; that belongs to the state. Indeed, this role must be carried out even when the wicked person is the pope, or a leader of one of the Anabaptist groups (see section on Radical Reformers below; cf. Luther's *Letter to Philipp of Hesse*), or a false prophet (cf. Luther's *Letter to Wenceslaus Linck*), or some other leader of the church.[13]

> Therefore, when necessity demands it, and the pope is an offense to Christendom, the first man who is able should . . . do what he can to bring about a truly free council. No one can do this so well as the temporal authorities, especially since they are fellow Christians, fellow priests, fellow members of the spiritual estate. Whenever it is necessary or profitable, they ought to exercise the office and work which they have received from God over everyone.[14]

The church has a job to do, and it should do it well. The state has a job to do, and it should do that job well. When the church fails in its work, the state is obliged to step in and to correct it. Given Luther's assumption that the state is filled with Christian-minded leaders, this makes sense. Yet Luther did not take account here of the possibility that the state's interests may be clouded by less-than-pure Christian motives.

Three years later, he realized how mistaken this assumption was. In a work titled *On Secular Authority* (1523), Luther complains that the rulers have not become sufficiently Christian. While affirming the state's God-given right to use the sword to punish the wicked (cf. Rom. 13), Luther nevertheless insists on the right of the church to oppose the state when that sword is used to compel obedience to a false god, religion, or church. Presumably, Luther argues, a righteous person does not seek to be wicked; therefore, such a person, as a member of God's kingdom, the true church, is subject to its rules more so than to those of the state. "For this reason these two kingdoms must be sharply distinguished, and both be permitted to remain; the one to produce piety, the other to bring about external peace and prevent evil deeds; neither is sufficient in the world without the other."[15] With this text, Luther reveals how quickly his concern grew for separating even further the two kingdoms of church and state. In an ideal world, the church would be under the state, but that only works if the state is led by good Christians. In the absence of that ideal, the two kingdoms need to remain more carefully within their respective spheres.

John Calvin and "Calvinists"

A little more than a decade after the Lutheran Reformation had taken hold in Germany, a similar reformation was taking shape in Geneva and the adjacent area of western Switzerland. This movement was led by John Calvin, a pastor who had earlier trained as a lawyer.[16] Not unlike Luther's theology, Calvin's theology was driven by the conviction that salvation came to otherwise hopelessly lost and sinful men and women by virtue of God's unmerited offer of grace. God's distribution of grace to individuals is a sign of his providential care of the world, for this ensures that a group of people will be present in the world to offer worship and praise to him as its creator. And because God providentially cares for the world, Calvin felt that it was time for men and women to entrust themselves more to God's leadership in every sphere of life. They can do so because God's providential care and leadership is over the church and the state just as much as it is over the divine grace in their own lives.

Calvin incorporated his ideas about God's sovereignty over the two king-doms in the fourth book of his *Institutes of the Christian Religion*. He titled chapter 20 "Civil Government," and in it the reader discovers several impor-tant points helpful to our concern with social ethics. Calvin benefited from a little bit of hindsight with regard to the Lutheran experience. Whereas it took Luther a few years to realize the need to separate the two kingdoms, Calvin starts with this sobering assessment. He says at the beginning of "Civil Government" that too often princes abuse their power and "do not hesitate to set them[selves] against the rule of God himself" (*Institutes* 4.20.1).[17] Having said that, Calvin insists that the state exists for legitimate purposes. One is for the maintenance of the basic needs of society's members, and he includes as duties related to this "that men breathe, eat, drink, and are kept warm." The state also exists for purposes beyond ensuring that the basic necessities are provided. It has a duty to ensure that the civic realm has a properly functioning religion, including preventing "idolatry, sacrilege against God's name, blasphemies against his truth, and other public offenses against religion." The state also has a duty to protect private property and the freedom of wholesome speech. "In short, it provides that a public manifestation of religion may exist among Christians, and that humanity be maintained among men" (*Institutes* 4.20.3).[18] All of this may seem like too much state involvement in church, but Calvin is only saying that the state has a duty to ensure that the Christian religion is preserved and able to function. What precisely constitutes Christian religion and its practices and beliefs belongs solely to the kingdom of the church and not to the state.

Underlying all of his teaching regarding the separate roles for the church and the state is divine providence. Both kingdoms exist to carry out God's own purposes. For this reason, the state is as much under God's authority as is the church. At God's pleasure, rulers are raised up and rulers are brought down. This is why Calvin says to leaders of the state, "Let the princes hear [the Bible's stories of God bringing down bad rulers] and be afraid" (*Institutes* 4.20.31).[19] Yet what are Christians to do when the state turns against

John Calvin (1509–64)

✓ Born in Noyon, France.

✓ Studied first for the priesthood in Paris, but his father moved him to the University of Orléans, then to the University of Bourges to study law.

✓ During 1533 he broke away from the Roman Catholic Church. After persecutions began against Protestants in France, in 1535 he fled to Basel, where he published the first edition of his famous *Institutes of the Christian Religion* in 1536. Later that year he began assisting with pastoral work in Geneva.

✓ Pastored churches in Strasbourg from 1538 to 1541, then moved to Geneva until his death.

✓ Married Idelette de Bure in 1540, who had two children from a prior marriage. The children born to John and Idelette all died in infancy. She died in 1549.

them? Since such an occurrence too must be part of God's providential care, the church's members are obliged to obey the state regardless of how much suffering they may need to endure. Calvin writes,

> But we must . . . be very careful not to despise or violate that authority of mag-
> istrates, full of venerable majesty, which God has established by the weightiest
> decrees, even though it may reside with the most unworthy men, who defile
> it as much as they can with their own wickedness. For, if the correction of
> unbridled despotism is the Lord's to avenge, let us not at once think that it is
> entrusted to us, to whom no command has been given except to obey and suf-
> fer. (*Institutes* 4.20.31)[20]

This obligation to obey and suffer, however, applies only to individual citizens. Calvin next says that those citizens who have the capacity to remove tyrants as a part of their role as officials within the state are obliged to fulfill their duties and to remove the tyrants. This is why it is critical for state officials to be Christian. Not only is it more likely that Christian leaders will refrain from becoming tyrants, but they will also accept the duty to remove tyrants regardless of what it might cost them personally to do so. And this brings Calvin's whole discussion of the two kingdoms full circle. Church and state have separate duties for the people, but both exist by God's good pleasure; God gives them their respective charges. The best way to align the functions of these two kingdoms in the world with what God intends for them is to have faithful Christians administering both kingdoms. If one or the other kingdom fails to fulfill its duties, Christians are to trust that God will eventually provide the necessary remedy.[21]

One of the matters threatening the integrity of the separate kingdoms was the church's practice of discipline and excommunication. Calvin argued that this fell within the bounds of the church; local officials, however, argued that these matters were best left to the state. To understand this, recall that Calvin had trained as a lawyer before taking up work as a pastor in Geneva. He drew on this training in seeking to reorganize the affairs of the new Protestant churches and to set down new guidelines for how they were to operate. One of the texts he produced in this regard was the *Ecclesiastical Ordinances* (1541). The text created a governance structure for the Genevan churches, and this included the creation of a body of elders known as the Genevan Consistory. The consistory was assigned the task of meeting regularly (every Thursday morning) to discuss disciplinary issues regarding members of the several churches in town.[22] They became known for meting out discipline that involved the closure of certain taverns and other businesses deemed unbecoming of a Christian society. This is where the state declared that the church had overstepped its proper bounds. It was okay for the church to discipline its members, but it could not, on pain of excommunication of the business owner, compel shops to close. So the state wrote legislation to give itself alone the right to determine who could and could not be excommunicated.

Calvin fought back, and in his fighting back one sees him working out the principles he wrote about in the *Institutes*. To stop the state from interfering in the church, it was incumbent on the state to respect God's sovereignty over the state. To do that requires the presence of Christians among the leadership of the state. Indeed, during 1543–45, Calvin worked to get Christians favorable to his position elected to the Council of 60, a Genevan legislative body. Those Christians eventually overturned the legislation that had given to the state alone the right to excommunicate.[23]

Calvin's theology and the other Protestant reforms at Geneva soon spread well beyond that city. Calvinist-minded Protestants soon emerged among the Dutch in the northern part of Europe and in Scotland. This is not the place to review their respective theological ideas and whether and how they differed from those of Calvin and the later Calvinists in Geneva.[24] Here we are interested in the texts that emerged in these circles that also addressed the two-kingdoms principle. The Calvinists in Scotland wrote about the two kingdoms in their Second Book of Discipline (1578), and the idea of the two kingdoms is assumed in comments about civil government in their Westminster Confession (1647). The Calvinists among the Dutch incorporated their assumptions into comments about civil officials in their Belgic Confession (1561), Heidelberg Catechism (1563), and Second Helvetic Confession (1566).[25]

The Scots' Second Book of Discipline addresses the topic in its tenth chapter, titled "The Office of a Christian Magistrate in the Kirk [church]." The title alone shows that it was assumed that local officials are Christian. Given Christians' faith and their role within the state, the Second Book of Discipline delegates to the state the shared obligation to advance the "kingdom of Jesus Christ" (10.1). They may do this by assisting and fortifying "the godly proceedings of the kirk," which means ensuring that the church exists as part of civil society (10.2). Specifically, the state is to protect the property of the kirk and to keep out of it false teachers, "dumb dogs and idle bellies" (10.3), the last of which refers to individuals who seek only to live off the church's welfare rather than to work for their food. The state is to maintain the schools and to provide for the needs of the poor (10.5). Furthermore, those whom the church has disciplined or excommunicated are to have the administration of their punishments enforced by the state, "always without confounding the one jurisdiction with the other" (10.4). Finally, the state is warned to "make the laws and constitutions agreeable to God's word, for advancement of the kirk" (10.7). If a conflict ever arises between the church and the state on these matters, the Second Book of Discipline gives priority to the church. Assuming that the church is rightly constituted of God-fearing persons, "all godly princes and magistrates ought to hear and obey their voice, and reverence the Majesty of the Son of God speaking by them" (10.7).

Similar ideas are found in the documents of the Dutch Calvinists. They affirm that God instituted civil government to provide peace and tranquility (Second Helvetic Confession 30.2), and they affirm that the state bears the sword for the sole purpose of punishing the wicked (Belgic Confession 36; Second Helvetic Confession 30.3; Heidelberg Catechism Q.105). Consequently, citizens are obliged to acknowledge the state as a gift from God (Second Helvetic Confession 30.6). Moreover, the state is best run when it is "truly seasoned with the fear of God and true religion," since this alone will ensure advancement of the faith and the protection of the kingdom of the church (Second Helvetic Confession 30.2).

Radical Reformers

The name "Radical Reformers" refers to any of a number of religious groups that emerged in southern Germany and in the eastern parts of Switzerland, especially in and near the city of Zurich, who felt that the Lutheran Reformers elsewhere in Germany had not gone far enough in their repudiation of the Roman Catholic Church's teachings and in their separation of the church's affairs from those of the state. There were a spectrum of positions within these communities. For example, Ulrich Zwingli, a Protestant pastor in Zurich, went further than did Luther in his repudiation of Catholic understandings of the sacraments.[26] Yet Zwingli retained the practice of infant baptism. This was unacceptable to others within the Radical Reformation movement, such as the several Anabaptist communities: driven by more narrow readings of the Bible, they felt that only those things explicitly taught in Scripture are to be done, and infant baptism is not one of them. Still, the Anabaptist communities were rarely of one mind themselves about how to interpret Scripture; consequently they divided into different groups, some of which still exist today, such as the Mennonites and the Hutterites. The founder of Methodism, the onetime Anglican pastor Charles Wesley, lived for a time among the members of one of these groups (at their commune on the land of Count von Zinzendorf), and he came away from that experience impressed by their piety and devotional practices. He later translated their ideas into a "method" for the spiritual life, and the Methodist Church was soon born.

Leading Members of the Radical Reformation

✓ Ulrich Zwingli (1484–1531)—led the reformation movement in Zurich.

✓ Conrad Grebel (1498–1526)—broke from Zwingli to become one of the founders of the Swiss Brethren movement among Anabaptists.

✓ Michael Sattler (1495–1527)—a onetime Benedictine monk, he helped to draft the Schleitheim Confession and led an Anabaptist community in Rottenberg.

✓ Menno Simons (1496–1561)—a onetime Catholic priest in his home region of Friesland in the Netherlands; led the Anabaptist movement among the Dutch from 1536 until his death. The Mennonites today are named after him.

✓ Jakob Hutter (ca. 1500–1536)—led Anabaptist communities first in Tyrol, Austria, then in Moravia (today part of the Czech Republic). The Hutterites today are named after him.

For all their diversity, the Radical Reformers shared a distrust of any association between the church and the state. Believers' prime loyalty to Christ and the church modulated their commitments to their country. Indeed, the Dutch Calvinists criticized the Radicals for their separatist mentalities (Belgic Confession 36; Second Helvetic Confession 30.5). Yet their separatist mentality was not without good reason, for the state, with the support of the Lutheran-minded church, had repeatedly tried to dismantle their communities by force, and many members of their communities were executed for heresy. One of the most practical causes of their view that church and state should have nothing to do with each other was their pacifism. They taught Christ's law of love and rejection of any recourse to violence. That at least was the ideal. The historical record includes events in which some members of these groups did, at times, take up arms for self-defense and at least once overthrew a city to establish a theocracy (cf. the short-lived takeover of Münster in 1534). In any case, their argument for the pacifist position was first made in the Schleitheim Confession (1527), a document composed during a conference in the city of Schleitheim, convened by members of several different Anabaptist groups.[27]

The text opens with the words, "The articles we have dealt with, and in which we have been united, are these: baptism, bans, the breaking of bread, separation from abomination, shepherds in the congregation, the sword, the oath."[28] Mention of the sword in this list refers to their pacifist stance. While admitting the state's right to bear the sword, Anabaptists wanted nothing to do with the duties associated with that right. Remarkably, according to the Schleitheim Confession, this rejection of violence even extends to the protection of one's own friends. "Thereby shall also fall away from us the diabolical weapons of violence—such as sword, armor, and the like, and all of their use to protect friends or against enemies" (Confession §4).[29] It also did not matter that the sword could be used against the wicked, or for the benefit of the common good, or for the sake of love (Confession §6).

The Anabaptists treated violence as so abhorrent an evil that no good that might emerge from employing it justifies the evil. Thus it necessarily follows that Anabaptists refused to serve as magistrates or in the military or in any other capacity of the state, since that might compel them to employ violence in carrying out their duties. "[It] is asked concerning the sword whether the Christian should be a magistrate if he is chosen thereto. . . . It does not befit a Christian to be a magistrate: the rule of the government is according to the flesh, that of the Christians according to the Spirit" (Confession §6).[30]

If it is not already clear by this point in the Schleitheim Confession just how separated the kingdoms of church and state ought to be, the section on pacifism concludes: "In sum: as Christ our Head is minded, so also must be minded the members of the body of Christ through him . . . so that his body may remain whole and unified for its own advancement and upbuilding. For any kingdom which is divided within itself will be destroyed" (Confession §6).[31] For the church to be successful in its own sphere, it needs to avoid any entanglements with the state, regardless of the consequences that may come. Indeed, Anabaptist communities went on to celebrate as martyrs those among its members who, without putting up a fight, accepted the right of the state to execute them.[32]

The Economy

While the two-kingdoms concept transformed the debate within Protestant communities over what constitutes proper social ethics from the sixteenth century onward, the Reformers also reflected on the economy and some of its proper functions. As we saw above, the Reformers assigned principally to the state the duty to maintain public order, and this included the maintenance of the poor. Samuel Torvend's book *Luther and the Hungry Poor* skillfully documents the connections between Luther's theology of grace and justification and thus the recognized obligations of civic and church officials to maintain community resources for collecting and distributing excess goods for the benefit of the poor.[33] Calvin's sermons on Deut. 15, delivered in October 1555, and on Deut. 24, delivered in February 1556, are a handful of prominent examples (among others) attesting his understanding of rich people's duties to alleviate the suffering of the poor.[34] Among the Radical Reformers, Peter Walpot's *True Yieldedness and the Christian Community of Goods* (1577) argues for communally owned resources to benefit the entire community. Walpot was a member of the Hutterites, and his text is both an explanation of Hutterite values and a rationale for the total sharing of goods among Christians.

The Reformation also addressed usury practices. Luther wrote about them in two sermons, in 1519 and 1520, later combined into one treatise, *Trade and Usury* (1524).[35] And Calvin wrote "A Letter on Usury" (1545).[36] Usury, or the loaning of money at interest, was forbidden within the Jewish community, and Christians in Late Antiquity and for much of the Middle Ages maintained the prohibition. During those eras, loans were typically only made to the poor, so charging them interest was rightly seen as unjustly compounding the problem of poverty. By the late Middle Ages, however, with the advent of a money-based economy and greater industrialization, loans were increasingly being made to businesspeople who used the money to increase their productive capacity. In other words, it was no longer just the poor who sought out the assistance of banks and wealthy individuals for the offer of a loan. The Roman Catholic Church began to allow the charging of some interest on loans at this point, but it was restricted to an amount in line with the costs associated with running the bank or of processing and maintaining the accounts associated with the loan. Fast-forward to the sixteenth century, and the Protestants' concern to align their teachings with the words of Scripture. Luther and Calvin were confronted with questions about moneylending practices and usury and whether they conformed to the teachings of Scripture.

Luther's treatise *Trade and Usury* situates usury within the broader economic system, which has too many incentives for merchants to maximize their wealth at the expense of the community. On the specific matter of loaning at interest, Luther was less than enthusiastic. He taught that interest should be limited to 5 percent, but he knew that loans were typically made at substantially higher rates. Therefore, ideally no one should stand in surety for a loan made to anyone else. Instead, the Christian should just give to the person who has a need what they need without expecting the gift ever to be returned or repaid. The Christian may graciously receive back what was loaned if it is repaid, but there should be no difficulties between the giver and the receiver if that does not happen. Thus Luther is much more in line with earlier Christians' disdain for the practice. Loaning at interest, regardless of its economic purpose, still puts the borrower in the position of a poor person. To Luther's mind, the poor person—not the economy—ought to be the central concern of Christians.

Somewhat in contrast to Luther's position, Calvin taught that usury can be put to a productive end. While admitting that "usury almost always travels with two inseparable companions: tyrannical cruelty and the art of deception" ("Letter on Usury"), he also recognized that society and its economic life had changed significantly since biblical and earlier Christian eras. "How do merchants increase their wealth? By being industrious. . . . No one borrows money from others with the intention of hiding it or not making a profit. Consequently, the gain is not from the money but from profit. . . . Hence, I conclude that we ought not to judge usury according to a few passages of Scripture, but in accordance with the principle of equity." Calvin did, however, limit his allowance of usury practices. He said that no one is to be in the usury business as a full-time occupation, loans with interest are not to be made to the poor, and the loan should be structured in such a way that the borrower is able to earn as much or more (by increased productive capacity) than the loan amount itself. Perhaps most interesting of all are his limitations: Calvin says lenders should not treat their loans as being between themselves and an individual, but between themselves and the common good. "Thus we should see that the contract will benefit all rather than hurt." Many later Protestants took from this and related teaching in Calvin's writings that it is the duty of Christians to be productive, to make an honest profit, and to cultivate a good work ethic. It would set the stage for Protestants in the Reformed tradition to struggle with understanding how to balance their desire to support capitalist-driven economies with their obligation to care for the poor that such economies necessarily leave behind.

Summary

Much more can be said and much has been written by scholars about particular teaching on the economy, health care, politics, and other features of Protestant teaching during the Reformations era. The focus here on the two-kingdoms principle offers insight into Protestant mentalities regarding just what civil society is, what it should be, and what responsibility Christians have for ensuring that civil society is ordered for the common good. Divergent views among Protestants about the different roles for the church and the state, and even whether Christians should be involved in the state, could not help but create differences among later Protestants in how they viewed their responsibility to solve problems in the wider culture, including especially issues centered on capitalism versus social democracy. These are subjects to which we turn in the next two chapters.

Main Points of the Chapter

» The kingdom of the church is to have unfettered authority over spiritual matters, doctrine, and correction of its members.

» The kingdom of the state is to use its power of the sword (Rom. 13) to ensure the maintenance of law and order, including the protection of private property and the institutions of the church.

» For Luther and Calvin, it is the duty of Christians to enter public service to ensure the state's fidelity to God's will. To the Anabaptists, the state's use of the sword makes it hopelessly irreconcilable with the church.

❄ 9 ❄

Post-Reformations Era

Learning Outcomes for This Chapter

» Summarize Enlightenment mentalities regarding religious authority and their impact on the Protestant communities in Europe and America.

» Contrast Protestant concerns to separate the church from the state with their concerns to integrate the church into society.

» Explain the contribution of the social gospel movement to Protestant thinking about the role of the church in society.

As we saw in chapter 8, the two-kingdoms ideas of the sixteenth-century Protestant Reformers revealed divergent views among Protestants about the different roles for the church and the state, including whether Christians should be involved in the state. These differences alone would have been enough to cause Protestants in later centuries to develop different social ethics. However, a shift in the intellectual landscape of Western culture proved more crucial to those differences that emerged. The Enlightenment shifted social ethics out of a church-and-state question and instead into a question of what elements of Christianity were any longer relevant to an increasingly secular culture. In the wake of this, different branches of Protestantism emerged, and each branch contributed something unique to Protestant social ethics.

Brief Historical Review

For our purposes, the post-Reformations period spans the latter part of the seventeenth century through the present day. Two features of this period have proved decisive in the construction of Protestant social ethics: (1) a separation of the state from the church, and (2) a promotion of scientific knowledge above theological knowledge. The first of these led to the church having to assume an outsider role in promoting policies of the state that could foster the common good. The second of these led to Western cultures no longer appreciating the sources of truth on which Christianity has traditionally been based.

The first of these two features, the separation of the church from the state, can be marked by at least two pivotal moments. One is the Peace of Westphalia (1648), which was a series of treaties signed toward the end of Europe's Thirty Years' War. They were the first to disconnect the work of the church from the work of the state. While the details of the war and its various combatants are worth studying in other venues, we will focus only on how the war was partially based on the rights of Christian communities to worship in the different parts of Germany where they had been previously restricted (e.g., Catholics wanted to worship in Lutheran regions, and vice versa). The Peace of Westphalia declared the rights of Catholics, Lutherans, and Calvinists (and only those three groups at that time) to worship wherever they chose. The state was no longer to be involved in deciding where or what people could worship, although rulers retained the right to support and to protect the religion of their choice.[1]

The second pivotal moment was the embrace of John Locke's (1632–1704) "social contract" idea by political leaders in Europe and America. Although it had earlier been articulated by Thomas Hobbes in his *Leviathan*, it was Locke's *Two Treatises on Government* that proved more influential on late eighteenth-century leaders.[2] Locke challenged the notion that political authority was dependent on religious authority. Rather, people contract together to form a government for the sole purpose of protecting their private property. Religion has no role in legitimizing such a state. In terms of social ethics, this new relationship with the state was both a blessing and a curse for the church. On the one hand, the church was now more free to speak prophetically about injustice it witnessed in the state. On the other hand, the church had to reframe its socioethical principles in terms that now were more conducive to secular values. The church could not rely solely on its distinctly Christian language, including its scriptural language, to promote its social ideals.

Having said that, the state's gradual extrication of itself from the affairs of the church certainly caught many Protestant communities off guard. Yet it was a

Key events and movements leading to . . .

✓ separating the church from the state
  • Peace of Westphalia
  • Locke's "social contract"
✓ divisions within Protestantism
  • Enlightenment mentalities
  • Higher criticism

welcome change from earlier policies for other Protestants, such as Baptists and the Radical Reformation communities.[3] They welcomed the opportunity it presented for the church to extricate itself from the state. This was especially the case for Protestants in America. The US Constitution's first amendment includes the following line, known as the establishment clause: "Congress shall make no law respecting an establishment of religion, or prohibiting the free exercise thereof." James Madison, later the fourth president of the United States, had drafted this and other language of the Bill of Rights. Also, in his first draft of what would later become the Second Amendment, on the right to keep and to bear arms, Madison added a concession to the nation's Quakers, Mennonites, Moravians, and other like-minded Christian citizens, "but no person religiously scrupulous of bearing arms shall be compelled to render military service in person." This was eventually dropped from the final language of the amendment.[4] These two texts reveal how Madison appreciated Martin Luther's earlier teaching on the two-kingdoms principle: to be genuinely human meant both a free exercise of religion and the free exercise of political rights.[5] Indeed, it was clear in 1789 that the United States would be a nation where religious practices were tolerated by the government.

Yet it was not entirely clear to some American Protestants that the government would steer sufficiently clear of their religious affairs. In 1801 the Danbury Baptist Association wrote to President Thomas Jefferson, inquiring about the government's intentions in regard to the establishment clause. Jefferson's reply incorporated the famous phrase that there is a "wall of eternal separation" between the church and the state.[6] Further, according to Jefferson, the First Amendment prevented any part of the American government from prescribing "even those occasional performances of devotion." The Danbury Baptists—and all religious communities—were free to set their own rules and their own devotions for their own sects. The government would neither intervene in their affairs nor establish any particular set of religious practices. The church was free to do what it wanted to do; the state was equally free to pursue its own ends.

The second feature of this period that proved decisive in changing Protestantism, which is not unrelated to the previous matter, was the emergence of the

Enlightenment. This intellectual movement fundamentally reshaped Protestant (and, for that matter, Catholic) Christianity from the late seventeenth century forward. Significant in this movement was the work of philosophers such as René Descartes (d. 1650). Descartes taught that the foundation on which a person may be certain about what is and is not true is the subjective realm of the mind. Thus one can doubt as true nearly everything once thought to be true; the only thing that one cannot doubt is that one is thinking at that moment. Thus the phrase *Cogito ergo sum* (I think, therefore I am) is often recalled to sum up what Descartes taught: a person is a thinking person.[7] Then, according to Descartes, what is necessary is for there to be a correspondence, on the basis of reason, between what one knows in the mind and what one senses in the natural world.

Statue in the Thomas Jefferson Memorial in Washington, DC.

Although Descartes was positive about such a correspondence, the Enlightenment project was instead a gradual separation of the world of thought (the world of mind) from the natural world around us (the world of matter).

A Wall of Separation

Believing with you that religion is a matter which lies solely between Man & his God, that he owes account to none other for his faith or his worship, that the legitimate powers of government reach actions only, & not opinions, I contemplate with sovereign reverence that act of the whole American people which declared that their legislature should "make no law respecting an establishment of religion, or prohibiting the free exercise thereof," thus building a wall of separation between Church & State. Adhering to this expression of the supreme will of the nation in behalf of the rights of conscience, I shall see with sincere satisfaction the progress of those sentiments which tend to restore to man all his natural rights, convinced he has no natural right in opposition to his social duties.

—Thomas Jefferson, Letter to the Danbury Baptist Association (1802)

Portrait of René Descartes (1569–1650) by Frans Hals.

These two worlds developed with two different languages. Study of the world of mind required the language of philosophy; study of the world of matter required the language of mathematics. Eventually truth was recognized in observations of the world of matter, and the correspondence between mind and matter had to proceed in the direction opposite that posited by Descartes. Now the mind needed to rethink its understanding of what is true to correspond with the truths discovered in matter.

Once the truths of matter, in the domain of the natural sciences, took preeminence over the world of mind, which continued to be the domain of subjects like philosophy and theology, Christianity quickly found itself in a difficult place, culturally and intellectually. Religion generally, especially the Christianity of Western cultures, was deemed an irrelevant producer of mental rather than scientific knowledge. It did not help that the Roman Catholic Church in 1633 had obliged Galileo to renounce his heliocentric theory of the cosmic realm.[8] Christianity could no longer command the respect it once assumed in the halls of academia. And if it was no longer trusted as a source of truth, for what purposes could it be trusted?

During the nineteenth and early twentieth centuries, Protestant communities took divergent paths in their response to what was then considered to be the challenge of modernism. One response was to embrace scientific knowledge and to reinterpret the Scriptures and the Christian tradition in order that they might better conform to that type of knowledge. One example of this response is the development of higher criticism, which is the study of the editorial processes by which the Scripture texts came to exist. Protestants who pursued this course did their academic work without any longer presuming a divine author or inspirer of the Scripture texts or presuming their internal consistency. Instead, the Scripture texts were studied as products of human ingenuity and editing in response to historical circumstances. This suggests that the Christian religion too was the product of fortuitous historical circumstances. Its texts and sources may be examined as products of human

Higher Criticism (or Historical Criticism)

✓ Higher Criticism is a movement among biblical scholars that began in the early 1800s.

✓ For the sake of an academic study of the Bible, it assumes that books within the Bible are solely the product of human authorship.

✓ Its aim is to understand the world, the author, the audience, and so forth that lies behind the text.

✓ It focuses on the sources that the author may have used in composing the text, on the form of communication used by the author (e.g., poetry versus letter), and on the extent to which the text was edited by its later readers.

ingenuity rather than divine agency. From an academic standpoint, then, the methods of higher criticism suggest that Christianity's truth claims are as historically contingent as those of any other religious movement. In terms of its impact on social ethics, higher criticism lent itself to some Christians sensing a need to articulate their values regarding the common good in terms that could be universally held rather than in terms based on principles gleaned from a text like the Bible, which too few still believed was divinely inspired.

Whereas this type of response embraced the culture's shift toward the preeminence of the world of matter, a second type of response to modernism among Protestants favored the validity of the world of mind. This response focused its efforts on personal conversion and renewal. The so-called Second Great Awakening in the nineteenth century (marked by the preaching of Charles Finney, Billy Sunday, and others) was one of several movements marking this type of response.[9] It exhorted men and women not to lose sight of their eternal destiny no matter the changes occurring as a result of a scientific worldview in the wider culture. While less a dismissal of scientific knowledge than it was an attempt at restoring interest in the world of mind, preaching like that associated with the Second Great Awakening eventually had to respond to concerns about the reliability and authority of Scripture. Leaders developed Bible and prophecy conference circuits, which sought to reeducate Protestants about the content of Scripture. Some of its leaders met regularly from 1876 to 1897 at an event known as the Niagara Bible Conference. In 1878 they issued a "Niagara Creed," which listed fourteen fundamental points of the Christian faith. That list was later distilled into five points and taught in a series of pamphlets by R. A. Torrey, C. I. Scofield, and others, and they were issued as

The Five Fundamentals of Fundamentalists

1. Inspiration and inerrancy of the Bible
2. Virgin birth of Christ
3. Substitutionary atonement of Christ
4. Bodily resurrection of Christ
5. Historicity of the biblical miracles

a statement of Christian fundamental beliefs at the 1910 General Assembly of the Presbyterian Church. Statements such as these revealed what was at stake in terms of Scripture's authority in Western culture's embrace of scientific knowledge. In terms of social ethics, this response to modernism, in keeping with its focus on individual conversion, lent itself well to the creation of charitable institutions and relief agencies.

A third response to modernism was a theological movement known as neo-orthodoxy. If the first type of response to modernism can be seen as an embrace of the world of matter and the second response a renewal of interest in the world of mind, then this third response can be seen as an attack on the assumptions of scientific knowledge, particularly as it relates to religion, in its own attempt at restoring the preeminence of the world of mind. In the wake of World War I (1914–18), neo-orthodox theologians felt the promise of scientific knowledge had not only proved incapable of "saving" humanity but had also promoted humanity's moral decline; there was no longer any pretense of inevitable progress in the human condition because of advancing scientific knowledge. Replacing this failed hope ought to be a renewed interest in a transcendent God who had offered grace and forgiveness in the midst of human sin and brokenness. Leading theologians in the neo-orthodox movement included Karl Barth, Emil Brunner, Rudolf Bultmann, and Reinhold Niebuhr (though Niebuhr preferred the term "Pauline realism" or simply "Christian realism" to "neo-orthodoxy").[10] Although more liberal Protestants frequently accused them of being "quietists" when it came to social ethics, this was decidedly inaccurate. Such a charge did not take proper account of Barth's Gifford Lectures in 1937–38, titled *The Knowledge of God and the Service of God according to the Teaching of the Reformation*, or of Brunner's *The Divine Imperative*, or of Reinhold Niebuhr's *Moral Man and Immoral Society*.[11] In terms of social ethics, their concern with sin would helpfully shape later Protestant thinking about sinful social structures.

In the American experience of Protestantism, these three responses to the challenge of modernism were reflected in what, throughout the twentieth century, was seen as a split between "mainline" (liberal) Protestantism and "fundamentalist" (conservative) Protestantism. Elements of neo-orthodox theology would find their way into both groups. Evangelical Protestantism,

Coercion and Justice

The stupidity of the average man will permit the oligarch, whether economic or political, to hide his real purposes from the scrutiny of his fellows and to withdraw his activities from effective control. Since it is impossible to count on enough moral goodwill among those who possess irresponsible power to sacrifice it for the good of the whole, it must be destroyed by coercive methods and these will always run the peril of introducing new forms of injustice in place of those abolished.

—Reinhold Niebuhr, *Moral Man and Immoral Society:*
A Study in Ethics and Politics (1932)

to the extent that it may be thought of as a group distinct from the other two, emerged out of the fundamentalist group in the mid- to late twentieth century. Evangelical Protestantism combines elements of both groups: with mainline Protestants, it shares an appreciation for scientific knowledge; with fundamentalists, it shares a preference for focusing on personal conversion and renewal. Thus one might think of three branches of Protestantism today: mainline, evangelical, and fundamentalist, although the boundary lines between them are fluid. There are also the Pentecostal and Holiness movements, which have exploded since the beginning of the twentieth century.

In addition, Mainline Protestantism has suffered a quickening pace of membership decline since the middle of the twentieth century. For a number of years, this decline among mainline Protestants meant growth for evangelical Protestants, but the most recent studies suggest that the pace of evangelical Protestant growth has now leveled off and might also be in decline. Only in recent decades has the reality of membership decline led to greater cooperation on social ethics among the diverse Protestant communities. Likewise, Protestants have recently expressed greater appreciation for the social teachings of and a willingness to cooperate on social projects with the Catholic Church (the subject of the next chapter).

Connecting Church and Society: Two Inspirations

Although the church began to enjoy a gradual separation from the state during the post-Reformations period, the church did not, by and large, seek to separate itself from society. Increasingly, social concerns became church concerns. During the nineteenth and later centuries, in particular, Protestants embraced a responsibility to build a more just society. In many corners of Protestantism, work toward social justice came to be understood as a constitutive expression of the gospel. In time, Protestant social justice work included abolitionism, the promotion of suffrage (voting) rights, temperance movements, worker rights, civil rights, and institutional counterweights to the negative effects of urbanization. To understand Protestant concerns about social justice in the nineteenth and later centuries, one needs to recognize two elements of Protestantism during the seventeenth and eighteenth centuries. The first was the legacy of Puritanism within England and, later, colonial America. The second was the preaching ministry of John Wesley.

"Puritanism" is a term with a complicated history. At various times in England during the first half of the 1600s, the term could be used to describe (1) separatists from the Church of England, (2) Radical Reformers within the Church of England, (3) promoters of the rights of Parliament against the rights of the king, and (4) promoters of a strict morality.[12] After 1660, with the restoration of the English monarchy, the term "puritan" took on almost exclusively separatist religious tones. Regardless, church-and-state issues were intricately connected to the protesting ideas of whatever type of "puritan" one happened to be.

The Puritans' influence on Protestantism in England and America was rather extensive. They promoted a work ethic that grounded one's right to private property in the presence (or lack) of personal labor. Puritans succeeded in making idleness a prison-worthy offense in England and colonial America.[13] They elevated the task of preaching. When their preaching was unwelcome in the Church of England or Presbyterian churches, they formed house churches. Heads of households became the "ministers" of Puritan theologies. One of their main theologies was the restoration of Sunday as a Sabbath day of rest. For one day each week, labor ceased; it was replaced with extended time of worship and community or family bonding. This regular renewal of social bonds helped to promote awareness of and compassion for those who were struggling.

In 1630 civil war broke out in England. Puritan ideas grew increasingly less welcome. So minister John Winthrop set sail aboard the *Arbella* from England to the New World. He and his community were the first of what would eventually be thousands of Puritans journeying to America's shores. They founded first one colony, then eventually four colonies, and these colonies populated what would become Massachusetts, Connecticut, and Rhode Island. Winthrop's vision was for a "city upon a hill," a place to which all the world would look for a model of the common good.

Indeed, in 1648 the Puritan leader Thomas Hooker wrote that the common good was the point of everything the Puritans were doing in the New

A City on a Hill

We must consider that wee shall be as a Citty upon a Hill, the eies of all people are uppon us; soe that if wee shall deale falsely with our god in this worke wee have undertaken and soe cause him to withdrawe his present help from us, wee shall be made a story and a by-word through the world . . . till wee be consumed out of the good land whether wee are going.

—John Winthrop, "Model of Christian Charity," sermon composed while sailing to the New World

World. "*Salus populi* [*est*] *suprema lex*. It is the highest law in all Policy Civill or Spirituall to preserve the good of the whole; at this all must ame, and unto this all must be subordinate."[14] This common good was built on a social covenant preached by its early leaders and ministers, a covenant that was to conform to the purposes for which God established government and civil society.[15] The social covenant called for everyone to accept their proper station and work in life. Numerous laws were written to ensure conformity to an ordered and structured lifestyle, including acceptance of slavery if such was the status of an individual.[16] That social covenant partially reinforced class distinctions brought over from England: members of the new aristocracy (the educated, landed, and religious individuals) were appointed to rule the Massachusetts Bay Colony, which the Puritans founded, as its governor and magistrates. By 1645 appointment to these offices was for life,[17] and this system remained in place until 1774, when the colony's residents overthrew both the governor and the English monarch he represented. The social covenant also obliged members to fulfill their economic calling by discerning the work that God assigned to them, using their labor to provide for their financial needs and contributing generously to the needs of the community.[18] Wealth was not to be accumulated for its own sake, since the involuntary and temporary poverty of others was to be alleviated from the financial excesses of others. In keeping with an appreciation of a divine calling for work, the sooner a poor person could be put back to work, the better. Economically speaking, the social contract was more concerned with "promoting morality than commerce."[19]

This Puritan image of building from nothing, by virtue of hard work and unwavering commitment to God, an ideal society based on a social contract has lingered long in Protestant memory in America. There is implicit within it an eternal optimism that one can accomplish anything if one puts one's mind

The Poor and Work

If the Poor will but *Work*, they would make a better hand of it in this country, than in almost any under the Cope of Heaven. What a pity it is, that such an *Hive* should have any Drones in it.

—Cotton Mather, "Concio ad populum [Sermon to the People]"

and labor to the task. This commitment to hard work and industry proved to be transformative in the American experience. The Industrial Revolution in nineteenth-century America brought vast new wealth to the country. But it also discouraged empathy for those suffering from racism, which contributed to a denial of access to meaningful education, proper housing, businesses, and work. The violations of the civil rights of Native Americans and of African Americans caused many white Protestants to dismiss their struggles as a lack of personal initiative and work. Rewriting the "social contract," whatever that might be, became necessary to change these social and structural sins.

John Wesley (left) speaking to William Wilberforce, an antislavery member of Britain's Parliament. Engraving from Selections from the Journal of John Wesley (1891).

The Protestant Work Ethic

The phrase "Protestant work ethic" took on new meaning with Max Weber's (1864–1920) publication of *The Protestant Ethic and the Spirit of Capitalism* in 1904–5. According to Weber, this idea of a Protestant work ethic is rooted in the shift among Calvinist-minded Protestants, including the Puritan communities that came to America, to think of secular work as vocation and a divine calling. Whereas the Catholic Church, it is argued, had previously only promoted religious work as a divine calling, Protestants promoted all work as capable of being done for God's glory. This mentality proved useful for constructing capitalist-driven economies, and economic success could then become a measure of God's blessing.

> Like the meaning of the word ["calling"], the idea is new, a product of the Reformation. This may be assumed as generally known. It is true that certain suggestions of the positive valuation of routine activity in the world, which is contained in this conception of calling, had already existed in the Middle Ages, and even in late Hellenistic antiquity. . . . But at least one thing was unquestionably new: the valuation of the fulfillment of duty in worldly affairs as the highest form which the moral activity of the individual could assume.
>
> —Max Weber, *The Protestant Ethic and the Spirit of Capitalism*

Joining these Puritan influences on American Protestantism was the preaching ministry of John Wesley (1703–91), a onetime minister in the Church of England who began a movement first called "the Holy Club," but later became known as Methodism. Wesley traveled widely in England, Europe, and colonial America, preaching his new brand of the Christian life, which combined "the teaching of justification by faith alone with an emphasis on the pursuit of holiness to the point of Christian perfection."[20] In his personal life as much as in his preaching, he taught social ethics. While still a college student at Oxford, he organized a school for the children of poor families. He taught the children, and he visited the families regularly for pastoral care. In addition, he used personal funds to provide charitable relief and, when personal funds ran low, he fasted in order to save money on food and gave the savings to the poor. This continued after college too. He and like-minded friends continued the work of organizing schools for the poor and providing financial assistance. Recognizing that the problems facing the poor were multifaceted, Wesley expanded his work substantially. He acquired some basic training in medicine and then began to travel the slums of London, offering free medical care and dispensing medicines to the residents. To expand the reach of his medical program, he even wrote a basic textbook on medicine, *Primitive Physic*, for use by fellow ministers working with England's poor. In addition, Wesley prevailed on businesses to hire the unemployed he met in the slums; when that failed, he began his own business of processing cotton in

---

The 1908 "Social Creed" of the Methodist Church

This creed was adopted May 30, 1908, at the Methodist General Conference in Baltimore.* Notice how it reflects many of Wesley's concerns about the conditions of the poor and about the social structures that limit advancement of the poor.

The Methodist Episcopal Church stands

- ✓ For equal rights and complete justice for all men in all stations of life.
- ✓ For the principles of conciliation and arbitration in industrial dissensions.
- ✓ For the protection of the worker from dangerous machinery, occupational diseases, injuries, and mortality.
- ✓ For the abolition of child labor.
- ✓ For such regulation of the conditions of labor for women as shall safeguard the physical and moral health of the community.
- ✓ For the suppression of the "sweating system."[21]
- ✓ For the gradual and reasonable reduction of the hours of labor to the lowest practical point, with work for all; and for that degree of leisure for all which is the condition of the highest human life.
- ✓ For a release for [from] employment one day in seven.
- ✓ For a living wage in every industry.
- ✓ For the highest wage that each industry can afford, and for the most equitable division of the products of industry that can ultimately be devised.
- ✓ For the recognition of the Golden Rule and the mind of Christ as the supreme law of society and the sure remedy for all social ills.

* See Methodist Protestant Church, *Constitution and Discipline of the Methodist Protestant Church: Revised by the General Conference of 1908* (Baltimore: Board of Publication of the Methodist Protestant Church, 1908).

order to employ the poor himself. Moreover, to help those who were capable of running their own businesses, in his estimation, he set up a microlending organization that assisted the poor in launching their own small businesses.

Starting schools. Raising charitable funds. Teaching. Preaching. Learning about medicine. Writing a medical textbook. Operating a job-training company. Beginning a microlending bank. And doing all of these in three major cities (London, Bristol, and Newcastle-upon-Tyne). That is more than enough work to fill the lifetimes of several people. Yet Wesley did all of these on top of overseeing the birth of a new church movement, Methodism, which required administering the affairs of churches, preachers, and the appointment of bishops and mission superintendents. Moreover, he managed all of this while maintaining a thoroughly demanding travel schedule (it is estimated that he traveled about 200,000 miles in his lifetime) and an equally demanding preaching schedule (he likely preached about 40,000 sermons). In terms of preaching, that would mean he averaged eleven sermons every single week of every single year of his entire adult life. Most preachers struggle to deliver one good sermon per week, not to mention a reticence to do all the other things Wesley was doing at the same time.

It should thus be unsurprising to discover that, while Wesley did not succeed in changing the social structures that trapped so many English families in poverty, he inspired thousands to join him in building structures that would alleviate the experience of poverty. In contrast to prevailing attitudes among the political class and even among fellow Protestants, Wesley frequently taught that the cause of poverty among the poor was not idleness or laziness. He knew from firsthand experience with the poor that their poverty was the result of prejudicial mentalities and economic structures that diminished their humanity. Thus Methodism was born out of a concern to link the life of faith with compassion for the suffering, and the Methodist community became an inspiring voice for many people concerned about social justice in nineteenth- and twentieth-century America.

Connecting Church and Society: Particular Expressions

Together, the Puritan values and the Wesleyan values were transformative for Protestant social ethics. Add to them the peace traditions of the Radical Reformation communities (i.e., the Moravians, Mennonites, Amish, Shakers, Hutterites, etc.) and the concern for a separation of church from state in those and Baptist communities—and a sense of the type of social justice work attractive to Protestant communities begins to emerge. Protestants embraced their duty to participate in the building of a society ordered toward a common good. This section of the chapter focuses on Protestants in America, yet the concerns and work of Protestants in this region compare favorably to what Protestants were doing elsewhere in the world.

From their beginnings, Protestants embraced the cause of education. Lutherans in Germany and Calvinists in French- and Dutch-speaking regions of Europe were convinced that widespread literacy would increase Bible reading and thereby decrease support for what were perceived to be Catholic superstitions. So when the Puritans arrived in New England, one of their early projects was to organize grammar schools in most of the towns in which they were located. Protestants in Boston soon opened the nation's first "public" school, the Boston Latin School, in 1635, and in 1647 the Massachusetts General Assembly passed a law mandating every town to build their own school and thereby counter "one chief point of that old deluder, Satan, to keep men from the knowledge of the Scriptures."[22] Where public education was not available—particularly in rural areas, needing children for farm labor during the week, and among the urban poor, needing children to support the family via factory work—Protestants in England and America developed Sunday schools. Wesley and other Methodists, along with Anglicans, were

Colonial-Era Universities and Their Protestant Founders

1636	Harvard College (later, Harvard University)	Congregationalists
1693	College of William and Mary	Anglicans
1701	Yale College (later, Yale University)	Presbyterians
1746	College of New Jersey (later, Princeton University)	Presbyterians
1754	King's College (later, Columbia University)	Anglicans
1764	College of Rhode Island (later, Brown University)	Baptists
1766	Queens College (later, Rutgers University)	Dutch Calvinists
1769	Dartmouth College	Congregationalists

some of its biggest proponents (Methodist Hannah Bell may have opened England's first Sunday school in 1769).[23] Sunday schools met before or after church services, and they taught the children of such families the basics of literacy, writing, and mathematics.[24] Moreover, this was done for white citizens as well as for free and enslaved blacks in England and America, at least as far as Methodist schools were concerned. In any case, Protestants continued to support and organize the expansion of free public education well into the nineteenth century, but a discernable shift in attitudes toward public education emerged after Horace Mann's mid-nineteenth-century education reforms led to age-graded schools and more secular content.[25] As a hedge, Protestants expanded Sunday school programs and shifted their curriculum increasingly in the direction of religious instruction. Yet by the early twentieth century, post-Enlightenment sensibilities in the public schools drove fundamentalist Protestants to build parallel institutions of primary, secondary, and postsecondary education.[26] By the twenty-first century, one of the principal associations of such institutions, the Council for Christian Colleges and Universities, could count nearly 120 member institutions in the United States alone (and another 60 abroad). Overall, the early history of American education is a story of Protestant education. Protestants deeply valued an educated citizenry for the building and maintenance of a strong state, a healthy economy, and a vibrant religious life.

Shifts in America's educational landscape during the nineteenth century mirrored changes taking place in the economic landscape. Capital resources were now directed almost exclusively toward industrial projects rather than

Decline of Religious Literacy in America

It has now become clear that this division of function between the public school and the churches has not been a success. The modern home is notoriously incompetent in this field. The Sunday school with its one hour a week of religious instruction, by volunteer teachers, under conditions of slack discipline, is barely more than a gesture toward education. It cannot command the respect of pupils accustomed to the vastly superior methods, discipline, and prestige of the public school. The result is that the curve of religious literacy and of respect for religion itself has been steadily downward for more than three-quarters of a century. American society has become a secular-minded society.

—Charles C. Morrison, "Protestantism and the Public School," *Christian Century* (April 17, 1946)

agricultural ends, and the experience of workers in these new conditions changed quickly. Labor conditions were hazardous, pay was low, workers and their families struggled to build wealth, and these families' transition to cities to find work created new problems for themselves and for the cities to which they moved. As Wesley did in eighteenth-century England, Protestants moved quickly to build institutions intended to alleviate the suffering of these new classes of (working) poor people. During the 1850s and 1860s, William and Catherine Booth preached to and provided support services for the urban poor of London. Their work led to the creation of a church-like community known as the Salvation Army. Even today, the social and employment needs of the poor remain the Salvation Army's chief orientation. Most people today think of the YMCA as a place where they hold a gym membership or participate in recreation activities, but in 1840s London, George Williams created the institution as a place where poor and working-class men could come for Bible study and recreation instead of resorting to the temptations and vices of city life. From the 1880s to the 1920s, Protestants participated in the settlement-house movement at places like Toynbee Hall in London and Hull House in Chicago. Settlement houses were places where middle-class, typically college-educated, Christian men and women would come to share living space with lower-class individuals in an economically depressed part of a city. The idea was that middle-class knowledge and culture would be transmitted to those in the lower classes and aid their quest to rise out of poverty.

Protestants also (belatedly) joined Catholics in building hospitals and training workers for those hospitals around the United States, particularly in the rural parts of western America. One example is the Methodists' Deaconess hospital system, which was organized to more capably distribute resources where needed among its member institutions. The Protestant mission organization Operation Mobilization maintains a unique ministry around the world with its Mercy Ships. These ships, which are floating medical centers, ferry medical staff and equipment to ports around the developing world, providing free medical care and education services to the poor and the underserved.

Education and institutions for poor relief came easy to Protestants. Some local problems could be solved by a local church or churches, with little government interaction or permission. Other social justice issues, however, proved more thorny and required changes in political, legal, or social structures. Protestants proved less united in their resolve to address them or even in how to address them. Here one thinks of the suffrage, abolitionist, temperance, and civil rights movements of the previous two centuries and of debate over the merits of capitalist and Marxist economic ideologies.

Henrietta Brewer and the Birth of St. Peter's Hospital

Henrietta Brewer, as the wife of the Episcopal bishop of the then-missionary diocese of Montana, Leigh R. Brewer, was thrust into a brutal frontier world after having spent much of her life in the urban centers of New England. Yet, embracing her husband's calling, she decided that her contribution to the Episcopal Church's mission work among the rough crowd of miners and their slowly expanding families in Montana would be the establishment of a hospital in Helena.

During 1883, Henrietta developed the plans and began fund-raising for the hospital. In 1884 she finally opened its doors. She got the Episcopal Church's Women's Auxiliary to furnish its rooms. She hired nursing staff and put together a board of trustees. Later she recruited a nurse administrator. Then in 1885 she began work on a newer, bigger facility—again raising funds, scouting for real estate, and hiring construction teams. In 1901 a fire partially destroyed the hospital, so once again Henrietta organized the affairs needed to rebuild the facility and to restore its services.

Episcopal Church records reveal that Henrietta was especially concerned to balance two aspects of the hospital's operations: financial solvency, for which she sought a substantial endowment, and care for the medical needs of the poor who could not pay their bills. Reverend Brewer wrote stories of the hospital caring for children whose parents had no resources whatsoever. He wrote of a desire to endow a "free room" in the children's wing where a patient could be cared for at no cost.

Although now a community hospital and no longer run by the Episcopal Church, a nod to its Protestant founder continues with the local Episcopal bishop having a permanent seat on the hospital's board.

Consider, for example, the movement to abolish the slave trade. Despite the early and consistent call by Radical Reformation groups and Quakers in England and the American colonies to end slavery—George Fox preached emancipation as early as 1671, a *Germantown Protest* pamphlet was printed by Quakers (and Mennonites) in 1688, the Quakers formally condemned slavery in 1727, and William Wilberforce tried (in vain) to formally end its practice by a decree of Parliament in 1791—the slave trade flourished in the two regions.[27] Eventually the practice pitted many Protestants in America's southern states against those in its northern states. Yet to southern Protestants the slave trade was less a religious question than it was one about the southern way of life. The rural economy of the South, like farming economies elsewhere in Central America that had imported slaves from Africa, depended on slave labor to produce its goods at a cheaper price than if they had been produced by paid laborers. In other words, without slaves working the fields, political leaders in the American South believed their economies would collapse. Sharing these same convictions, Protestant leaders in those states propped up slavery with religious arguments. Yet again, those arguments were secondary to the economic and cultural arguments for slavery. In the North, however, the argument worked the other way for Protestants. Not sharing the South's economic and cultural view of the world, the religious mentalities of Protestants—particularly their appreciation for the dignity of all persons—led them to conclude that the slave trade was a pernicious evil. Efforts by Protestants in the northern states to abolish slavery coalesced around organizations such as the American Anti-Slavery Society and the American Colonization Society, the latter of which sought to relocate slaves to Africa in places such as Liberia. Still, by the time of America's Civil War, three of the largest Protestant communities in America split over the practice of slavery: northern Baptists split from southern Baptists; southern Presbyterians split from the "Old School" Presbyterians—later, the PC(USA); the Methodist Episcopal Church split into

How the Liberty Bell Got Its Name

Visitors to Philadelphia invariably stop to visit the Liberty Bell and the nearby Constitution Hall. As the bell at the top of the Pennsylvania State House, where the Declaration of Independence was adopted on July 4, 1776, the bell is thought to be a symbol of that call to independence by the American colonists.

Yet the bell earned the name "Liberty Bell" not because of its association with the Declaration of Independence. It was given that name by abolitionists who used images of the bell in their pamphlets denouncing slavery. While historians have yet to pinpoint who first coined the term "Liberty Bell," the New York Anti-Slavery Society was the first to print this name alongside an image of the bell in one of their pamphlets, dating to 1837. The bell used to announce liberty for white Americans in 1776 would become known as the "Liberty Bell," calling for liberty for all Americans.

northern and southern conferences. Other Protestant denominations that did not split—such as the Episcopal Church, the United Church of Christ, and the Disciples of Christ—nevertheless after the Civil War admitted their complicity in the slave trade by failing to sanction their members who owned slaves. What is more, the wounds left by the Civil War took decades to heal. Reckoning over complicity in the practice of slavery among every one of these denominations would not take place until well into the twentieth century. Some of these splits would never heal, although the reasons for the current divisions no longer have anything to do with slavery (e.g., Southern Baptist churches no longer are confined to the southern states, and their presence as a separate group within the Baptist community of America is for theological reasons).

Social Gospel Theology

No survey of the history of Protestant social ethics in the post-Reformations era would be complete without mention of the social gospel movement that dominated Protestant discourse for much of the late nineteenth and early twentieth centuries. The names Washington Gladden, Francis Peabody, Walter Rauschenbusch, Charles Sheldon, and Ernst Troeltsch are no longer household names among Protestants, but they were in the first half of the 1900s; their ideas continue to inspire Protestant social teaching documents today. Gladden, Rauschenbusch, and Sheldon were preachers of a social gospel theology; Peabody and Troeltsch (and later Rauschenbusch) were academics who supplied social gospel proponents with the necessary rigor and historical evidence to promote their ideas. In brief, social gospel theology highlighted Jesus's ministry among the poor and the marginalized. It emphasized his constant refrain that he had come to "proclaim the kingdom of God" on earth. It identified Christian commitment to this same type of ministry as a constitutive expression of genuine Christian preaching. Such a commitment demanded that Christians address structural injustices in society, since those structural injustices hindered the proclamation and the work of building God's kingdom here on earth.

Gladden, a Congregationalist minister in Ohio, helped to launch the social gospel movement in the 1880s by promoting concern for the conditions of the poor in his home of Columbus. Similarly, Rauschenbusch, a Baptist minister in New York City in the 1880s and 1890s, discovered that the poor community among whom he ministered struggled because of the increasing concentration of capital in the hands of too few individuals. That concentration of capital created not only a downward pressure on wages but also too many incentives for the abuse of workers. As with Gladden and Rauschenbusch, so too Sheldon, a Congregationalist minister in Topeka, Kansas, witnessed unjust treatment of workers and the lack of openness by those with excess wealth to distribute that excess to the poor. Along with similarly minded men and women throughout America, each man in his own way expressed the frustrations he found with these conditions. Their frustrations were magnified when fellow Protestants, some of whom were the owners of this capital, were part of the very problems they exposed. Gladden preached frequently on the subject and wrote several books and articles. Sheldon wrote a novel, *In His Steps*, that crystallized his concern with the needs of the poor by exploring the lives of average men and women who asked themselves the question "What would Jesus do?" when confronting the needs of those who were suffering. Rauschenbusch wrote several theological treatises, most notably *Christianity and the Social Crisis* (1907) and *Christianizing the Social Order* (1912), countering the unbridled capitalism of his age with a sophisticated biblical hermeneutic and a systematic understanding of the kingdom of God.

Earlier historians of the social gospel movement often linked the movement with the socialism of Karl Marx. Besides the movement's embrace of the word "social" to describe the gospel they preached, it was argued that the movement's concern with unjust economic structures and the rights of

What Would Jesus Do?

During the mid-1990s, many evangelicals had a particular fascination with clothing and accessories with the letters *WWJD* imprinted on them, which stood for the question "What Would Jesus Do?" The question came from the book *In His Steps*, by Charles Sheldon. In this excerpt from the book, the fictional Rev. Henry Maxwell laments to his congregation the recent death of a transient man whom he had turned away after the man asked him for assistance. Reverend Maxwell was determined not to make the same mistake again.

> Our motto will be, "What would Jesus do?" Our aim will be to act just as He would if He was in our places, regardless of immediate results. In other words, we propose to follow Jesus' steps as closely and as literally as we believe He taught His disciples to do. And those who volunteer to do this will pledge themselves for an entire year, beginning with today, so to act.
>
> —Charles Sheldon, *In His Steps* (1896), 21

workers betrayed such sensibilities. Yet historians' more recent assessments of the movement suggest something else. Since "socialism" can mean a number of different things (a reference to a "social spirit," to economic socialism, to socialist political parties, or to movements of workers), it is now best to conclude that the social gospel proponents were socialists only to the extent that they appreciated socialism's concern with justice and human solidarity.[28] Peabody had gone out of his way to separate himself and other social gospel theology proponents from any association with Marxism, since the latter was decidedly irreligious and degraded the dignity of individual persons.[29] As will be discussed in part 3 of this book, justice and solidarity are foundational principles of Protestant social ethics. To the extent that politically oriented socialists share these concerns with Christians, they may have common cause with social gospel proponents, but there is no necessary connection between the two.

In any case, the social gospel movement began to pass from favor starting in the 1920s, and the decline accelerated in the 1940s. The first signs of change came with the shift among fundamentalist Protestants away from social concerns toward revivalism. Although mainline and fundamentalist Protestants initially shared many of the social gospel movement's concerns (and had joined together to build the types of institutions described earlier, such as the Salvation Army), by the 1920s fundamentalists had come to value more the type of work that was done by earlier evangelists such as D. L. Moody. Moody had argued that preaching for personal transformation was a more effective use of an evangelist's time than the longer horizon required of those seeking changes in social structures. This decline in the social gospel movement camp from the departure of fundamentalists accelerated in the 1940s with the departure of some even in the mainline Protestant communities. Neo-orthodox theologians shifted Protestant interests still further away from positivist views of human society with a renewed appreciation for the reality of sin and toward a concern with God's transcendence as an ordering principle of individuals' lives.

Still, the social gospel movement never went away. Protestants in civil rights movements (be they rights for racial minorities, for women and, in some corners, for sexual minorities) continue the use of social gospel language. Baptist minister Martin Luther King Jr. specifically credited Rauschenbusch as a significant influence on his thinking.[30] The evangelical Protestant organization Sojourners, founded in 1971 and led still today by Jim Wallis, continues to promote the ideals of those in the social gospel movement through its monthly publication, *Sojourners*. Also, the work of educators such as Glen Stassen (at Fuller Theological Seminary until his death in 2014) transmits the language of the social gospel movement's concern about economic and social justice to new audiences of Protestants.[31]

Summary

Protestant social ethics in the post-Reformations era was marked by two significant splits. First, the Enlightenment shifted the intellectual climate of Western culture away from any appreciation for the sources of authority in religious traditions, particularly in the Christian tradition. This prompted Protestants to consider different paths in how best to respond. Mainline Protestants embraced the new scientific worldview that came in the Enlightenment's wake; fundamentalist Protestants dismissed the scientific worldview and focused instead on personal conversion and renewal; neo-orthodox theologians rejected the scientific worldview's priority over the world of mind and reignited interest in the transcendence of God. This intellectual split within the Protestant community manifested itself, second, in its divergence over social ethics in the late nineteenth and twentieth centuries. During this time, Protestants split over the extent to which they felt called to change the social structures that propped up racial, economic, and social injustice in Western society. Mainline and fundamentalist Protestants found common cause in institutional forms of charity and poverty relief, but when it came to structural changes, mainline Protestants embraced a social gospel theology, while fundamentalists continued to focus on personal conversion. The emergence of evangelical Protestantism out of the fundamentalist community in the twentieth century perpetuated some of these same splits. Some evangelicals believe that they are called to build the kingdom of God on earth through attention to social justice and calls for structural change, while other evangelicals have focused instead on reestablishing personal faith in a post-Enlightenment intellectual culture.

Main Points of the Chapter

» The intellectual movement known as the Enlightenment led to divisions in the Protestant community during the eighteenth through twentieth centuries.

» Initially these intellectual splits within the Protestant community did not translate into differences over concerns about the poor and the marginalized. Protestants of all communities combined their efforts to build institutions of charitable relief. Eventually differences emerged over whether and how to advocate for structural changes to address social injustice.

» Mainline Protestants embraced a social gospel theology, which thought of work toward structural change as a constitutive expression of Christian ministry.

» Fundamentalist Protestants embraced a theology of personal conversion, which, they believed, would lead to the types of social changes that social gospel proponents sought.

» Evangelical Protestants, a group that emerged out of fundamentalist communities in the mid- to late twentieth century, includes those who advocate for structural changes and those who advocate for personal conversion.

⊰ 10 ⊱

Contemporary Catholic Social Ethics

Learning Outcomes for This Chapter

» Summarize key events in the recent history of the Catholic Church.

» Introduce principal documents in Catholic social teaching since the publication of *Rerum novarum* in 1891.

» Identify lessons Protestants might glean from the Catholic Church's experience of sharing its social vision with a pluralistic world.

By this point it should be clear that Protestant social ethics did not emerge in a vacuum. Besides the history of Christians' reflection on justice, just societies, and what it takes to help build a just society, Protestants have also benefited from some developments in the social teaching of the Catholic Church since the nineteenth century. In many areas of social ethics, the Catholic Church has acted sooner than Protestants in offering prepared statements on topics of social concern. In part, this is because the Catholic Church has a more centralized governance structure by which such statements can be drafted and published with a modicum of speed. The consequence of this is that often prepared statements from Protestant communities on social ethics reflect earlier work done by Catholics. Therefore it behooves the student of Protestant social ethics to have some acquaintance with what the Catholic Church has done and how it goes about doing it.

Brief Historical Review

The Catholic Church of the late twentieth century, and certainly of the twenty-first, bears very little resemblance to the Catholic Church of the Reformations era or even of two or three generations ago. Protestants often discover this after taking the time for lengthy dialogue about their faith with Catholic friends or even with Catholic clergy. Gone are the days of thinking of Protestants as heretics. Indeed, Catholics and Lutherans agreed to a common definition of "justification by faith" in the 1990s.[1] Gone are the days of criticizing members of our world's other religions. Catholics are as much, if not more, integrated in interfaith dialogue as many Protestant groups. Gone are the days of separating themselves from scientific advances. Catholic universities are generally marked as some of the most progressive academic institutions in the world today.

How did this happen? To understand this, one must back up to the early nineteenth century. Biblical studies was only then beginning to embrace the assumptions of the Enlightenment era, and the product of that work was a general state of questioning the veracity of the biblical texts. Soon the practice of religion itself became the subject of scrutiny as it came to be seen as a merely human phenomenon. These developments coincided with discoveries in the natural sciences that led many in Western cultures to choose scientific "knowledge" over and against religious "knowledge." The Catholic Church fought back against this sensibility of the modern age. It embarked on a campaign that Catholic Church historians label as "antimodernism."[2]

The Campaign against Modernism

✓ During the 1800s, the Catholic Church grew increasingly concerned about post-Enlightenment mentalities in Western cultures. These mentalities privileged reason over religion. They were drawing people away from an interest in religious life.

✓ Pope Pius IX, in 1864, issued *Syllabus errorum* (Syllabus of Errors), which challenges numerous claims of modernism.

✓ Vatican Council I, in 1870, issued *Pastor aeternus* (Eternal Shepherd), which renews the call for fidelity to the pope as the protector of Truth in the modern world.

✓ Pope Piux X, in 1907, issued *Pascendi dominici gregis* (Feeding the Lord's Flock), which thoroughly summarizes and critiques the mind-set of modernist thinkers.

The high point of that campaign was Vatican Council I, which convened during the years 1869–70. Among its several pronouncements was one that it believed would help the Catholic Church weather the storms of the modernist age. This was fidelity to the pope. The document *Pastor aeternus* declared the pope's doctrinal teaching to be infallible, or not prone to error. Catholic faithful were obliged to consent to any teaching that the pope declares ex cathedra, "from the chair" of St. Peter. In other words, no matter how intellectually difficult the scientific world might make the practice of religion seem, Catholics can trust by faith that the bishop of Rome has insight into truth far deeper than that accessible to the scientists.[3]

For the next ninety years, the Catholic Church suffered along with so much of Europe during the Franco-Prussian War and the two World Wars. In 1960 the experience of rebuilding Europe led a new pope, Pope John XXIII, to consider convening a new council of the church's bishops. But, in a change from earlier convention, the roughly twenty-five hundred bishops invited to this new meeting, to be called Vatican Council II, were not given an agenda for the meeting: they were asked to submit requests for what they wanted on the agenda. By this and other moves, Pope John XXIII signaled a shift toward something called *aggiornamento* (bringing up to date) in the Catholic Church. It was time for the world's bishops to tell the Vatican what the church needed to be concerned about rather than have the instructions flow the other way. John XXIII felt this would enhance the capacity of the Catholic Church to spend more of its energies talking about God's love for people than God's judgment, more about God's concern for the poor than about doctrines and religious formulas.[4]

Vatican II, which met during the years 1962–65, indeed covered a tremendous amount of cultural and theological ground. Discussion of much of it is best left to other books, yet here it is important to point out that a common theme in the council's documents is a need for the church to reengage the world.[5] The antimodernism campaign was deemed a failure. One example of just how new was the direction the church took under John XXIII's leadership was that, for the first time since the Reformation, the council called Protestants "fellow Christians," and the council even invited Protestant leaders to attend and to contribute their voices at every session. Another significant theme was the call to shift more of the duties of the Catholic Church to laity. The bishops at Vatican II rightly assessed that the recent steep declines in church membership, in men and women choosing the religious life, and in men accepting a call to the priesthood would only worsen in the years ahead, and it did.[6] The laity needed to take up the responsibility to study Scripture and to lead their parish churches. The history has yet to be written on just how much responsibility the Catholic Church has ably passed to its laity, but suffice it to say that what John XXIII began continues. The Catholic Church still struggles to navigate the new waters into which Pope John XXIII steered it.

One of these new waters includes greater attention to Christianity in non-European contexts, especially the experiences of Christians in Central and South America. The longest-serving pope in the decades after Vatican II, Pope John Paul II, expended much energy supporting the lay piety of Catholics in these parts of the world, even as he also sought to clamp down on some of its liberation-minded theology. The election in 2013 of Pope Francis, a long-serving bishop in Argentina, also marked a nod to the strength of Catholicism in South America, in contrast to its decline in Western contexts. This feature of the post–Vatican II Catholic Church could not help but impact the Church's social teaching.

Catholic Social Ethics

Most scholars consider "modern" Catholic social ethics to have begun in 1891 with the publication of a document titled *Rerum novarum* (ET: Rights and Duties of Capital and Labor), by Pope Leo XIII.[7] It is a scathing critique of the Industrial Revolution's negative effects on the dignity of humans, on the rights of workers, and on the promotion of wealth and profit above concern for the poor. It accurately assesses that society's love affair with capital and wealth led to a diminishing respect for the worker as anything but a replaceable part in a factory.

> The following duties bind the wealthy owner and the employer: not to look upon their work people as their bondsmen, but to respect in every man his dignity as a person ennobled by Christian character. They are reminded that, according to natural reason and Christian

Pope Leo XIII, author of *Rerum novarum* (1891).

philosophy, working for gain is creditable, not shameful, to a man, since it enables him to earn an honorable livelihood; but to misuse men as though they were things in the pursuit of gain, or to value them solely for their physical powers—that is truly shameful and inhuman. (*Rerum novarum* §20)

Rerum novarum is a foundational text insofar as it put the world on notice that the Christian community—at least in the Catholic Church—would no longer stand idly by and watch the dignity of humans be degraded by supposedly invisible, inhuman forces of capital. *Rerum novarum* proclaimed the judgment of Jesus against the degrading of persons in this way. The Christian church, which for centuries had stood up for the poor, the suffering, and the marginalized, but which had in more recent decades lost some of its cultural footing, was now reasserting its moral voice.

Rerum novarum was a significant shot in the arm for the Christian world. As discussed in the previous chapter, within a few short years Protestants found themselves joining Catholics in their critique of society and their critique of society's degrading of human persons. The Catholic Church too took seriously its newfound role in being a voice of moral conscience to the world. It followed *Rerum novarum* forty years later with another text in 1931 called *Quadragesimo anno* (After Forty Years). In some ways this text was among the boldest of the Catholic Church's many documents on social ethics. It was the first to address the subject of how best to order the affairs of the state, advocating for a principle of subsidiarity (§79): a principle of social ethics teaching that problems within society should be addressed by those closest to those situations. More will be said about this topic in chapter 15. More important, *Quadragesimo anno* crafted an alternative economic model for society. It promoted what came to be known as

Human Dignity in the Workplace

In the following quote, society's increasing distaste for the Christian religion is linked to its willingness to reduce the dignity of humans in the workplace:

Public institutions and the laws set aside the ancient religion. Hence, by degrees it has come to pass that working men have been surrendered, isolated and helpless, to the hardheartedness of employers and the greed of unchecked competition.

—*Rerum novarum* §3

> ## Right Ordering of Economic Life
>
> The right ordering of economic life cannot be left to a free competition of forces. For from this source, as from a poisoned spring, have originated and spread all the errors of individualist economic teaching. Destroying through forgetfulness or ignorance the social and moral character of economic life, it held that economic life must be considered and treated as altogether free from and independent of public authority, because in the market, i.e., in the free struggle of competitors, it would have a principle of self direction which governs it much more perfectly than would the intervention of any created intellect. But free competition, while justified and certainly useful provided it is kept within certain limits, clearly cannot direct economic life.
>
> —*Quadragesimo anno* §88

"corporatism," at the time thought to be a middle-ground position between capitalism and Marxism.[8] Neither unregulated capitalism nor Marxism can direct economic life because both pay no heed to the first principle of human dignity. A "corporatist" model would have the employees, not invisible shareholders or an impersonal central government, be the sole owners of the corporations for which they work. Further details of that economic model are best studied elsewhere. What is important for the purposes of this text is an appreciation for the shock the world experienced at having a religious institution get into the nuts and bolts of economic models! Many at the time wondered what expertise a church had in economic theory. Yet such concerns miss the point. The Catholic Church was speaking up for the rights of workers who continued to be oppressed by capitalist-driven, industrialized societies that privileged profits over people. That the Catholic Church offered these critiques of capitalism at the very dawning of a worldwide economic depression awakened many to just how damaging unfettered capitalism might actually be.

Still, the Catholic Church later abandoned its corporatism proposal in *Quadragesimo anno*. It even went so far as to say that the Catholic Church oversteps its bounds when it becomes too prescriptive about economic and political models. What the Catholic Church excels at is the propagation of the message of Jesus and the knowledge of God's compassion for the poor; people of goodwill can take that message and apply it in whatever way they sense is best for the particular economic or political situation in which they find themselves. Evidence of this shift in social teaching is found in the Catholic

Church's next major social pronouncement, a document published in 1961, *Mater et magistra* (Mother and Teacher).

Mater et magistra and a social teaching document that followed a couple years later in 1963, *Pacem in terris* (Peace on Earth), were published by the same pope, John XXIII. Considering his legacy, discussed earlier, it is no surprise to find in *Mater et magistra* and in *Pacem in terris* a less prescriptive approach to economic life and more concern with general principles of justice and solidarity. Both documents deal with international relations, and they build on the Declaration on Human Rights that emerged from the United Nations in 1948. *Mater et magistra* focuses on the growing interdependencies of people in the world. Remaining mindful of the principle of subsidiarity, it recognizes a growing role for the state in confronting the abuses of economic and labor systems.

> A sane view of the common good must be present and operative in men invested with public authority. They must take account of all those social conditions which favor the full development of human personality. Moreover, we consider it altogether vital that the numerous intermediary bodies and corporate enterprises—which are, so to say, the main vehicle of this social growth—be really autonomous, and loyally collaborate in pursuit of their own specific interests and those of the common good. (*Mater et magistra* §65)

While defending the rights of workers to organize and to collectively bargain for their wages, these abuses were then on such a global scale that they had eclipsed the power of any one individual or labor organization to prevent them. So *Pacem in terris* directs its concern to the topic of solidarity. Solidarity is no longer only between and among individual persons or labor organizations: it also must be fostered between and among states. Organizations with a global impact must take greater responsibility to foster this solidarity and to protect against the exploitation of one people group for the benefit of another. Combined, *Mater et magistra* and *Pacem in terris* tell a story of the Catholic Church's ongoing concern with industrialization's seemingly insatiable capacity to reduce both wages and human dignity around the world.

In 1965 Vatican Council II produced a text that has also taken its rightful place among the preeminent documents of Catholic social teaching. It is titled *Gaudium et spes* (Joy and Hope; ET: On the Church in the Modern World). The substantial length of *Gaudium et spes* is one reason for its extensive reach into the world's economic, political, militaristic, and cultural affairs. Noteworthy for the purposes of this chapter is a phrase from

Basic Human Rights

Pacem in terris (§§11–14, reworded) lists the following as rights to which every human is entitled:

- ✔ to live
- ✔ to have bodily integrity
- ✔ to have the means needed for the proper development of life, particularly food, clothing, shelter, medical care, rest, and finally, the necessary social services
- ✔ to be looked after in the event of ill health; disability stemming from one's work; widowhood; old age; enforced unemployment; or whenever through no fault of their own they are deprived of the means of livelihood
- ✔ to be respected
- ✔ to have a good name
- ✔ to be free to investigate the truth
- ✔ to have freedom of speech and publication
- ✔ to be free to pursue any chosen profession
- ✔ to be accurately informed about public events
- ✔ to share in the benefits of culture
- ✔ to receive a good general education
- ✔ to worship God in accord with the right dictates of their own conscience

Gaudium et spes that has taken on something of a life of its own among Catholics. That is the document's exhortation for its readers to "read the signs of the times."[9] On the one hand, the phrase suggests that Catholics be careful observers of what is going on around them, to pay attention to the news, to take advantage of their right to vote, to be politically engaged, and to cultivate a sense of where their culture (or the world's cultures) is heading. On the other hand, the phrase was more aggressive. To read the signs of the times is also to identify those places where injustice may be found, to step into those places, and to try to reshape them for the better. In other words, reading the signs of the times might require civil disobedience, and so it is as much about action as it is about the comparatively more passive notion of just reading.

Consequently, *Gaudium et spes* is something of a watershed moment in the history of Catholic social teaching. Recalling this document, Catholics in diverse parts of the world began to challenge the unjust practices of political

Catholic Social Teaching: The Major Documents

Year	Text	Principal Subject(s)
1891	*Rerum novarum*	Labor conditions; workers' rights
1931	*Quadragesimo anno*	Corporatism model of economic life
1961	*Mater et magistra*	Global, economic inequality; reforms of social life/organization
1963	*Pacem in terris*	Human rights; a global notion of the common good
1965	*Gaudium et spes*	Call to read the "signs of the times"
1967	*Populorum progressio*	Human development and solidarity
1987	*Sollicitudo rei socialis*	Renews concern for solidarity; identifies obstacles to development
1991	*Centesimus annus*	Updates concerns of *Rerum novarum*; constructive critique of capitalism
2005	*Compendium*	Systematic summary of Catholic social teaching
2005	*Deus caritas est*	Balancing charity and justice
2009	*Caritas in veritate*	Love for others reveals uncomfortable truths of inequities in economic life
2013	*Evangelii gaudium*	Needs of the poor demand more just economic and social institutions
2015	*Laudato si'*	Concern for the environment

and economic leaders in their particular corners of the world. Catholic bishops in the United States, for instance, took *Gaudium et spes* as the inspiration for their own reflection on the unjust economic policies of the Reagan administration in the 1980s[10] and on the highly dangerous practice of nuclear proliferation in which the United States was participating during the 1970s and 1980s.[11] In the preamble to their pastoral letter titled "Economic Justice for All" (1986), the US bishops wrote, "Our faith calls us to measure this economy, not by what it produces but also by how it touches human life and whether it protects or undermines the dignity of the human person. Economic decisions have human consequences and moral content; they help or hurt people, strengthen or weaken family life, advance or diminish the quality of justice in our land" (preamble §1). The bishops acknowledge that, in the United States, economic freedom is highly valued (I.8), but that the market must be limited by fundamental human rights. A rightly functioning economic system allows everyone to share in its success. Leaving anyone behind makes the system unacceptable.

Likewise, the bishops in Central and South America responded to *Gaudium et spes* by issuing a series of documents, starting in 1968 and continuing into the 1990s, that had significant theological and economic consequences.[12]

> ## Poverty and Social Justice
>
> We brand the situation of inhuman poverty in which millions of Latin Americans live as the most devastating and humiliating kind of scourge. . . . This poverty is the product of economic, social and political situations, and structures. . . . Hence this reality calls for personal conversion and profound structural changes that will meet the legitimate aspirations of the people for authentic social justice.
>
> — Consejo Episcopal Latinoamericano (CELAM), Puebla §29

These documents named the many sins of economic and political oppression throughout their countries, and they promoted a vision of the gospel that inextricably linked the task of preaching and evangelism with the task of enabling the poor to rise up against their oppressors. The documents also facilitated the creation of "base ecclesial communities," small groups of believers meeting to study Scripture while also thinking of how they might restore justice to oppressed people.

They also spawned the work of theologians such as Gustavo Gutiérrez, whose influential 1973 book *A Theology of Liberation* jump-started an entirely new approach among Central and South American Christians—indeed, among Christians around the world—to think of sin not just in individual terms but also in terms of social structures propped up by the state.[13] Liberation theologians argue that one expression of the preaching of the message of Jesus is the liberation of oppressed people. Yet liberation theology came at a steep price. Many priests, nuns, bishops, and lay Catholics, because of their work, were assassinated by those in power. An even greater number were thrown into jail and lost their livelihoods in the decades-long struggles against oppression.[14] Today many say that the work of liberation theology is far from concluded in this and other parts of the world. Even so, the Catholic Church in the 1980s, under the leadership of Pope John Paul II, reined in some of the more outspoken voices of liberation theology in Central and South America. The Catholic Church replaced such bishops with more moderate voices, but at the same time, it accepted that working for justice is a constitutive element of evangelism. This compromise allowed liberation theology to proceed, yet not with so much of its prior militaristic elements.[15]

In addition to the documents emerging from regional bishops' conferences, the Vatican too issued its own document similarly inspired by *Gaudium et spes*'s call to read the signs of the times. It was the 1967 document *Populorum progressio* (The Development of People). It argues that human development has not proceeded with equal attention to all members of the human family. The poor are forgotten in the race for development and wealth. Solidarity among humans has broken down. So this text explores the contribution of justice language to several areas affecting human development around the world, including topics as diverse as foreign aid, international trade, property rights, workplace conditions, proper role of unions, rights of migrant workers, and the need to protect family cohesion.

> It is not just a question of eliminating hunger and reducing poverty. It is not just a question of fighting wretched conditions, though this is an urgent and necessary task. It involves building a human community where men [and women] can live truly human lives, free from discrimination on account of race, religion or nationality, free from servitude to other men or to natural forces which they cannot yet control satisfactorily. It involves building a human community where liberty is not an idle word, where the needy Lazarus can sit down with the rich man at the same banquet table. (*Populorum progressio* §47)

Notice how far-reaching is the assessment of human development. Citizens of developed nations cannot be content simply with sending money abroad or even circulating it at home to eliminate hunger or to reduce poverty. What is to be done is to devote one's energy to the building of a genuine human community.

Whereas *Gaudium et spes* helped to devolve some of the decision making to lay Catholics and to regional groups of bishops about whether and how to respond to injustice, the papacy of John Paul II offered something of a return to Vatican-initiated reflections on social teaching. It helped that John Paul II served as leader of the Catholic Church for twenty-seven years, one of the longest tenures of any pope in modern history. Under his leadership, the Vatican issued several social teaching documents, including *Familiaris consortio* (1981), *Sollicitudo rei socialis* (1987), *Centesimus annus* (1991), and

The Social Message of the Gospel

The social message of the Gospel must not be considered a theory, but above all else a basis and a motivation for action. . . . Today more than ever, the Church is aware that her social message will gain credibility more immediately from the witness of actions than as a result of its internal logic and consistency.

—*Centesimus annus* §57

Preferential Option for the Poor

The phrase "preferential option for the poor" is often used in recent Catholic social teaching documents, though it may well be argued that its roots extend much deeper in Christian history. It means the needs of the poor ought to come first in any decision we make, individually or collectively as a society. It is especially concerned about decisions that relate to economic life—such as where and by whom goods are manufactured, the prices at which goods are sold, and our consumer habits—yet also with government policies that affect things like education, zoning ordinances, policing, and so forth.

In brief, the phrase is a shorthand way of saying the wealthy will always find a way to meet their own needs, so our job as citizens is to build a society that, first and foremost, works better for the poor and others on society's margins.

a *Compendium of the Social Doctrine of the Church* (2005). These joined dozens of speeches and homilies in which John Paul II expressed solidarity with one group or another or challenged unjust practices in disparate corners of the world. In addition to reminders of the Catholic Church's ongoing concerns about unfettered capitalism and humanity-degrading communist collectives, these documents introduced new concepts. *Familiaris consortio* (ET: The Family in the Modern World) celebrated the family as a "domestic church,"[16] and it defended marriage and family from what it saw as negative cultural encroachments. *Sollicitudo rei socialis* (On Social Concern) aligned its vision for social justice with human development by promoting human dignity. According to the document, people are more than laborers for goods or services in the world's economies. The notion of solidarity among human persons is a drumbeat that permeates every section of the text. *Centesimus annus* (Hundredth Year), as the name implies, celebrates the one-hundredth anniversary of *Rerum novarum* and updates that earlier text with a new list of things that the Catholic Church is concerned about in the more technologically advanced societies of the late twentieth century. Such societies shed traditional labor-intensive jobs and thus have the prospect of leaving even more people behind economically than ever before. Consequently *Centesimus annus* gives particular prominence to a concept known as a "preferential option for the poor," which was first used by Catholics in Central and South America two decades earlier. It says that decision makers have an obligation to consider what their policies will do to the poor and for the poor, and this includes not merely their economic well-being but also their spiritual and cultural well-being.

The more recent popes, Benedict XVI and Francis, continue to reinforce the long legacy of Catholic social teaching, and they have offered still further directions for that teaching to go. Benedict XVI, in a 2005 document called *Deus caritas est* (God Is Love), renewed the discussion among social ethicists about the proper balance between justice and charity (a topic to which we will return in the next part of this book). His 2009 document *Caritas in veritate* (Love in Truth) reflects on the concept of the common good and updates the Catholic Church's concerns about the potential for a technology-driven, knowledge-driven society to actually impair global human development. The document avoids prescribing particular antidotes, choosing instead to invite those in power to think ethically, to consider the potential for injustice from profit-motivated behavior alone, and to weigh carefully their organization of economic life so that it might give special attention to the needs of the poor.

In 2013 Francis published a document called *Evangelii gaudium* (Joy of the Gospel), which continued the Catholic Church's now long-standing practice of shining a moral light on the economic behaviors of the world's people. It is yet another critique of unfettered capitalism and a critique of powerful nations that disrupt development work among majority-world countries by their abuse of those countries' natural and agricultural resources. Francis also extended the Catholic Church's social teaching into yet another new area with his 2015 document titled *Laudato si'* (ET: On Care for Our Common Home), which is a call to action among the world's developed and developing nations to stop the advance of human-caused climate change. In this text Francis even says that nature itself is among the world's poor, and it cries out for justice just as much as they do.

Summary

The Catholic Church paved the way for Protestants to interject their biblically derived ideas about God and God's justice into increasingly secular and sometimes morally tone-deaf cultures. Indeed, the world's people have shown a willingness to make space for a Christian voice on matters of social concern. The Catholic Church has stood for the rights of workers amid calls for unregulated free markets. It reminds societies that labor is more important than capital, that workers are more important than profits, and that corporate responsibility entails a concern for how their products impact the poor, including the environment. The bishops in Central and Latin America have further directed Christian attention to the social and especially political structures that contribute to repression of the poor. They ask Christians to look at whether and how societies prop up industries and corporations that are harmful to workers, families, and the environment. Combined, Catholic social ethics has proved to be an exceptionally rich resource for Protestant social ethics. It will not be surprising to discover, then, that principles and themes in Protestant social teaching, which are discussed in the third part of this book, adhere closely to principles and themes found in Catholic social teaching.

Main Points of the Chapter

» The rights and dignity of workers are more important than the profit motive of corporations.

» The technology-driven, knowledge-driven economy of the present has even greater potential than the industrial age to imperil the dignity of workers.

» Equal to the concern about the dignity of workers is the plight of the environment in the face of damaging human activity.

» Committing oneself or one's church to work on behalf of justice is a constitutive expression of the gospel.

Part 2 Summary

The first part of the book introduced Scripture's invitation to join God in the work of restoring order out of the chaos in the lives of individuals, in society, and throughout the world. This second part documented how Christians have responded to this invitation from the earliest days of the community's history. The work of God through Jesus indeed left a strong impression on his followers. This part of the book traced that story through the periods of Late Antiquity, the Middle Ages, the Reformations, and in the centuries since the Reformations.

Christians in the earliest centuries took seriously their responsibility to collect funds for the maintenance of the needs of the poor, the sick, the widows, orphans, prisoners, and the families unable to pay the burial expenses of their deceased relatives. They did this for members of their church community and for those who were not members of their community. With the freedom from imperial persecution that came in the middle of the fourth century, the Christian church could organize itself more effectively for the collection and distribution of these resources, among other benefits. Soon thereafter, institutions such as hospitals, schools, and *diakonia* were built to support the needs of those on society's margins in even more effective ways.

To this trajectory, Christians during the Middle Ages added even more. Monastic communities were formed that embedded the church more deeply into the lives of ordinary people. The monks shared in the toil of managing the agricultural landscape. They copied texts and by so doing preserved the wisdom of earlier cultures. Together with them, and with support from the ruling class, the church built new educational institutions that expanded knowledge about medicine, law, the arts, and theology. The church offered guidance to rulers about what constituted civil society, what constituted a just state, and how their laws might best correspond to the natural law that God implanted in every human person.

Christians in the Middle Ages never quite found their way toward building a Christian society, but their work on the proper roles for the church and the state would not be squandered by the Protestants. Indeed, so much of what constitutes a framework for social ethics in Protestantism is derived from one theory or another about the proper relationship between the church and the state. Some Protestants responded by largely separating themselves from the state, as one sees in Amish, Hutterite, and even some Mennonite communities still today. Others felt that Christ had come to fundamentally reshape culture; thus Christian participation in the state is paramount. Others taught something between these poles. Putting these ideas into action, nondenominational Protestant organizations such as the Salvation Army, Mercy Ships, World Vision, and Compassion International have provided mechanisms for Protestants to redistribute their wealth to alleviate the suffering of the poor and, hopefully, to build a more just world.

Along the way, Protestants have received more than a few hints about how to do this well from the Catholic Church, whose program of social teaching exhorts all persons of goodwill to give greater thought to the world's poor and marginalized persons. Individual Protestant churches have issued statements of their own on various matters, and occasionally Protestants have created umbrella organizations to make joint statements in order to increase their impact. However, even these Protestant statements lack the economic sophistication and global breadth of the Catholic documents.

Given the important contributions of both Protestant and Catholic thinkers to social ethics, readers interested in Protestant social ethics would do well to draw from the insights not only of their particular tradition but of the church universal. Indeed, it may ultimately be more helpful to think not in terms of developing *Protestant* (as opposed to Catholic) social ethics but rather in terms of developing *Christian* social ethics—social ethics that are faithful to one's particular tradition while drawing from the wealth of resources from across the church. In part 3 we will discuss five general principles that can help readers develop such a Christian social ethic. How these principles are applied may differ in various contexts, but they are principles that every student interested in social ethics should take seriously.

Principles for Protestant Social Ethics

⚜ **11** ⚜

Human Dignity

Learning Outcomes for This Chapter

» Define "human dignity" and its contribution to social life.

» Summarize the contribution of biblical and later Christian literature to understanding the importance of human dignity.

» Examine challenges societies face in protecting the dignity of their individual members.

This third part of the book introduces the reader to five principles of social ethics. As discussed in the part 2 summary, these principles are not exclusive to Protestant social ethics but are common in Catholic social ethics as well. Understanding these principles is important for forming Christian thought about the world and its social order. The first principle is human dignity. It is the first principle because from it flows every other principle. It seems so obvious to say, but society is a collection of humans. Humans create societies for themselves because societies provide things for individuals that those individuals cannot acquire alone, or certainly cannot acquire alone without too much difficulty or without risking other needs. Put another way, societies exist for the benefit of humans, not the other way around. For this reason, human dignity may be considered a *why* principle in social ethics. It explains why Protestants ought to be involved in social ethics.

Definition of Human Dignity

Human dignity is the status held by humans entitling them to respect from the moment life begins to the time of natural death.[1] The word "dignity" is derived from the Latin *dignitas*, which means ornament or decoration. Thus all beings possessing a human nature are necessarily ornamented, or decorated, with dignity, which entitles them to be respected. It is an intrinsic part of who we are. Consequently, dignity is presupposed of human life. It is also presupposed of social ethics. Everything . . . absolutely everything . . . to which social ethics addresses itself starts with the presupposition that humans possess dignity; social ethics is about organizing social life in such a way that dignity is enhanced, not diminished.

Classical understandings of dignity locate it within the reasoning capacity of an individual. That reasoning capacity enables one to make choices about the type of life one wants to lead, and one's capacity to act on those choices—one's agency—also reveals the presence of this dignity. Reason and agency collectively grant individuals the capacity to live the type of life they wish to lead, and human dignity involes respecting the right of persons to decide how they choose to live even if those lifestyles conflict with one's own beliefs and practices.

Yet one encounters a richer, or thicker, understanding of human dignity within the Christian tradition. The human capacities to reason and choose freely are merely expressions of the dignity of persons created in God's image. But since humans do not always use reason (e.g, when asleep) nor act freely (e.g., when under the sway of a strong emotion), human dignity must be identified with something more intrinsic—with our very being as bearers of God's image. Humans are created bearing God's image, are created with a divine purpose, and maximize their experience of intrinsic dignity when they live in accordance with that purpose. In what way can we live in accordance with that purpose? Jesus's answer to the scribe who asked him about God's commands is instructive: we are to love God and to love our neighbors (Matt. 22:36–40; Mark 12:28–34). That is the reason we were endowed with dignity by God. Jesus taught his followers that they will be known by their love for one another.[2] We have intrinsic dignity in virtue of being human, but that dignity also comes with a responsibility to live in accordance with God's purposes.

> **Definition: Human Dignity**
>
> The status held by humans entitling them to respect from the moment life begins to the time of natural death.

Thick and Thin Ethics

Ethicists tend to refer to the evaluation of moral judgments in terms of thick versus thin. A thin concept is one that can be talked about at a general, or nonspecific, level. Thin concepts evaluate actions or individuals without further descriptive information. A thick concept describes an activity in a more specific way. Thick concepts both evaluate and describe an action or individual. For example, the terms "good" and "bad" can be used to evaluate an action or individual, but they do not tell us why or how the action or individual is good or bad. Thus they are ethically thin concepts. Thicker words like "courageous," "honest," "cruel" or "callous" tell us both that an action or individual is good or bad while also describing why or how the action or individual is good or bad.

Thick notions of human dignity go beyond speaking of an individual as respect-worthy. Thick notions describe what it is that humans possess which makes them deserving of respect. Thus, one thinks both of the reasoning capacity of human persons and also of their agency, their capacity to will and to act.

Cf. Brendan Cline, "Moral Explanations, Thick and Thin," *Journal of Ethics and Social Philosophy* 9 (2015): 1–20, esp. 7.

The implication of our definition of human dignity for social life is rather profound. For the will to be free to select the type of life a person wishes to lead, it is imperative that the society of which that person is a part organizes the resources sufficiently to make the available choices available as broad as possible. One thinks here of resources like education, health care, libraries, infrastructure, and a functioning government. Access to these resources increases the range of choices available to a person in terms of things like employment, housing selection, political participation, and where to go on vacation. Again, society exists for humans, not the other way around. Society's resources are to be organized in such a way that they maximize human agency.[3]

In connection with this, society must protect an individual's right to access society's resources in the first place. Ideally, a society can rely on the goodwill of every citizen to allow every other citizen the freedom to make these choices. Yet, this being unrealistic, societies have chosen instead to foster human dignity through the protection of rights.[4] The questions then become which rights are to be protected and how ought they to be guaranteed. There are many lists of these rights in our modern world. The United Nations published a

> ## Thank You, Tax Collector!
>
> Have you ever thought about what you need to thrive? A stable home life helps tremendously. Stable parents or guardians. Access to food. Clean water. Unpolluted air. Education. Health care. Infrastructure to facilitate mobility. Safety services such as fire and police departments. And so on.
>
> In order not just to survive but to thrive, you may also need access to things like parks, museums, art, music, and entertainment venues as well as friends and colleagues and bosses who look out for your best interest.
>
> Things such as these cannot easily be provided by yourself. You need the help of others. Societies exist precisely because they provide things for individuals that those individuals cannot acquire alone. Societies do this most efficiently through systems that redistribute their available resources, such as through tax collection systems and through charitable organizations. Next time you pay a tax bill, consider thanking the tax collector for ensuring your access to things you need to thrive!

list of human rights in 1948, its Universal Declaration on Human Rights. The Catholic Church published a list of rights in, among other texts, *Pacem in terris* (Peace on Earth). These are listed in the previous chapter. The US Declaration of Independence summarizes many rights under the broad umbrella terms of life, liberty, and the pursuit of happiness. Additional rights are listed in its first ten amendments to the Constitution, a list referred to as the Bill of Rights. Western cultures have added many new rights beyond these, including rights for passengers on airlines, rights for prisoners, rights for postsecondary students to the protection of their academic record, and so on. Even John Calvin enumerated rights due to every person.[5]

Brief Review of the Sources

Naturally, a central text in any discussion of human dignity in Protestant social ethics is Gen. 1:26, in which God is reported to say, "Let us make humankind in our image." There is a corollary passage to this at Gen. 9:6. So Gen. 1:27 and 9:6 suggest what distinguishes human beings from other beings created by God: humans alone bear something called the image of God, the *imago Dei*.[6] The texts do not tell us what this *imago Dei* is, but they do say it is possessed by males and females and that it is sufficiently important to justify capital punishment for those who kill a fellow human. Through the centuries most commentators on Genesis have linked the *imago Dei* with the intellectual, or rational, capacity of human beings. This is not an unhelpful link, yet modern scientific discoveries have revealed a host of beings within the animal kingdom that possess a rational capacity. So perhaps what one is to understand here is that rationality is something of a spectrum, along which may be located human beings and many other beings.[7] Humans' higher-order reasoning processes, which have yielded moral codes and a capacity to dominate other beings within the environments in which they find themselves, attest to their particular location along that spectrum.

Imago Dei in the Bible
Gen. 1:27
Gen. 9:6
Isa. 40:18
Eph. 4:24
Col. 1:15–16; 3:10
1 Cor. 11:7; 15:49
2 Cor. 3:18; 4:4
James 3:9

For this chapter, we gloss over many texts in the Old and New Testaments that attest to human dignity, particularly the Torah codes that reveal how society can be organized to maximize the dignity of humans. Instead, here we consider a text often overlooked in discussions of social ethics. This is Paul's teaching, in Col. 1 that Jesus is the *imago Dei*. Paul says nothing here about other humans bearing God's image too. Instead, Paul links Jesus's being the *imago Dei* to his capacity to create and to sustain all that exists. Paul writes that Jesus "is the image of the invisible God, the firstborn of all creation; *for* in him all things in heaven and on earth were created" (Col. 1:15–16, emphasis added). Other humans did not create the heavens and the earth, so at this point one would be right to ask Paul what he believed was the difference between humans bearing God's image and Jesus bearing it.

The answer lies in the Christian doctrine of the incarnation, and this is perhaps the most important element to Christian understanding of human dignity. Christianity's doctrine of the incarnation is its teaching that God, in the person of Jesus, took on human flesh. God became human. Henceforth

Incarnation

Latin: *In* + *carnem* (into flesh)

A term used by Christians to refer to the event of the birth of Jesus. It implies that this event was more than the birth of a human being; it was the moment when the Second Person of the Trinity, the Son of God, took on human flesh.

the divine nature inextricably linked itself to human nature. As the early Christians testified, God did this so that humans might become like God. This is salvation, and this is the beauty of the incarnation doctrine. God became human in order to divinize—to save—humans. What God did to Jesus, Christians believe, Jesus does to them as a consequence of faith. Thus Paul writes in Rom. 8:29, "For those whom he foreknew he also predestined to be conformed to the image of his Son." There is the word *imago* again. Salvation is about being conformed to the *imago* of Jesus.

To state the matter bluntly, the *imago Dei* within an individual human, for whatever reason, is stunted. Some Christians would say this is a consequence of sin, or even of an original sin passed down from Adam to the whole human race.[8] Regardless of how the *imago Dei* was initially stunted, by faith men and women have the opportunity to be conformed to the fully formed *imago Dei* in Jesus. And Jesus is the one to whom men and women should want to be conformed, because Jesus is God himself.

Original Sin

Genesis 3 relates a story of Adam and Eve who, while living in the garden of Eden, were tempted by a serpent to eat the fruit of a tree from which they had been forbidden to eat. After they gave in to that temptation, God sent them out of Eden. They no longer had access to the food of this garden, including the fruit of a "tree of life." Their situation had become far more precarious.

To make matters worse, their children were born into this more difficult situation and would not get to experience Eden. They would not have their turn with the serpent, to succumb to its temptations or reject them. Adam and Eve's decision to give into temptation necessarily affected their children. And as the problems associated with life outside Eden mounted, there was an increasing propensity among humans to reject God and to live life on their own terms.

This experience of human life—our birth into a world struggling against God and our own initial rejection of God—is what is meant by original sin. Augustine of Hippo, a leading Christian theologian of the early fifth century, argued that it is because of this stain of original sin in our lives that we are in desperate need of God's grace. Grace washes away this stain of Adam and Eve's sin. Grace renews our capacity to love God again. Grace is God calling us to a new life and a new relationship with himself.

Thus dignity is an ornament or decoration that entitles humans to respect because they are bearers of God's image, and the entire reason for God taking on human nature was to provide humans with the capacity to conform that image as nearly as possible to God. This understanding of human dignity is unpacked further by later Christian writers such as Augustine and Thomas Aquinas. Augustine identified the *imago Dei* in humans with their threefold capacity of memory, understanding, and will (*The Trinity* 15). He further argued that the existence of a will reveals the existence of the other two. In *Free Will* 3, he says the will allows humans to experience delight in the world.[9] The exercise of one's will increases appreciation for one's agency. To this idea, Augustine adds the notion of grace. God's offer of grace to an individual invites him or her to delight not only in the beauty of this world but also in the beauty of God himself. God's grace, then, improves our agency—in this case, our capacity to will to love God.

In a similar way, Thomas Aquinas, in the preface to his *Summa Theologicae* II-I, discusses the *imago Dei*. He writes,

> Since, as [John of Damascus] states [*The Orthodox Faith* 2.12], man is said to be made in God's image, in so far as the image implies "an intelligent being endowed with free-will and self-movement": now that we have treated of the exemplar, i.e., God, and of those things which came forth from the power of God in accordance with His will; it remains for us to treat of His image, i.e., man, inasmuch as he too is the principle of his actions, as having free-will and control of his actions.[10]

Here Aquinas links the *imago Dei* with understanding and then this understanding with freedom of the will in exercising it. Yet even more important, as Aquinas will demonstrate in the articles that follow in this part of the *Summa*, understanding is given by God in order that humans might order their lives toward that God. Thus, to Augustine and Aquinas, the end (purpose) of human dignity is relationship with God. It is not simply the maximization of agency within society. Society's end (purpose) is the enhancement of human dignity, which itself exists for the purpose of drawing each person closer to God, their creator.

During the Reformations, John Calvin too wrote of human dignity rooted in the *imago Dei* of each person. Yet his view is a bit more complex. The will of a person had been corrupted by sin, and grace was necessary to restore it. Calvin writes in his *Institutes*, "Even though we grant that God's image was not totally annihilated and destroyed in him, yet it was so corrupted that whatever remains is frightful deformity" (*Institutes* 1.15.4). The very fact that human will (along with understanding, but not memory since Calvin did not agree with Augustine's trinitarian conception of the soul)[11] had not been obliterated is proof that God preserved the nobility of the human condition throughout. Human dignity rests on God's work, and it is not removed or vitiated even when the cause of its existence, the presence of the *imago Dei*, is itself vitiated by the experience of sin.

In applying these biblical and historical Christian sources to the study of human dignity, the upshot is that society is obliged to organize itself in such a way that human dignity is enhanced rather than diminished. Society does that by making the needs of humans central to any decisions about civic, economic, cultural, and political affairs. Persons with financial or political means already have at hand the tools by which to ensure that their dignity is protected. Thus, more accurately, it is not the needs of humans, generally, but the needs of humans on the margins of society that are paramount.

Illustrations of the Principle

In order to begin thinking like a social ethicist, one should consider some illustrations of the principle of human dignity in practice. In one illustration, human embryos have been frozen in fertility clinics around the world. Thousands of these embryos will go "unclaimed" during the lifetimes of those who put them there. Some of the couples who placed them there are no longer together. Some of the individuals have died. Still other couples have, for various reasons, decided that they are done having children, and these remaining embryos are no longer wanted. How ought a social ethicist think about this matter?

The first issue is to determine whether these frozen embryos are human beings.[12] If they are, they deserve dignity. Their dignity is intact regardless of their present state of human development. Suppose one concludes that they are human beings; the next question is what can be done to enhance their dignity. Since there is no legal tool to oblige the couples who deposited the embryos to claim them, and no such tool is likely to be forthcoming, one might want to seek other means by which the embryos could be brought to a more mature state of human development. For example, the state could seek adoptive parents for the embryos, or perhaps a surrogate mother could birth the child and allow it then to become an orphan, a ward of the state. Indeed, if these are priorities, then one way society can organize itself to enhance the dignity of these frozen human beings is to provide the financial, medical, and emotional resources required for adoptive parents and surrogates to embrace this as a genuine possibility. The state too would need to find enough foster

Frozen Embryos

✓ There is no official record of embryos, but it is estimated that hundreds of thousands of them are preserved in tanks of liquid nitrogen in clinics around the United States.

✓ Approximately 1.5 percent of all births in the United States are attributable to the implanting of once-frozen embryos.

✓ Unused embryos are stored at a cost of $300–$1,200 per year, which is paid by the individual who placed them there.

Tamar Lewin, "Industry's Growth Leads to Leftover Embryos, and Painful Choices," *New York Times*, June 18, 2015, A1.

Embryologist freezing embryos for storage.

parents to house the nonadopted newborns until their emancipation into adulthood. All of these things would have to be a priority, and it is not hard to imagine a state or a culture deciding that this is too much to ask, given other social concerns. So, what if no adoptive parents or surrogates can be found? It certainly makes little sense for a clinic to be obliged—indefinitely—to lease buildings, pay electric bills, and own freezers solely in order to keep "alive" these frozen human beings. Corporations do not live forever, and they certainly are not going to be convinced by the idea that they should retain these embryos "until Christ returns." Thus it makes the most sense to figure out some way to let these embryos experience a natural death. It is not inconceivable that a social ethicist would conclude that, having exhausted all means to sustain the lives of these human beings in a natural state, the best thing to do would be to move the unclaimed embryos out of their freezers, allow them to thaw, and thereby allow them to experience a natural death.

Still, this is not enough. Recall our definition of human dignity: a status held by humans entitling them to respect. A social ethicist may well conclude it is appropriate to let unclaimed embryos thaw and so experience a natural death, but this act alone does not mean society has treated the embryo in a respectful way. There must be some recognition that the deceased embryo was human. This means its death was not to be sought for a malevolent purpose. That is to say, its death could not be sought simply because others wanted it for medical testing, for example. Nor can its death be sought for the sake of convenience for the state or even for those who placed it there. We must find a way to honor its life by not misusing it. It would even be conceivable to consider holding a funeral for it much as one would honor other humans after their deaths.

An illustration closer to the field of social ethics would be the risk to human dignity posed by the decisions of a society regarding affordable housing. From the principle of human dignity is derived the right of every person to basic necessities of life. Safe, reliable, affordable housing is surely one such necessity. Yet one need not travel far through the urban centers in our world to discover that the poor have great difficulty accessing this type of housing. To understand why, consider the situation faced by urban centers. The property needed for building large housing structures is expensive, and then come the high costs of building code-compliant structures on that property. The corporations that assume the financial risk in building housing structures rightly expect to be repaid for their investment, so they have an incentive to charge the highest possible price the market will bear for their apartment or housing units. Very quickly the poor are displaced from urban cores as affordable housing supplies diminish.

At this point several options suggest themselves to the social ethicist. One option is for the government to acquire the property and to assume the costs of construction. In more centrally planned economies of our world, this does happen. Governments accept the responsibility to ensure affordable housing for the poor. The challenge with this option is in ensuring the government's commitment to maintain the structures, to continue to subsidize the rents, and not to show politically motivated favoritism in the selection of individuals allowed to rent units in the first place. Less centrally planned economies, such as the United States, prefer to incentivize private industry to build affordable housing by offering tax credits on their future rental profits and direct subsidy payments to the corporation to offset the lower rents. The housing units made available under this type of program in the United States are generally referred to as "Section 8 housing," or HUD-approved housing. (HUD stands for the federal department of Housing and Urban Development.) Typically, apartment structures built with HUD support will make some or all of their units available at below-market, subsidized rates. This seems like a good solution; however, in reality few corporations take up the government's offer of these tax and subsidy incentives. They are afraid the presence of "the poor" in their building will lower the attractiveness of the structure to higher-class renters or buyers, and they are further convinced that they can make more money from higher-class renters than the rent earned from poor tenants, even with the government's incentives calculated into the mix. There was even a case in New York in 2014 in which owners of a large, high-end apartment building agreed to incorporate into their building some apartments for subsidized housing. But to make sure that these tenants did not have access to all the building's high-end features and that they would not have contact with the higher-class tenants in the building, the structure was designed in such a way that those living in the subsidized portion of the building (i.e., the poor) would not have any contact with those living in the nonsubsidized portion of the building. The building's developers even created a separate entrance for tenants in the subsidized portion of the building. Activists in the New York area dubbed the separate entrance "the poor door," which began a conversation about affordable housing in the city.

Section 8 Housing

(a) Authorization for assistance payments

For the purpose of aiding low-income families in obtaining a decent place to live and of promoting economically mixed housing, assistance payments may be made with respect to existing housing in accordance with the provisions of this section.

(b) Other existing housing programs

(1) **In general.**— The Secretary [of Housing and Urban Development] is authorized to enter into annual contributions contracts with public housing agencies pursuant to which such agencies may enter into contracts to make assistance payments to owners of existing dwelling units in accordance with this section. In areas where no public housing agency has been organized or where the Secretary determines that a public housing agency is unable to implement the provisions of this section, the Secretary is authorized to enter into such contracts and to perform the other functions assigned to a public housing agency by this section. . . .

(c) Contents and purposes of contracts for assistance payments; amount and scope of monthly assistance payments

(1) An assistance contract entered into pursuant to this section shall establish the maximum monthly rent (including utilities and all maintenance and management charges) which the owner is entitled to receive for each dwelling unit with respect to which such assistance payments are to be made.

—"Section 8" of the Housing Act of 1937 (42 U.S. Code §1437f)

Another option that would seem to sidestep many of the concerns about the reliability or the attractiveness of government intervention and the high cost of constructing and maintaining housing units is moving the poor to the less desirable and cheaper parts of the cities. These parts are typically between the downtown core and the suburbs (because suburban communities price out the poor through zoning ordinances that require lower-density housing and thereby increase the cost of real estate). This option falls within the "let the market decide" category, since the personal choices of home buyers and renters have led them to dwell either in downtown centers or in suburbs, but not in these middle regions. As a result, housing stock becomes cheaper in these middle regions. To a social ethicist, however, this is a solution with its own set of difficulties. While it is true that affordable housing can more easily be found here, it is less likely that the housing will be safe. It is less likely that the community's infrastructure will be properly maintained. For these reasons, few jobs actually exist in these regions. The poor, who typically will not own or have regular access to a working vehicle, will need to rely on public transportation to get to desirable jobs in other parts of the city or suburbs. However, this is precisely where most public transit fails: few cities sufficiently fund their public transit systems to facilitate the employment prospects of the poor. Besides that, public transit can lengthen commuting time considerably, assuming that it even takes one to where one needs to go for desirable work.

Whether one seeks to resolve the problem of housing insecurity for those on society's margins through government programs or through private market incentives, the point is that society does not have a choice but to work toward solving the problem. The people affected by housing insecurity have dignity as bearers of God's image. It would be a sin to turn a blind eye to their suffering. More to the point, we express the realization of our own dignity when we conform our lives to the purposes God intended, and this requires loving well those whom God specially loves, our neighbors who are suffering.

Summary

Human dignity is an intrinsic quality of individuals that entitles them to respect from others. Its intrinsic quality is rooted in humans bearing God's image, and this divine image obliges all people to conform their lives to God's purposes, which are to love God and neighbor. To the extent we take seriously our call to love our neighbors well, the concept of human dignity draws us into the realm of social ethics.

More is to be gained by living in community than by living alone. Consequently, communities provide resources that enhance an individual's choices, and they protect the right(s) of each person to access those choices. Social life, then, is to be entirely organized on the basis of what enhances human dignity rather than diminishes it. For this reason, it is the first principle in social ethics. At the same time, society cannot make available every *conceivable* choice to every individual. There are limits to a society's resources, and social life is not to be construed in this self-centered way. This is where the second principle in social ethics, the common good, enters the discussion.

Main Points of the Chapter

» Human dignity is the status held by humans entitling them to respect from the moment life begins to the time of natural death.

» Human dignity derives from humans being created in God's image, which obliges us to love God and others in return.

» Human dignity is further revealed by human exercise of reason and human capacity to make rational choices.

» Human dignity is revealed further still through human agency, the human capacity to act on rational choices.

» The existence of human dignity demands that societies order their resources (and their protection of rights to those resources) to maximize each individual's agency.

⊰ 12 ⊱

Common Good

Learning Outcomes for This Chapter

» Define "common good" and its contribution to social life.

» Summarize the contribution of biblical and later Christian literature to understanding the importance of the common good.

» Examine challenges societies face in organizing themselves in accordance with the common good.

The next foundational principle in social ethics is the common good. Whereas human dignity concerns itself with the status of individual persons in society, the principle of the common good widens our focus to the status of the whole society. This is what makes the common good another *why* principle in social ethics. Protestants need to think about social ethics because the good of society is at stake. A proper orientation toward the common good should inspire Protestants to take increasing ownership of public life. It should encourage Protestants to ensure its many civic, political, and cultural institutions address the suffering of those on society's margins.

Definition of Common Good

The common good is the set of conditions within society that enables everyone to have the opportunity to flourish. Several parts of this definition require further explanation. First, the "set of conditions" refers to the controllable features of society. For example, education is a feature that members of society can decide whether to provide. Geographic location and the topography of a region are not controlled by society, so they would not be part of that "set of conditions" that a social ethicist would measure in terms of human flourishing. Second, "opportunity" in the definition suggests that the common good is measured by whether everyone has

> **Definition: Common Good**
>
> The set of conditions within society that enables everyone to have the opportunity to flourish.

a *chance* to flourish, not whether everyone *actually* flourishes. For example, if education is one of the conditions within society, then its availability to all is an important measure of the common good. However, if some members of society freely choose not to avail themselves of education, the common good is not at risk.

Finally, "to flourish" may variously be understood as "to be happy" or "to live an authentic, human life." It suggests that the common good is measured by the extent to which the social conditions provide individual members of society with the ability to become the type of people that they ought to become. Some individuals will define flourishing as the ability to pursue a certain career; others may say they are flourishing if they can spend as much time outdoors as possible; still others might define it in economic terms. Yet not all definitions of flourishing are valid. It is not acceptable, for example, for individuals to define their flourishing in terms of a lifestyle that harms others. Consequently, this is the point in the definition of the common good where social ethicists defer to the resources within other branches of ethics, such as virtue ethics, since other fields help individuals determine healthy from unhealthy understandings of their own flourishing.[1]

Brief Review of the Sources

Scripture provides a wealth of resources for thinking about the organization of society. There are the law codes that are intended to organize Israelite society and fill so much of the Torah narratives. There is an extensive criticism of kingship in 1 Samuel and repeated criticisms of individual kings throughout the historical narratives and the Prophets. The Prophets also proclaim God's message of judgment against Israel and its neighbors for their failure to organize society in such a way that everyone—especially the poor—have an opportunity to flourish.

Kingship in the Old Testament

After the Israelites fled Egypt, Deuteronomy records a warning against appointing a king over their new nation. The king could well turn the people in a wrong direction:

> When you have come into the land that the LORD your God is giving you, and have taken possession of it and settled in it, and you say, "I will set a king over me, like all the nations that are around me," you may indeed set over you a king whom the LORD your God will choose. One of your own community you may set as king over you; you are not permitted to put a foreigner over you, who is not of your own community. Even so, he must not acquire many horses for himself, or return the people to Egypt in order to acquire more horses, since the LORD has said to you, "You must never return that way again." And he must not acquire many wives for himself, or else his heart will turn away; also silver and gold he must not acquire in great quantity for himself. When he has taken the throne of his kingdom, he shall have a copy of this law written for him in the presence of the levitical priests. It shall remain with him and he shall read in it all the days of his life, so that he may learn to fear the LORD his God, diligently observing all the words of this law and these statutes, neither exalting himself above other members of the community nor turning aside from the commandment, either to the right or to the left, so that he and his descendants may reign long over his kingdom in Israel. (Deut. 7:14–16)

Centuries later, those warnings proved prescient. In a veiled rejection of God, the Israelites formally requested a king from Samuel, the prophet and priest ministering in Israel during the early-ninth century BC:

> The elders of Israel gathered together and came to Samuel at Ramah, and said to him, "You are old and your sons do not follow in your ways; appoint for us, then, a king to govern us, like other nations." But the thing displeased Samuel when they said, "Give us a king to govern us." Samuel prayed to the LORD, and the LORD said to Samuel, "Listen to the voice of the people in all that they say to you; for they have not rejected you, but they have rejected me from being king over them. Just as they have done to me, from the day I brought them up out of Egypt to this day, forsaking me and serving other gods, so also they are doing to you. Now then, listen to their voice; only—you shall solemnly warn them, and show them the ways of the king who shall reign over them." (1 Sam. 8:4–9)

The New Testament also adds to these critiques. Jesus proclaimed God's love and compassion for the Jewish people suffering under not only the oppressive Roman regimes but also the burdens of the oral law tradition. Jesus also complained about the organization of Jewish religious life, because it fleeced the poor with temple taxes and money-changing operations during festivals. More positively, Jesus invited society's greatly marginalized persons into a relationship with God—tax collectors, prostitutes, half-Jews such as Samaritans, and even non-Jews such as Roman soldiers; Jesus was really providing the vision for a new type of society in which his followers were to be invested.

The apostle Paul appreciated what Jesus had been doing, and he committed the last decades of his life to sharing God's love, mercy, and grace to people from all walks of life, within and without the Jewish community. He wrote to the church in Corinth,

> To the Jews I became as a Jew, in order to win Jews. To those under the law I became as one under the law (though I myself am not under the law) so that I might win those under the law. To those outside the law I became as one outside the law (though I am not free from God's law but am under Christ's law) so that I might win those outside the law. To the weak I became weak, so that I might win the weak. I have become all things to all people, that I might by all means save some. (1 Cor. 9:20–22)

He also urged that those with excess wealth should share resources with those having less than they needed, identifying these gifts with the fellowship (*koinōnia*) that exists between Christians (cf. chap. 5).

Related to this, texts like the Acts of the Apostles and the Letter of James further highlight how early Christians organized the church community around the sharing of excess wealth and not discriminating among people based on their wealth. For example, Acts 2 records that the earliest followers of Jesus were willing to redistribute their resources to meet everyone's basic needs (see Acts 2:44–45). James warns his readers against treating wealthy Christians differently than they treat poorer Christians: "Do you with your acts of favoritism really believe in our Lord Jesus Christ? . . . Has not God chosen the poor in the world to be rich in faith and to be heirs of the kingdom that he has promised to those who love him? But you have dishonored the poor" (James 2:1, 5–6). Despite the many constraints of Roman life, each text reveals a concern to organize society, at least the church's society, in such a way that people either have what they need to flourish or the opportunity to acquire that.

In Late Antiquity, one discovers at least three ways in which Christians incorporated language about the common good into their writings. The first, not surprisingly, is in discussions about the common good of the Christian community. Romans 12:4–5 (also 1 Cor. 12:12) compares the Christian community to a body, and each member of the community has an obligation to support the other parts. In his commentary on this passage in Romans, Theodoret of Cyrus, a pastor and leader in the Christian community in the fifth century, says that the support each member gives to the community contributes to the common good (*koinon ōpheleia*). Moreover, this unity of the Christian community is a consequence of the grace of God, a grace that itself is acknowledged to be a gift given by God for the common good of all people.[2] The Christian message is most effectively distributed for common benefit to the world after the Christian community itself is in theological agreement.

Second, writers in Late Antiquity spoke about the common good in economic terms. Healthy economic activity was built around the continuous movement of capital: from buyers to merchants, merchants to producers, and producers to employees, with the employees themselves being buyers again. In this way, everyone has a share in the common good of an economic system. Basil of Caesarea, in his *Homilies* 6, writes, "Riches grow useless left idle and unused in any place; but moved about, passing from one person to another, they serve the common good [*koinōphelēs*] and bear fruit."[3] The context for Basil's homily is the appropriate disposition of an abundant harvest, yet the homily has in view something called redemptive almsgiving.[4] This is significant, for it reveals that Basil understood that the poorest citizens and the feeble were not equal participants in the constant rotation of money within an economic system. They were unlikely to be earning a regular wage; thus it was the obligation of those with greater financial means to inject more of their financial capital into the economic system via direct financial assistance to those on the economic fringe. In this way, both the rich and the poor may more equally share in the economic common good.[5]

Third, the writers in Late Antiquity incorporated common-good language into their political discourse. Admittedly, their comments are often brief, and one should not approach them as harbingers of historical accuracy. Even so, one may be impressed at the depth of understanding found in Gregory of Nazianzus's remarks about the "common benefit" (*koinon ōpheleia*) derived from a "government administered with moderation, the lowering of taxes, the judicious choice of magistrates, the punishment of embezzlers"—this list continues for two more paragraphs.[6] More widely known is Augustine's *City of God*, which situates language about the common good within the framework of pride. Augustine writes, "Accordingly, two cities have been formed by two loves: the earthly by the love of self, even to the contempt of God; the heavenly by the love of God, even to the contempt of self. The former, in

Redemptive Almsgiving

Inspired partly by James 2:5, "Did not God choose the poor in the world to be rich in faith and heirs of the kingdom?" (NET), Christian writers in Late Antiquity sometimes wrote of the practice of almsgiving (i.e., the giving of one's money or other resources to aid the poor) in terms of a spiritual exchange. Wealthy people are rich in money; poor people are rich in faith. When rich people help poor people with money, poor people then help rich people get to heaven by praying to God on their behalf. In other words, the more you help the poor, the more likely it is you will be welcomed into an eternal rest.

The redemptive aspect to this exchange was based on the assumption that people who gave alms did so because they cared about their relationship with God. They gave alms as an expression of contrition for the sins they committed after baptism. One's pastor might have even recommended an appropriate amount to give in accordance with the gravity of sin for which one sought God's forgiveness.

As Cyprian of Carthage wrote: "As in [baptism] the fire of Gehenna is extinguished, so by almsgiving and works of righteousness the flame of sins is subdued. And because in baptism remission of sins is granted once for all, constant and ceaseless labor, following the likeness of baptism, once again bestows the mercy of God" (*Works and Almsgiving* 2).

a word, glories in itself, the latter in the Lord. For the one seeks glory from men; but the greatest glory of the other is God, the witness of conscience. . . . The one delights in its own strength, represented in the persons of its rulers; the other says to its God, I will love You, O Lord, my strength."[7] The hallmark of the heavenly city is the common good, for in that city there is no pride. The earthly city could also exhibit the common good, but the pride of its rulers prevents this.

Fourth, Christians in Late Antiquity also anticipated some of the judicial language associated with the common good that would flower in the scholastic age. For example, Irenaeus of Lyons (*Against Heresies* 5.24) writes, "Earthly rule . . . has been appointed by God for the benefit of nations, . . . conducting themselves after a quiet manner, so that under the fear of human rule, men may not eat each other up like fishes; but that, by means of the establishment of laws, they may keep down an excess of wickedness among the nations."[8]

Here Irenaeus reflects on the implications of Rom. 13, a text in which Paul both calls his readers to submit themselves to the rule of the state and also defends the right of a state to use force to punish evildoers. "Whoever resists authority resists what God has appointed, and those who resist will incur judgment" (Rom 13:2). Irenaeus's comments underscore the contribution of the state to fostering the common good. Lack of contentment leads many unjustly to acquire the goods of others. The state has a role in quelling such misbehavior and restoring good order.[9]

Turning to the Middle Ages, it may be surprising to discover that the common good is less central to Thomas Aquinas's thought than matters of law and virtue.[10] The common good nowhere emerges as a separate topic of discussion in his *Summa*. Jean Porter, who has studied Aquinas's views on the common good, locates his thought about it in two areas. One is in his contrast between private and public goods. The other is in his view of political authority, which exists to direct society toward the common good. The only piece missing is a definition of the common good itself. Consider

---

Rulers Are Robbers

Set within a wider argument about the injustices of the early days of the Roman Republic, Augustine of Hippo articulates the necessary connection between the legitimacy of a state and its propagation of justice. Citizens of a state immediately sense changes in the winds of justice, and they have every right to demand either that their state reverse its course or that a ruling be set aside in favor of another system:

> Justice being taken away, then, what are kingdoms but great robbers? For what are robbers themselves, but little kingdoms? The band itself is made up of men; it is ruled by the authority of a prince, it is knit together by the pact of the confederacy; the booty is divided by the law agreed on. If, by the admittance of abandoned men, this evil increases to such a degree that it holds places, fixes abodes, takes possession of cities, and subdues peoples, it assumes more plainly the name of a kingdom, because the reality is now manifestly conferred on it, not by the removal of covetousness, but by the addition of impunity. Indeed, that was an apt and true reply which was given to Alexander the Great by a pirate who had been seized. For when that king had asked the man what he intended by keeping hostile possession of the sea, he answered with bold pride, "What you intend by seizing the whole earth; but because I do it with a petty ship, I am called a robber, while you who do it with a great fleet are styled an emperor."

—Augustine, *City of God* 4.4

Humans Naturally Seek Society

Because in man there is first of all an inclination to good . . . inasmuch as every substance seeks the preservation of its own being. . . .

Secondly, there is in man an inclination towards things that pertain to him more specially, . . . such as sexual intercourse, education of off-spring and so forth.

Thirdly, there is in man an inclination to good, according to the nature of his reason, which nature is proper to him:

Thus man has a natural inclination to know the truth about God, and to live in society.

—Thomas Aquinas, *ST* I-II.94, art. 2

Aquinas's comments in his *Summa*. He is evaluating the hypothetical situation of whether a political structure of rulers and ruled would have emerged in a world without sin, and he concludes,

> Lording it [over others] can be taken in two ways; first, as opposed to slaving it, and in this sense we call someone a lord who has someone else subjected to him as a slave. Secondly, lording it can be taken as relative to any sort of subjection in general, and in this sense even the man who has the office of governing and directing free men can be called a lord. . . . Someone lords over another as a free man when he is directing him to his own, the free man's, proper good, or to the common good."[11]

Although his interlocutors believed that sin was the cause of some people needing to be ruled by others, Aquinas argued that this is true only in the case of slaves being subject to masters. The other kind of rule is that of cities, in which the ruler guides those being ruled toward the common good, which is a far more benevolent course than the type of rule needed for the cause of restraining sin. Thus everything that a ruler does in this case, including the production of law, is to be directed toward the common good.

During the Reformations era, reflection on the common good coincided with the Reformers' teaching on the two kingdoms. To John Calvin, the political community is a continuous outworking of God's providential care of the world. Thus, by its very existence, a common good is presumed to be its proper end. Civic officials exist to maintain the common good, and they do so in concert with the church.[12] Somewhat differently, Martin Luther taught that the common good begins with an individual's commitment to others; secondarily, it lends itself to one's support of the state. For example, in his

Freedom of a Christian, Luther writes, "The good things we have from God should flow from one to the other and be common to all, so that everyone should 'put on' his neighbor and so conduct himself toward him as if he himself were in the other's place."[13] Since the state is the chief instrument of God by which resources are collected and redistributed to make sure everyone has what they need, support of the state for its role in the common good is essential. Luther writes in his work *On Secular Authority*,

> Christians, among themselves and by and for themselves, need no law or sword, since it is neither necessary nor profitable for them. Since, however, a true Christian lives and labors on earth not for himself but for his neighbor, therefore the whole spirit of his life impels him to do even that which he need not do, but which is profitable and necessary for his neighbor. Because the sword is a very great benefit and necessary to the whole world, to preserve peace, to punish sin and to prevent evil, he submits most willingly to the rule of the sword, pays tax, honors those in authority, serves, helps, and does all he can to further the government, that it may be sustained and held in honor and fear. Although he needs none of these things for himself and it is not necessary for him to do them, yet he considers what is for the good and profit of others, as Paul teaches in Ephesians 5:21.[14]

Christians support the state because the state is ordained by God and exists for the common good. Ideally, Christians would be content with what they possess and not rely too much on the state, but Christians pay taxes and support government because they know it is helpful to others.[15]

In more recent centuries, some political philosophers thought about the common good in terms of the greatest good for the greatest number of people, a view called utilitarianism.[16] Since that understanding would unfortunately oblige us to accept that some minority percentage of persons may not enjoy the goods of society, that their being left behind should be tolerated in order that the greatest number of people can enjoy those goods, it behooves Protestants to look beyond politically motivated theories alone for a richer understanding of the common good. Fortunately, the resources of the Christian tradition have provided a thicker ethic and thus a more robust understanding of the common good.

Illustrations of the Principle

In democratic countries, every time people go to the polls to vote, each citizen is making a judgment about the common good. There are choices among candidates representing different political parties, and these parties have formed and continue to exist because they offer different visions about how society ought to be organized. Usually decisions about party affiliation correspond with one's views of resource distribution. This is because some parties believe federal or state governments are best suited to collect, organize, and then redistribute the resources of a society, to build or to otherwise provide the sets of conditions needed for human flourishing. Other parties advocate less of a government role in managing resources. Instead, they believe private markets can organize a society's resources more efficiently and effectively to provide the services required for human flourishing.

One of the problems individuals face when considering these big questions regarding the roles of government and private markets in distributing society's resources is the problem of free ridership. "Free riders" are those who benefit from a resource without having done anything to create that resource. For example, a community's infrastructure, such as its roads and parks, are susceptible to the free-rider problem. Most residents of a city, if asked about individual projects, "Will you pay money to build park x or to make repairs to road y or to build a new elementary school?" will quite likely say no. Few people agree to part with their money for projects that they estimate they will use infrequently or not at all. However, given the existence of that park x or road y or new elementary school building, they will be happy to use it and will enjoy the benefit of the higher property values it may yield as a result. The free-rider problem is precisely why most private markets do not work

Who Votes?

According to the U.S. Census Bureau, between 1978 and 2014 on average fewer than 50 percent of eligible voters ever cast a ballot.

In 2014, for example, only 41.9 percent of the voting-age population voted in that year's midterm election. Who did vote that year?

Age of eligible voters	Percent who voted	
18 to 34 years	23.1	
35 to 44 years	37.8	
45 to 64 years	49.6	
65 years and older	59.4	

Source: U.S. Census Bureau, "Who Votes? Congressional Elections and the American Electorate" (July 2015), 3, 6. www.census.gov.

for building or maintaining institutions required to produce the common good. Private markets do not have the legal authority that governments have to compel contributions (via taxes) from individuals to pay for things like parks or roads or schools, which they might claim they would never use; yet when those assets are in place, they will still be able to enjoy the benefit of a higher property value or a higher standard of living.

To further this discussion of the role of voting, its impact on the common good goes beyond a general sense of which party has the right idea about the distribution of society's resources and how best to resolve free ridership. Voting also demonstrates a preference for one "set of conditions" over the opposing candidate's, or party's, alternative "set of conditions" for the common good. Voting demonstrates this preference because different candidates promote different visions of what society *owes* its members in order to help them succeed. For example, United States citizens have long supported government-funded education for the K–12 academic years. That is guaranteed for every citizen in every state. Individual states are free to expand that government-backed education guarantee, and some states have expanded it to include pre-K education programs as well. Thus K–12 or pre-K–12 education is widely regarded as one condition required for everyone to have the opportunity to flourish. In recent years, however, it has become increasingly clear that a bachelor's degree holds roughly the same value for a person's economic future as a high school degree held a few decades ago. So some Americans argue that the government should now expand its definition of free public education to include postsecondary studies. Proponents argue that this is the minimum level of education needed today for people to flourish; a high school degree is not enough. Indeed, citizens in European countries arrived at this conclusion a few decades ago, and they have provided either free or substantially subsidized postsecondary education for their citizens ever since.

Is a college degree necessary for human flourishing in our day? Let us assume that it is, for the sake of argument. On that basis, the common good is not being achieved in societies where the opportunity to access postsecondary education is not being met, and it is incumbent on voters in those societies to elect individuals who will align the government's spending priorities with making sure college-level education is accessible to everyone. Yet something complicates such illustrations: what makes education accessible (or inaccessible) to one person is not what makes it accessible (or inaccessible) to another. For example, the cost of postsecondary education might make access to it prohibitive for some. For others, cost may not be the issue, but the distance one has to travel to be in a postsecondary institution might be prohibitive. For still others, the problem is not cost or distance but one's family situation.

Resourcing the Common Good

What resources ought a society to provide to its members in order for that society to be in accord with the common good? What are you willing to pay for with your taxes? Do you agree with some of the items below? What should be removed from the list? What should be added?

✓ Pre-K education
✓ Primary education
✓ Secondary education
✓ Postsecondary education
✓ Fire services
✓ Police services
✓ Court system
✓ Water rights / access to water
✓ Water testing / inspection
✓ Natural resource management
✓ Emergency medical care
✓ Chronic disease management
✓ Medical research
✓ Health insurance
✓ Road construction

✓ Snow removal
✓ Railroads
✓ Bus system
✓ Military services
✓ Weapons research
✓ Flood insurance
✓ Workplace safety regulations
✓ Food benefits for the poor
✓ Daycare for children of working parents
✓ Oil stockpiles
✓ Automobile safety standards
✓ Cleanup services after natural disasters

Perhaps an individual is a single parent or has responsibilities to care for an ill family member that makes accessing classes prohibitive.

Thus it is easy to conclude that education is one of the conditions necessary for everyone to have an opportunity to flourish. It is far less easy to organize society in such a way that everyone's access barriers are reduced. There are different needs. Reducing the cost of college to "free" would certainly be nice, but it would not ensure that everyone could go to college. Finding solutions that would lower the access barriers for all persons requires individualized approaches, and so it is reasonable for a voter to conclude that state or local governments are better equipped to address this than the federal government. Thus it is conceivable that someone might vote for a candidate at the federal level who has no interest in making college free while voting with precisely the opposite interest in mind for candidates vying for state or local offices.

The same calculations need to be made for other societal conditions that facilitate the common good. Here one thinks of access to health care, to arts and culture, to an impartial judiciary, to the provision of national defense, to strong families, to a well-functioning electric grid, to mitigation of devastation from natural disasters, and to the provision of disaster-relief supplies. The questions of just what exactly is owed to each member of society to ensure access to these things, whether that access is guaranteed by the state or by private markets, and what further conditions one might want for human flourishing—each of these issues is the subject of debate. Such questions make study of the common good so enriching for social ethicists and their audience.

Summary

There is no feature of civic life on which the common good does not touch: employment, housing, food security, wages, health care, political party affiliations, and virtually everything else. This is because the principle of common good asks Protestants (indeed, everyone) to consider whether society has been sufficiently structured to give everyone an opportunity to flourish. More to the point, it asks whether society has given this opportunity especially to those on the margins, because people with financial and political means will always find a way to get their needs met. Protestants bring to this discussion the wisdom of their scriptural and historical witnesses. These texts reveal that God was pleased to establish political life, for it contributed to his own purposes of helping to bring order out of chaos. They also reveal God's ongoing, providential care of both the church and the state, in order to maintain unity among people and to provide for the needs of every person.

Main Points of the Chapter

» The common good is the set of conditions within society that enables everyone to have the opportunity to flourish.

» The common good is measured not by whether everyone is flourishing but by whether everyone has access to the things necessary to flourish.

» The Christian tradition first thought of the common good in terms of unity and the sharing of resources. During the Middle Ages and later, the common good became increasingly the subject of the political sphere.

» Utilitarian ideas about the common good are insufficient insofar as they tolerate the prospect of some persons being left behind in the wake of society's economic or technological progress.

⟨ 13 ⟩

Justice

As stated in chapter 11, human dignity is the first principle of social ethics. On that principle depends all the others. The common good is the second principle in social ethics, since it elevates concern for an individual's dignity to the level of protection and promotion of that dignity in the organization of civil society. Both principles explain *why* Protestants are to be concerned with social ethics. Justice is the third principle in social ethics, and it is dependent on the first two. Justice is a virtue regarding the treatment of others. Because each person has dignity, all deserve to be treated justly. Because civil society seeks the flourishing of each of its members, just treatment of individuals is constitutive of the common good. In this way, justice expresses the *what* of social ethics. It is what ought to be done in order to strengthen human dignity and the common good.

Definition of Justice

Justice is the virtue of giving people what is due them as a consequence of their God-given dignity.[1] Since it is a virtue, it is possible to analyze its presence or absence in both individuals and in civil society. In other words, there are just and unjust individuals, much as there are just and unjust societies. Also important are the various ways in which individuals may be given what is due them. These variations have encouraged social ethicists to divide justice into different categories, not unlike the divisions of justice made by Thomas Aquinas (see chap. 7). One way of giving individuals their due is to ensure that the benefits and burdens of society are fairly distributed. Social ethicists label such thinking distributive justice. Another way of giving individuals their due is to ensure fairness in the relationship between persons, which social ethicists call commutative justice. When fairness in those relationships breaks down, there is punishment for those who seek to harm others. Social ethicists label this retributive, or punitive or corrective, justice. In cases where retributive justice has run to excess, social ethicists speak about restorative justice, in which healing of the offended rather than punishment for the offender is the goal. One can also speak about procedural justice within a judicial system for all those who are party to a legal proceeding. To the extent that each of these particular expressions of justice—distributive, commutative, retributive, restorative, and procedural—is concerned with improving society, they can be summed up in the term "social justice." Our actions on behalf of social justice, then, are an exercise in virtue. And as with any virtue, the cultivation of justice depends on our repeatedly acting in a just way. It depends on our repeatedly honoring the dignity of others.

> **Definition: Justice**
>
> The virtue of giving people what is due them as a consequence of their God-given dignity.

Extending the Definition

Although people immediately think of police, courts, and judges when they hear the word "justice," the word is not necessarily connected to the practice of law. Instead, as a virtue, justice is the manner in which we ought to live. Legal mechanisms such as police, courts, and judges may facilitate the correction of injustice and the restoration of justice, and their presence certainly encourages individuals bent on behaving unjustly to curb their tendencies long enough to avoid being punished. Yet we would not call a person just whose desire is to behave unjustly but who does not act on those desires simply out of fear of punishment. Likewise, we would not call a society just if it desires injustice toward members of its own or neighboring societies. In other words, virtue is expressed in doing the right thing for the right reason rather than doing the right thing for the wrong reason.

There are several theories about what is the right reason for behaving justly. For example, do we treat others justly, as free rational agents, out of duty to them as fellow humans? Or out of a desire to maintain a certain rule of law? Or perhaps out of a desire to restrain our own selfish impulses? These and related questions have invited speculation among philosophers, theologians, ethicists, and political theorists about the proper way of speaking about the virtue of justice. The following list summarizes some of the positions that have emerged. These are not mutually exclusive positions but overlapping ones. Each articulates valuable ways we may be habitually disposed to giving people what is due them.[2]

1. *Justice as duty*. The Christian tradition has often spoken of justice as an obligation owed to fellow humans because they are created in God's image and therefore are deserving of dignity. The obligations become very personal, even when talking about relationship to others through social structures such as education, wage and employment contracts, and housing policies. Just behavior in these social structures is intended to produce a common good enjoyable by every person.

2. *Justice as law*.[3] States and international bodies create legal frameworks by which justice can be measured and restored if violated. Lawful behavior, then, is just behavior, and the right reason for behaving lawfully is the establishment of a just society. Furthermore, as cultures develop new understandings of what constitutes a just society, laws can be changed in order to reorient behavior. The legal framework is attractive to cultures that value the idealistic language of a "just" society but who seek to minimize dependency on religious language regarding human dignity.

3. *Justice as restraint of self-interest*.[4] Accepting the reality of sin, some in the Christian tradition have argued that justice will never be more than a pale version of the love for others that Jesus asked of his followers. To experience even this pale version, each person must value the interests of others as being equally or more important than one's own interests. This requires restraint of one's own prideful and self-interested impulses. Still, the best one can expect is a relative experience of justice, and that as a result of systems that balance power, coerce certain behaviors, demand equal treatment of others, and promote freedom.

4. *Justice as fairness*.[5] If the right reason to behave justly is the creation of a good society, then to theorists of "justice as fairness," justice is less about

individual behavior and more about social organization. In that case, what justice demands in social organization is fairness. This involves distributing fairly, though not necessarily equally, among a society's members its benefits and burdens, its rights and duties.

5. *Justice as virtue*.[6] In contrast to justice theories, such as that of fairness, that dilute individual contributions in favor of viewing justice purely in social terms, this theory argues that the right reason for behaving justly is that it increases one's own claim to being treated justly. Individuals who support the community's pursuit of the common good are living virtuously. Living virtuously increases one's merits with respect to justice. Thus the greater an individual's cohesion with the community, the greater his or her claim to just treatment from others.

6. *Justice as participation*.[7] This theory looks ahead to Christianity's vision of the eschatological age. That is the age in which God has promised to fashion a new kingdom out of a new heaven and a new earth. Scripture passages such as Mic. 5 and Rev. 21 portray life in this new kingdom: there will be no more suffering, pain, weeping, warfare, or death. In short, it is an age in which justice will be restored. Yet there is no reason to live as though that age is entirely out of reach. Jesus proclaimed the arrival of the kingdom of God, and his followers have been invited to carry on this work while awaiting his return. Justice as participation argues that the right reason for behaving justly in this world is to participate in the proclamation of the arrival of that beautiful kingdom. Living in this participatory way creates "an in-breaking future city of justice and peace."[8] One's fellow citizens experience something of what that future city will be like in this present world.

Latent in each of these theories of justice are those elements of social life that hinder the attainment of justice for all persons. Christian social ethicists typically label these elements "social sins" or "structural sins," depending on whether the "sin" is a mentality or the "sin" is embedded in the processes by which political and civic decisions are made. They reveal that the reason justice does not exist for all persons is that some members of a society have organized the society in such a way that its other members do not share properly in its goods or benefits. One obvious example is racism: the belief that it is acceptable for the goods of a society to be distributed unequally on the basis of race. One structural feature of racism is the myriad ways in society restricts the opportunities of racial minorities to flourish. For example, those in power in American society have restricted the access of African Americans to voting booths, written racial covenants into mortgage deeds preventing African Americans from moving into certain parts of cities or suburbs, and disinvested businesses in those areas in which African Americans were largely concentrated. None of this was or is done by accident. Sinful mentalities about the value of other persons were and are responsible. Those mentalities were and are followed up with sinful structures that embed injustice more deeply into the culture. It is incumbent on Protestants to pay attention to these features of society when they talk about justice.

Brief Review of the Sources

The New Testament word for "righteousness," *dikaiosynē*, is derived from the Greek word for "justice," *dikē*.[9] So when Scripture speaks of someone who is righteous, they are speaking of someone who is just. To be declared "righteous" by God is nothing other than being declared "just," or being the type of person who shares God's view of the world. Paul links the righteous/just with being ordered toward God when he says in Rom. 1:17, "The one who is righteous will live by faith." "The just person" and "the righteous person" are two ways of talking about the same thing.

With this in mind, the Bible has much to say about the ways that just people live. Of course, they live by faith, as Rom. 1 indicates. Micah 6:8 says they "*do* justice," love mercy, and walk humbly before God. The Ten Commandments (Exod. 20) say they worship God alone, devote time to worship him, and treat their neighbors and family well. A man who was an expert in these and the other commandments of the law code once asked Jesus which of all these laws he thought was the most important. Jesus told him that everything about the righteous can be summed up in two things: they love God, and they love their neighbors as themselves (Mark 12:28–34). When you consider also Jesus's listing of the Beatitudes in his Sermon on the Mount (Matt. 5:3–12), it becomes increasingly clear that just persons manifest their love for God and love for others in particular actions.

The same is true with a just society. Proverbs 21:15 suggests that one of those consequences is a willingness to maintain law and order: "When justice is done, it is a joy to the righteous, but dismay to evildoers." Likewise Amos 5:24 says, "Let justice roll down like waters, and righteousness like an ever-flowing stream." At the same time, the maintenance of law and order should never lend itself to tyranny. A just society lets God take revenge on one's enemies. "Beloved, never avenge yourselves, but leave room for the wrath of God; for it is written, 'Vengeance is mine, I will repay, says the Lord'" (Rom. 12:19). A just society waits for God even when that wait is longer than anyone would want.

> Therefore the LORD waits to be gracious to you;
>   therefore he will rise up to show mercy to you.

> For the LORD is a God of justice;
>   blessed are all those who wait for him. (Isa. 30:18)

In sum, just societies are just because they allow God, the paragon of justice, to be the focal point of their community. They live out their justice by following his direction. For the early Jewish community, this was to be lived out in the context of a covenant-bound nation. Jesus showed his followers how this can be accomplished even within societies harboring no particular love for God or even for justice.[10]

In Late Antiquity, Augustine wrote much about a just society. Three of his many contributions deserve mention here. First, within a Christian setting, Augustine situated the classical definition of justice that its demand is to give all people their due (akin to the justice-as-duty theory described earlier). In his treatise *De moribus ecclesiae catholicae* (*The Way of Life of the Catholic Church*), in the context of discussing the four cardinal virtues, he writes, "Justice is love serving God only, and therefore ruling well all else, as subject to man" (15.25).[11] Giving each person his or her due should be natural since that is how one expresses love for God while managing the earth's goods well. Consequently, second, a just society is ordered toward God. This was the problem with the Roman Empire, as Augustine asserts in his devastating critique of its immorality in his *De civitate Dei* (*The City of God*). It no longer deserved the right to be an empire, since from its foundations it had rejected the true God.[12] Third, the unjust laws of unjust societies, such as those of the Roman Empire, are not, properly speaking, laws at all. Therefore, as Augustine argues in *De libero arbitrio* (*Free Will* 1.5), they need not be followed.[13] What is just is exactly that because it derives from God and is ordered by God. We sense what is just or unjust when we are rightly ordered toward God ourselves.

This puts Augustine in the trajectory of later Christian thought on justice as duty and in its trajectory of thought regarding natural law—both subjects covered earlier, particularly as it related to the work of Thomas Aquinas (see chap. 7) and the Protestant Reformers (see chap. 8). Here it is worth stressing that, in agreement with Augustine, Thomas and the Reformers viewed the natural law as undergirding just forms of human law.[14]

In the aftermath of the Enlightenment, however, different ideas about justice began to emerge, which de-emphasize reason and instead put the passions at the center. For example, in chapter 6 of his text *Leviathan* (1640s), Thomas Hobbes articulates the "social contract" theory of justice. A person's passion for self-preservation encourages oneself to "contract" with other similarly minded individuals for a society in which everyone's respective rights are preserved. A person agrees not to harm others so long as they agree not to harm oneself.[15] In his *Enquiry concerning the Principles of Morals* (1751), David Hume argues that justice is based on "public utility" (2.17).[16] Justice is sought simply because it has utility: it is useful to humanity. Its usefulness is proved by its capacity for helping people who behave justly to win the approval of others. Likewise, Immanuel Kant locates justice within his categorical imperative of universality, particularly the universality of freedom. In his *Groundwork of the Metaphysics of Morals* (1785), he writes, "For as morality serves as a law for us only because we are rational beings, it must also hold for all rational beings; and as it must be deduced simply from the property of freedom, it must be shown that freedom also is a property of all rational beings" (§3).[17] Where the freedom of one's will is able to coexist with the freedom of others' will, there is justice.

Most recently the work of John Rawls (1921–2002) has been influential in promoting the justice-as-fairness theory described earlier. This has proved to be transformative in political and ethical discourse. His 1971 book *A Theory of Justice* and his later *Political Liberalism* (1993) establish three principles for this theory: (1) Society ensures each citizen an equal claim to rights and liberties. (2) The structures of society ought to ensure fair equality of opportunity. (3) Socioeconomic inequality should benefit the least advantaged members of society. When presented with these principles, Rawls argues, individuals would choose this type of society to live in more than they would choose one governed by utilitarianism or other social contracts that are about rights only or freedom only.

The Christian tradition's contribution of identifying just societies with those that are rightly ordered toward God is changed by these more recent, nonsectarian proposals for justice. These proposals (such as those by Hobbes, Hume, and Rawls) replace an ordering of society toward God with an ordering of society in accordance with what is best for the individual. In the push and pull of social life, what is deemed best for the individual is that which can be done without jeopardizing the rights, freedom, and liberty of others. The reality is that this requires accepting a fair share of society's burdens while also enjoying a fair share of its benefits.

Illustrations of the Principle

It is said that the only two things sure in this life are death and taxes. The former is distributed equally to all; arguably, the burdens of the latter are not. Consequently, tax systems in our world are excellent candidates for exploring the principle of justice. In the widest sense, a just tax system gives each person their due. This means that tax systems are to be as least restrictive as possible. Governments should tax only the amount required to maintain the common good and not one penny more. Obviously, the least restrictive tax system of all is a nonexistent one, but no one wants to live in a world composed entirely of private goods. If nothing else we want governments to exist in order to protect our private property rights. At a minimum, this requires taxes to pay for a judicial system to protect those rights. We also want our liberty protected, so the government should provide some form of national defense, which requires taxes too. To the extent that we also want things like well-maintained roads for transit, or access to green space for outdoor sports, or assurance that our drinking water is free of pollutants, or access to health care in our old age when private insurance companies refuse to offer us coverage, and so on—then it behooves each one of us to share the costs of these services through a tax system.

The existence of taxes, then, is not a problem for measuring justice. Taxes are clearly a burden at any amount, but they are a necessary part of building the common good. For this reason, whether a tax system is just depends instead on the system's ability to distribute its burdens fairly. This is the principle behind progressive tax systems such as those found in most of the developed world. Progressive tax systems charge higher rates of tax on higher incomes. In other words, the more you earn, the greater the percentage in tax that you pay. Now, on the one hand, progressive tax systems are about one's ability to pay. Those with higher incomes can pay more, so they should be taxed more. Yet, if ability to pay were the only reason for higher taxes on higher earners, then it would be right to challenge the justness of such a system, since it may be unfairly distributing society's tax burden on a small group of people. So, on the other hand, progressive tax systems are built on an assumption that higher-income individuals benefit to a greater extent than lower-income individuals from society's resources, and thus the higher-income persons *should* (instead of just *can*) pay more.

Consider, for example, a society that offers its members access to free public education for a period of time during one's youth. In general, those who take advantage of this resource will have higher incomes over their lifetime than those who do not take advantage of it. Since the higher income is linked, in part, to access to a public resource, it stands to reason that those who benefited more from that resource should bear a greater burden of maintaining it for future generations. Consider also the individuals who build businesses. To move their goods to market, such individuals benefit from a transportation network (such as roads, bridges, shipping lanes, etc.) that they themselves did not build, but that the wider society built. Even those whose business is information technology, moving their goods to market requires a technological infrastructure (such as the internet) that, again, they themselves did not build, but that was built with the help of government resources in the form of research grants given to scientists decades ago. The more successful one's business, the greater one's reliance on the physical or technological infrastructure built by others in society. Society applauds the work of its successful businesspeople, and it allows them to be rewarded with as much income as they can possibly earn. At the same time, society also asks that the successful businesspeople support the building of new infrastructure (which they will get to enjoy) with higher tax rates on their higher incomes.

Thus tax systems are weighed as just to the extent they fairly distribute society's financial burdens to maintain the common good. In principle, progressive tax systems do this better than other systems. Yet every society has difficulty in achieving this. There are, for example, many regressive taxes in American society. Sales taxes on food and goods are among them. Lower-income Americans spend a higher percentage of their income on food and goods than do higher-income Americans; thus on such things lower-income Americans are taxed *at a higher percentage of their income* than higher-income Americans. Some American states try to counter this regressive tendency in sales taxes by exempting certain items from these taxes that lower-income Americans are more likely to buy (e.g., prepackaged foods), but this is far from a perfect system. Another way in which tax systems disrupt the fair distribution of a society's financial burdens is by building behavioral incentives into tax codes. For example, America incentivizes home ownership, charitable giving, adoption of clean energy sources, and other lifestyle choices by offering tax deductions for them. It discourages things like high-frequency stock trading with higher tax rates for income earned from that activity.

In sum, the justice of a tax system is weighed by asking fundamental questions about what type of society we want to live in. How many services do we expect the government to provide? How much of those services do we expect the government to provide? What is the responsibility of citizens toward maintaining the society for the benefit of themselves and future generations? Finally, at what rate does each individual most justly pay for the benefits received from the society? Ideally, tax systems would be based as much, if not more, on one's lifestyle choices and behavior than on one's income. Yet most citizens agree that it is not only too intrusive for a government to evaluate such things, but it is impracticable to build so complicated a tax system to accommodate such vast differences in the population. Thus even though tax systems based solely on income necessarily create some injustice, the alternative is even more undesirable.

Summary

Justice expresses the *what* of social ethics insofar as it translates our commitments to human dignity and the common good into conceptions of what ought to be done. The Christian tradition, from the Scriptures and some of its key thinkers, supposes that a person or a society rightly ordered to God will necessarily produce a virtuous, or just, individual—or a virtuous, or just, society. This is because loving God cannot help but translate into genuine love for one's neighbors. Yet the reality of sin prevents us from properly loving God well, and so human history is littered with many illustrations of unjust societies. Protestants are rightly skeptical of societies that seek to be ordered to God as a guarantor of justice. Instead, Protestants join with recent theorists of justice who now concern themselves with practices of justice that nevertheless ensure each person is given his or her due (such as social justice expressed in distributive, commutative, retributive, and restorative terms). This creates opportunities to stress the dignity of humans while advocating for the common good and preserving an opening for Christians to continue to speak of their hope for an eventual restoration of justice and an overturning of every injustice at Christ's return.

Main Points of the Chapter

» Justice is the virtue of giving people what is due them as a consequence of their God-given dignity.

» Social justice is the establishment of social structures that justly distribute society's benefits and burdens.

» Terms such as commutative justice, retributive justice, restorative justice, and procedural justice highlight different aspects of a vibrant, social justice.

» In the course of time, philosophers, theologians, ethicists, and political theorists have developed different theories of how justice works and the reasons why someone would choose to behave in a just manner.

» Scripture and the Christian tradition emphasize that the role of social justice is a function of a society being rightly related to God.

» Post-Enlightenment writers emphasize theories of justice that accommodate human reason, such as a state that protects freedom, or liberty, or the fair distribution of its resources.

《 14 》

Solidarity

Learning Outcomes for This Chapter

» Define "solidarity" and its contribution to social life.

» Summarize the contribution of biblical literature to understanding the importance of solidarity.

» Examine challenges societies face in organizing themselves in accordance with solidarity.

If the principles of human dignity and common good express the *why* of social ethics, and if justice expresses the *what* of social ethics, the principle of solidarity (along with subsidiarity) expresses the *how* of social ethics. Solidarity answers the question of how one ought to live in response to concerns raised by the other principles. Solidarity challenges us to ask whether the social organizations of which we are a part strengthen the bonds of human friendship, especially the bonds between those with and those without sufficient resources. If the social organizations do not do this well, we ought to ask how they might be improved to facilitate such bonds. Solidarity also invites us to consider whether our own behaviors and mentalities demonstrate a concern with those on society's margins.

Definition of Solidarity

Solidarity is unity among persons within a social organization.[1] Naturally, the word "unity" in the definition requires greater clarification. It is, as the Catholic Church's 1987 document *Sollicitudo rei socialis* teaches, "not a feeling of vague compassion. . . . On the contrary, it is a firm and persevering determination to commit oneself to the common good" (§38).[2] Unity among persons stems from a commitment to the good of everyone. This commitment is rooted in the appreciation of every person's dignity. A social organization committed to unity recognizes that any diminishment in the dignity of one person is a diminishment in the dignity of all persons. Thus solidarity may be thought of as both an individual and a civic virtue, since it is the result of a demonstrated commitment to the good of everyone.

> **Definition: Solidarity**
>
> Unity among persons within a social organization.

At the civic level, solidarity often takes the form of mutual associations. Trade unions, for example, are a mechanism by which individuals can express solidarity with one another within the social organization of a particular business. They are not built on feelings of vague compassion, but they are determined to provide for the good of all of their members. Farm and energy cooperatives are another solidarity movement. They assist member farms and energy suppliers with the collection, sale, and distribution of their goods for the benefit not only of their member institutions but also for the larger society. Not-for-profit insurance companies, particularly the health insurance "mutualities" in European countries, are concrete expressions of solidarity between persons insofar as they spread the financial risk of medical crises among large groups of people without diluting those benefits by profit taking. Such structural elements within society to ensure the maintenance of solidarity are important: they obligate individuals to act virtuously toward others even when those individuals might, at times, not wish to do so.

At the individual level, solidarity is an exhortation to behave in a certain way. When we learn that an individual or a group of individuals is being oppressed, the virtue aspect of solidarity spurs us to take concrete steps to stop the oppression. Such steps might include political action, public protests, community organizing, letter-writing campaigns, or simply showing up at events organized by others. Since, not infrequently, people claim that they did not know such-and-such an oppression existed, another practical element of living out the principle of solidarity is simply being informed about the culture and the world around you. Being a consumer of news and

Health Care before Insurance Companies: Mutual Aid Societies

Not unlike today, bills for health care outpaced the earnings of most American and European families during the late nineteenth and early twentieth centuries. In that age, before the preponderance of health insurance companies, Americans and Europeans paid for their health care by joining mutual aid societies: organizations like the Oddfellows, the Moose Lodges, the Elks Club, the Shriners, and the Order of Saint Luke. One's race, gender, or religious affiliation might dictate which mutual aid society a person would join, but the dues an individual paid would be redistributed to members of the society on the basis of financial need for health care, burial expenses, or perhaps the maintenance of one's spouse or orphaned children in the event of one's death.

In addition to providing financial support for health crises, mutual aid societies also provided a social network for their members. Each society had its own initiation rituals and ethical obligations for their members. They organized regular events that brought their members together socially, and often those events would be used to raise additional funds for the use of the society.

While most Americans and Europeans now use insurance companies instead of mutual aid societies for their health care costs, mutual aid societies still exist and contribute to the maintenance of institutions such as hospitals and orphanages and for the care of families of injured or deceased employees in certain professions, such as police, firefighters, and those in the military.

being aware of the needs of others is a first step toward living in solidarity with others.

Extending the Definition

Because solidarity is one of the *how* principles in social ethics, several concepts introduced in earlier chapters come to bear on the understanding of solidarity's role in shaping social organizations and civil society. One of these is social sin. Social sins are those mentalities and things that societies do to hinder the progress of or to otherwise oppress others. Social sins include things like racism and ethnocentrism. By their very definition, the dignity of a group of people is not recognized as equal to the dignity of one's own group. Solidarity is the antidote to such mentalities. It exposes and then invites repentance for social sins.[3] Solidarity orients us to recognize the inherent dignity of the members of the other group. It then prompts us to admit that the success of one's own group depends on the success the other groups. It demands that members of the group in power give up that power, or at least share that power, for the sake of building cohesion across all the groups. The goal is the elimination of distinctions between and among individuals that would cause there to be unequal distributions of a society's benefits across members of all groups.

Sometimes the unequal distribution of society's benefits is due to the presence of structural sins.[4] These include laws, contracts, and social norms that prevent unity among persons of different groups. For example, laws enabled the institution of slavery to be practiced in many countries over the centuries. Even when those laws were repealed, racism continued to be expressed in the oppression of the former slave communities by employment and housing contracts that restricted their access to certain jobs or to homes in certain parts of town.[5] And when those things were addressed, social norms ensured that the oppressed community felt unwelcome in civic institutions, in private businesses, at the voting booth, and at other social venues. Again, solidarity is the antidote to structural sins. Because solidarity redefines one's relationship with others as a matter of unity, it quickly reveals these dark corners of civil society. Structural sins are more quickly exposed, and the opportunity for public discourse about how to change them can begin.

Hence, exposing—and subsequently repenting of—social and structural sins demonstrates one's concern for those on society's margins. Very often repentence will require sacrifice, such as sacrificing our own good and comfort to unite ourselves to those on society's margins. Inevitably the very existence of social margins becomes unacceptable. This is where solidarity connects with the exhortation that Christians ought to maintain a "preferential option for the poor," a concept mentioned in chapters 2 and 10. When the needs of the poor and the marginalized become the first consideration in decisions about matters such as public policy, urban planning, business development, and social organization, there is a greater likelihood of unity among all persons.[6] In other words, solidarity ought to be a structural element of decision processes. Again, the reality of human sin in the social sphere reminds us of our propensity to marginalize others for the sake of personal gain. Failing to account for this sin from the beginning of a design process (be it within a public or private enterprise) will likely disrupt unity within the social sphere.

One of the ways decision makers may account for the likelihood that their policies will adversely affect the lives of the poor and marginalized is to ask to what extent their decisions respect the idea that the earth's goods belong to

How to Rob a Poor Person

According to Thomas Aquinas, if you withhold your excess resources from those who have less than they need, you are robbing the poor; and if they take from you some of those excess resources in order to meet their basic human needs, they are not stealing from you. They are merely taking back what is rightfully theirs! (See *ST* II-II 66.7.) Consider for a moment just how radical this idea is to citizens of modern, Western countries. Then consider these words from Prov. 6:30: "Thieves are not despised who steal only to satisfy their appetite when they are hungry."

all. Christians in Late Antiquity called the natural things of the earth—like air, water, and land—universal goods.[7] They were created by God to serve the needs of the creation; therefore, they do not belong privately to anyone. This means that public policy and private industry decision makers must ask themselves to what extent their plans presume on a right to claim as private some goods that more justly belong to everyone, including future generations.[8] The world's poor and marginalized need access to as many goods as they can get; even minor restrictions on their ability to access needed goods necessarily deepens their deprivation and marginalization. This is why, for example, Western legal traditions throughout the Middle Ages, inspired by the writings of Ambrose, Augustine of Hippo, and Thomas Aquinas, treated differently the stealing of food by a person desperate for self-survival compared to the stealing of food by those whose survival is even somewhat more secure.[9] The former are not judged guilty of theft, while the latter are. In the former case, Augustine even says the real thief here is the person who keeps the excess food locked away.

As a practical matter, there are good reasons for protecting the right to private goods, and public policy and private industry decision makers need to retain some goods as private. Business owners need private goods such as physical buildings and equipment to carry out their trade. Citizens need access to private spaces for shelter and for their home life. Yet the Christian tradition has never taught that the right to private goods is absolute. Goods desperately needed by another cease to be the private possession of the one who currently holds them.[10] "Eminent domain" laws are one holdover of that tradition; they allow for the forcible transfer of the private goods of one person to another person who has a greater need for them. However, enforcement of eminent domain laws is always messy, and relying on the goodwill of a person to share his or her excess goods with those in need is not realistic.

It is far better, then, to employ the principle of solidarity, which prompts us to organize society's goods in such a way that all have access to what they need. Individuals and businesses can have private property and goods, but that property and those goods should not restrict the ability of the poor and the marginalized to flourish. Urban planners would be right to restrict how much land may be held privately in order to provide more public space for everyone. Restricting the size of land plots also helps to hold down property values, which should make property ownership, or at least rental prices, accessible to a wider range of individuals.

Brief Review of the Sources

The Bible's witness to solidarity is seen both in texts that spur individuals to seek the good of others and in texts suggesting that an individual's lack of concern for others hinders that individual's relationship with God. In the Old Testament, the Abrahamic covenant says that the blessing of Abraham was not for him and for his family alone. The blessing of Abraham was for the sake of blessing all the world's people. Abraham is told, in Gen. 12:2–3, "I will make of you a great nation, and I will bless you . . . so that you will be a blessing. . . . And in you all the families of the earth shall be blessed." In the same way, the Mosaic covenant promises that Israel will be a kingdom of priests (Exod. 19:6). The "congregation" for this kingdom of priests is other nations, with whom they are obliged to share the love that God has for each person.[11]

The Abrahamic and Mosaic covenants invite readers to see other nations as extensions of themselves. The New Testament more typically frames the other-as-oneself idea in personal terms. Consider Rom. 12:4–5 and 1 Cor. 12:12–26. In these texts, Paul writes about the church as the body of Christ. Just as human bodies have multiple parts and just as only the healthy functioning of every part together ensures the success of the human body, so too are social organizations, like the church, dependent on individuals working in sync with one another. No one person is to be disparaged just because his or her contribution to the community is less visible, and no one person is to be overly praised because his or her contribution is more visible. Each person's contributions are critical and are to be appreciated. Poignantly, Paul writes, "If one member suffers, all suffer together with it; if one member is honored, all rejoice together with it" (1 Cor. 12:26). We rise and fall together as a community.

The Bible offers further evidence of a need to think in terms of solidarity with others. Jesus lists several dispositions of those who are "blessed," and among them are people who treat others mercifully and those who seek peace (Matt. 5:7, 9). Jesus also taught that his followers are to seek reconciliation before coming to worship (Matt. 5:21–24), and this exhortation is extended by Paul both in 1 Cor. 11, in which he says we are to seek reconciliation before receiving communion, and in 2 Cor. 5, where he teaches that Jesus left to his followers the ministry of reconciliation with others.[12] That Jesus and Paul link solidarity to proper worship is reminiscent of Ps. 122. There the psalmist prays for the peace of Jerusalem because it is a sacred space within the Israelite community. Its peace and sacredness ought not to be disturbed by internal divisions within the community; therefore, the psalmist writes,

> Pray for the peace of Jerusalem. . . .
> For the sake of my relatives and friends
>   I will say, "Peace be within you."
> For the sake of the house of the LORD our God,
>   I will seek your good. (Ps. 122:6a, 8–9)

To these types of texts one can add those that exhort Jesus's followers to love one another (Matt. 5:44–45; Rom. 12:10; 13:8–10) and those that tie this love to a recognition that God has loved his people first (John 13:34–35; 15:12–13; 1 John 4:7–8). As far as it depends on us, Paul writes in Rom. 12:18, we are to live at peace with one another. We are to clothe ourselves in love, according to Col. 3:14, since it helps to bind everything together in harmony. Once we have chosen to love, we may "let the peace of Christ rule in [our] hearts, to which indeed [we] were called in the one body" (Col. 3:15).

After Scripture, sustained reflection on solidarity as a principle does not emerge again until the Catholic Church issued its document *Sollicitudo rei socialis* in 1987.[13] It explains three features of solidarity from which Protestant social ethics can benefit. First, the church must lead society in the practice of solidarity. Arguably, few other cultural institutions would be better suited to the task. Its practice of solidarity should be marked by standing with the poor, listening to their requests, and seeking to satisfy them as best as possible within the bounds of the common good. "By virtue of her own evangelical duty the Church feels called to take her stand beside the poor, to discern the justice of their requests, and to help satisfy them, without losing sight of the good of groups in the context of the common good" (*Sollicitudo rei socialis* §39). Second, interdependence among people and among nations, to which solidarity points, depends on an agreement that the goods of the earth belong to everyone. Those who apply their own labor to molding and shaping the goods of the earth into something marketable are justly able to be rewarded. However, what they produce and the extent to which they are rewarded must be within the bounds of what is "equally for the good of all" (§39). The greater one's wealth, the greater one's moral responsibility to ensure that everyone else has an equal opportunity to flourish. Third, solidarity trains one to see fellow humans as neighbors, not objects. "Solidarity helps us to see the 'other' . . . not just as some kind of instrument, with a work capacity, . . . but as our 'neighbor'" (§39). Unfortunately, the objectification of people is deceptively easy to do, particularly when one is preoccupied with the profit motive of a business enterprise.

Illustrations of the Principle

In defining solidarity earlier in the chapter, we pointed out that mutual associations such as unions, cooperatives, and some nonprofit insurance systems are examples of mechanisms necessary to foster unity among persons. We need mechanisms or systems for solidarity because we are prone to the sins of selfishness and self-promotion. These mechanisms are positive tools for solidarity. There are also negative instruments, such as laws and judicial systems to enforce them. Consider, for example, the solidarity function of traffic signals. Every time one approaches a red light while driving, one has an opportunity to appreciate how laws force one to be in solidarity with others. Most drivers want to keep driving to get to their destination and do not wish to be delayed by others. Yet every other driver has the same interest. Left to themselves, every driver wants every other driver to get out of the way! To balance these competing interests, we oblige drivers to form a line at places where many people want to go and then to wait their turn before continuing to drive. No one is happy about needing to wait, but drivers should appreciate that waiting for each driver to take a turn actually makes the entire trip go more smoothly. This is solidarity in action; this is solidarity for the common good.

The government's issuance of licenses for diverse behaviors is also an expression of solidarity. Law-abiding hunters and fishers queue up each year to purchase a license to engage in hunting or fishing. These licenses oblige the license holders to constrain their behavior by hunting for only a certain number of animals or to fish only for a certain number and certain size of fish. This too is an act of solidarity. Again, all hunters and fishers, if left to their own devices, would want to hunt or fish for any desired amount of game or

Solidarity with the Environment

Aldo Leopold (1887–1948) is thought of as the founder of modern forestry management and of environmental ethics. A longtime naturalist and professor at the University of Wisconsin, Aldo promoted greater solidarity between humans and the land—in particular because he stressed that humans rely on the land for survival.

There are two spiritual dangers in not owning a farm. One is the danger of supposing that breakfast comes from the grocery, and the other that heat comes from the furnace. To avoid the first danger, one should plant a garden, preferably where there is no grocer to confuse the issue. To avoid the second, he should lay a split of good oak on the andirons, preferably where there is no furnace, and let it warm his shins while a February blizzard tosses the trees outside. If one has cut, split, hauled, and piled his own good oak, and let his mind work the while, he will remember much about where the heat comes from, and with a wealth of detail denied to those who spend the weekend in town astride a radiator.

—Aldo Leopold, *A Sand County Almanac* (1949), 6

fish. Yet it is also known that overhunting or overfishing in any one year will limit the opportunity to engage in the same activity in the following year or, worse, eliminate the game or fish altogether. Thus hunters and fishers willingly restrain their self-centered impulses to ensure that there is enough game or fish for everyone with a license and that enough stock of game and fish will remain for future years. (Incidentally, this is why poaching is so despised by hunters.) For the sake of the common good, solidarity must be enforced on hunters and fishers with mechanisms like licenses and fees.[14]

A less mechanistic example of unity among persons is what those in the Christian tradition have called a "consistent ethic of life." The phrase refers to the attitude among Christians that all life is sacred and that every life is worthy of protection from birth to natural death. It is a corrective to Christians whose view of the sanctity of life is, for all practical purposes, limited to the issue of unborn children and the practice of elective abortion. A consistent ethic of life would say that, yes, the unborn child is worthy of our concern, but so too—and equally so—is the life of the mother who finds herself with an unwanted pregnancy. That mother might well represent a host of failed social policies (such as antipoverty programs) or social norms (such as the hookup culture), or she might be in an abusive relationship that made the sexual act leading to the pregnancy seem like a proper course of action at the time.

Christians with a consistent ethic of life will want to be in solidarity with that woman as much as they would want to be in solidarity with the unborn child.

Solidarity with others expressed in terms of a consistent ethic of life takes an interest in the social policies and social norms that do not enhance life. It challenges government officials and programs that do not help to mitigate the effects of poverty. It seeks to fix, rather than merely to expose, failing public schools. It moves people to financially support or to build from the ground up organizations that will actually help pregnant women to choose life for the baby rather than abortion. Such women might need shelter if they are kicked out of their homes, or they may need assistance in finding employment, or money to pay medical bills, or day care for the baby so they can finish their schooling, or perhaps help in the process of choosing adoption, or some combination of these. A consistent ethic of life is a holistic approach to the needs of humans, regardless of the circumstances in which they now find themselves.

Solidarity, of course, is also illustrated in the willingness of individuals to stand alongside those who are being oppressed. In America during the 1960s, marches in support of the civil rights of African Americans were held in many cities. When white men and women—that is, those of the dominant class—joined those marches, their presence communicated an interest in being unified with the struggle of African Americans for equality. Whether one participated in a march or in some other way spoke favorably of the right of African Americans to be treated equally, solidarity—being committed to unity among persons—was being expressed. In many cities around the world, recent years have witnessed civil rights marches in support of the right of same-sex couples to marry. Christian communities have struggled over whether and how to participate in supporting same-sex couples or even members of sexual minorities generally. No Christian should want any person to be the object of violence or abuse, as members of sexual minorities too often are, but how to express this concern for safety and protection without sanctioning the practices of sexual minorities is something many Christian communities have yet to figure out. The principle of solidarity can lead the way in helping Christians navigate these issues too.

Summary

Solidarity informs *how* one ought to act in light of a concern with social ethics. It directs one to cultivate unity within society. In a general sense, the cultivation of unity is the commitment to the common good. Practically speaking, it is the actions taken every day to inform oneself about the needs of others and then to consider the one or two ways in which one may help to meet those needs. Sometimes those needs can be addressed with an act of charity. More often, however, the need or needs (unemployment, housing discrimination, etc.) stem from deeper structural problems in society. In such cases the actions to be taken require coordination with many other individuals and organizations. This is where solidarity too often breaks down. What may be needed to solve structural problems can be daunting. Those who are honest with themselves will admit that they really do not want to give up their time, money, or energy to be involved. This is where the principle of subsidiarity proves useful. It breaks down structural problems into more manageable tasks, and so it is to this final principle of social ethics that we turn in the next chapter.

Main Points of the Chapter

» Solidarity is unity among persons within a social organization.

» The unity among persons is a commitment on the part of every person to the common good.

» Solidarity is the principal antidote to social and structural sins, especially in light of Scripture's concern to align our interest in being rightly related to God with our being rightly related to the people around us.

⟨ 15 ⟩

Subsidiarity

Learning Outcomes for This Chapter

» Define "subsidiarity" and its contribution to social life.

» Summarize the contribution of biblical and later Christian literature to understanding the importance of subsidiarity.

» Examine challenges societies face in organizing themselves in accordance with subsidiarity.

Like solidarity, subsidiarity is one of the *how* principles in social ethics. It is a principle for *how* social ethics might be done. Subsidiarity too answers the question of how one ought to live in response to concerns raised by the other principles. Better yet, subsidiarity answers the question of *who* ought to be deciding how one ought to live in response to those concerns. This is because subsidiarity presses one to think of who (or what entity) is ideally suited to respond to a social problem and then holds that individual (or entity) responsible for solving the problem. Thus subsidiarity holds sacred individual responsibility and the preservation of autonomy whenever possible, and subsidiarity accepts that the state has a role in strengthening both.

Definition of Subsidiarity

Subsidiarity holds that problems within a social organization ought to be solved at the lowest possible level of that social organization.[1] The "lowest possible level of society" can be as low as an individual person. It may be a particular family or a neighborhood or subdivision of homes. Sometimes the social problem is so intertwined with other issues that the lowest possible level may be a city, state, or federal government, or perhaps even an international body such as the United Nations.

Extending the Definition

Social ethicists say the principle of subsidiarity is needed because no one individual can provide entirely for oneself on one's own. Every day, in hundreds of ways, we experience dependence on someone else for the provision of something that helps us to meet our needs. For example, the moment an individual requires use of a vehicle or a bicycle or public transit to get to work, that individual reveals a desperate need for a well-organized, well-administered social life. Because of this need, individuals seek out associations with others and, if necessary, build such a cooperative from scratch. Subsidiarity suggests that these associations are best organized and properly administered when those who are closest to a problem are held responsible for solving that problem.

> **Definition: Subsidiarity**
>
> Problems within a social organization ought to be solved at the lowest possible level of that social organization.

To understand how this is done, we must recognize that subsidiarity incorporates both negative and positive duties for every institution within a social organization. Subsidiarity is a negative principle in the sense that it restricts the behavior of some groups, and it is a positive principle in the sense that it encourages the participation of other groups.

First, consider its negative aspect. Negatively, subsidiarity says that a higher level within a social organization either *should not* or *cannot* intervene in a problem if a lower level within that organization either *should* or *can* solve the problem. Additionally, in the United States at least, where the Constitution delineates a separation of powers among different branches of government and even between different levels of government (i.e., federal versus states), subsidiarity might even imply that higher-level organizations *cannot* intervene in certain problems, even if lower-level organizations refuse to do so, because they have not been given the power to intervene.

This negative aspect, the notion that a higher-level institution within a social organization *should not* or *cannot* intervene, reveals subsidiarity's link to the principles of human dignity and justice. Higher-level institutions that intervene in problems take away from lower-level institutions, including individuals, the opportunity to express their dignity in taking responsibility to respond to the problems themselves. The assumption of responsibility is a constitutive expression of dignity, since it is an expression of what individuals (or lower-level institutions) recognize they can or should do. By distributing responsibility for action to solve social problems, subsidiarity fairly distributes society's benefits and burdens, which enhances justice.

Second, consider subsidiarity's positive aspect. It stresses the duty of the higher-level institution to intervene (that it *can or must* do so) in a social problem if the lower-level institution is not able to do so or chooses not to do so. Of course, again, there are some political contexts (such as the United States, with its constitutional separation of powers) where higher-level institutions cannot intervene regardless of the behavior of the lower-level institution. Even in such contexts as this, however, there is no doubt vigorous debate among citizens about just what circumstances merit such restraint and which ones demand action regardless of what the law proscribes. Having said this, subsidiarity's positive aspect reveals its link to the principle of the common good. This is because the positive duty of a higher-level institution to intervene in a social problem is to bring about a particular end for the society as a whole. This end is to maximize the opportunity for everyone to flourish. Where lower-level institutions have proved to be incapable of creating the necessary social conditions for human flourishing, a higher-level institution is obliged to step in for the common good.

These negative and positive duties inherent within subsidiarity explain *how* this principle responds to concerns about human dignity, the common good, and justice in order to solve social problems. Yet any answer one gives to this *how* question invites one to consider another question: Just how centralized or decentralized ought political power to be within a sociopolitical organization such as a nation? This is not an easy question to answer, especially when you consider just how much we value mobility in our contemporary (American and European) societies.

Since, as we have already said in previous chapters, political jurisdictions exist to facilitate the common good, any one political jurisdiction exists to serve the needs of its population. But if that population no longer sees itself as part of just one political jurisdiction but a mobile member of multiple jurisdictions, then that population benefits by an increasing seamlessness in the benefits and burdens across those jurisdictions. Thus highly mobile cultures benefit most from more centralization and less decentralization of decision making. More centralization reduces conflicts for people over such things as acceptance of academic degrees earned elsewhere, the acceptance of work-related licenses and certifications acquired elsewhere, tax collection on money earned elsewhere, the portability of health insurance, the delivery of mail, the ease of public transit between suburban and urban areas, the use of properly maintained infrastructure for travel, or even the use of a driver's license across multiple jurisdictions. Nations and states initially set up to value decentralization will suffer growing pains as their citizens enjoy increased mobility across political jurisdictions. At the same time, increased centralization reduces autonomy, and societies are well advised to develop a conversation around just how much autonomy they wish to preserve and how much they are willing to give up for the sake of reducing the burdens of things like mobility.

Brief Review of the Sources

The main biblical text on subsidiarity is Exod. 18. Moses is in the midst of leading the Israelites in their exodus from Egypt. They are traveling in the Sinai Peninsula and heading to Mount Sinai, at which place they will receive the law code from God. Transit across the Sinai Peninsula has proved to be taxing for interpersonal relationships among the Hebrews. Fights, squabbles, and disagreements over matters large and small abound. Since Moses is the leader of the community, and the one purportedly in touch with God, the people turn to Moses to settle every dispute. Meanwhile, Moses has invited his wife's extended family to visit him from nearby Midian. During the visit, Moses's father-in-law, Jethro, witnesses how much time is spent (rather, wasted) by Moses sitting to judge every single dispute. He tells Moses that he will suffer an early death if he continues in this manner (Exod. 18:18). As a solution, Jethro proposes that Moses instead set up a judicial system with lower courts and appellate courts. Moses will preside as judge over only the highest-level appellate court. Cases that can be solved by appointed judges at lower-level courts should be solved at that level without Moses's involvement. Exodus 18:24–26 reports that Moses does precisely as Jethro suggests. "Moses chose able men from all Israel and appointed them as heads over the people, as officers over thousands, hundreds, fifties, and tens. And they judged the people at all times; hard cases they brought to Moses, but any minor case they decided themselves" (Exod. 18:25–26). We may safely conclude that Jethro's proposal not only saved Moses's psychological and physical health; it also reduced frustrations in the community by resolving disputes more quickly.

A case for subsidiarity is also found in the New Testament's instructions on how to deal with a wayward member of the Christian community. Jesus tells his disciples in Matt. 18:15–19,

If another member of the church sins against you, go and point out the fault when the two of you are alone. If the member listens to you, you have regained that one. But if you are not listened to, take one or two others along with you, so that every word may be confirmed by the evidence of two or three witnesses. If the member refuses to listen to them, tell it to the church; and if the offender refuses to listen even to the church, let such a one be to you as a Gentile and a tax collector. Truly I tell you, whatever you bind on earth will be bound in heaven, and whatever you loose on earth will be loosed in heaven. Again, truly I tell you, if two of you agree on earth about anything you ask, it will be done for you by my Father in heaven.

If you have a problem with someone, first deal with the offense one-on-one. Only when this lowest level of the social organization fails to accomplish its goal does one move up the organizational chain to seek the assistance of others. In the last resort, God takes over and solves the offense, with its concomitant eternal consequences.

Similar exhortations on how to deal with an offending Christian are found in other New Testament texts. Galatians 6:1 says spiritually minded people should do the correcting "in a spirit of gentleness." Titus 3:10–11 says the offending Christian should be given at least two warnings before being removed from the church. And 1 Tim. 5:19 says Christians should not resort to removing a pastor from the church until a charge of sin has come from at least "two or three witnesses." The point of these and the Matthew texts is that Jesus wanted his community to work toward peace and reconciliation as much as possible and that this work should begin at the lowest possible level of relationship: one person to one person.

Although a general sense of the subsidiarity principle has been a part of social organization going back at least to Moses's day, and although use of the Latin word *subsidium* (or, as Thomas Aquinas differentiated higher and lower social institutions, *gradus et ordines*, "degrees and orders")[2] may be traced through many writers of Late Antiquity and the Middle Ages, particular interest in subsidiarity as a principle of political life emerges next

---

Communities as Concentric Circles

Una congregano vel communitas inclusavit aliam, i.e., one social body or community includes another, naturally smaller one, as in a system of concentric circles. This applies to both secular and sacred association.

—Thomas Aquinas, *Commentary on the Sentences* 25.3.2.3.3

in the seventeenth century. Johannes Althusius (1563–1638), a law professor and German politician, wrote a treatise on politics titled *Politica methodica digesta* (1603). In it, he writes the following on the subject of subsidiarity:

> In this life, truly no man is self-sufficient. . . . Nor in his adulthood is he able to obtain in and by himself those outward goods he needs for a comfortable and holy life, or to provide by his own energies all the *requirements* [*subsidia*] of life. . . . An aid and remedy for this state of affairs is offered him in symbiotic life, he is led, and almost impelled, to embrace it if he wants to live comfortably and well, even if he merely wants to live. (*Politica* 1.3–4)[3]

According to Althusius, subsidiarity's role in social life, then, is to assist each individual in meeting basic needs. We need subsidiary institutions to help us not only to live but also to live well. Althusius later connected the subsidiarity idea with the need for a confederation of states, or federalism, which American political theorists recalled after liberation from Britain.

Also during the seventeenth century the political theorist John Locke (1632–1704) incorporated the principle of subsidiarity into his text *Second Treatise of Government*. Whereas Althusius spoke of the positive duty of institutions within a social organization to provide the resources needed for life, Locke instead stressed the negative duty of the state. The state derives its existence from the consent of those governed, so it is obliged to refrain from interfering in those individuals' lives except where positively permitted to do so. To Locke, the government's only real role in individuals' lives is the protection of their property.

A somewhat similar view of the state's negative duty is found more than a century later in the writings of Wilhelm von Humboldt (1767–1835). He argued that the state cannot intervene in situations where lower-level institutions possess the capacity to solve the problems themselves. Although Locke and Humboldt drew different lines regarding what justified a state's intervention, their shared concern with overreaching governments reminds social ethicists that increasing government power may be less about human welfare than the pursuit of power itself.[4]

A tempered view of this concern may be found in the statements regarding subsidiarity in Catholic social teaching. In his 1931 document *Quadragesimo anno*, Pope Pius XI acknowledged that industrially and technologically advanced societies require the involvement of larger associations of people. Yet he also said that it is a "grave evil" to take away from lower-level institutions the responsibility and obligation to do what they can to solve social problems (§79). Pius XI offered two tests for when higher-level institutions ought to and ought not to get involved in a social problem. They should ask themselves whether the activity "would otherwise dissipate its efforts greatly" and whether "it alone can do them" (§80). If its efforts would be dissipated because of too many layers of bureaucracy or if a lower-level institution *can* do it, then the higher-level institution is obliged to stay out of the problem.

The Catholic Church's 1965 statement *Gaudium et spes* went a step further. In the midst of warning against the encroachment of higher-level institutions on the lives of individuals, it says,

> Every day human interdependence grows more tightly drawn and spreads by degrees over the whole world. As a result *the common good . . .* today takes on an increasingly universal complexion and consequently involves rights and duties with respect to the whole human race. . . . At the same time, however, there is a growing awareness of the exalted dignity proper to the human person, since he stands above all things, and his rights and duties are universal and inviolable. . . . Hence, *the social order and its development must invariably work to the benefit of the human person if the disposition of affairs is to be subordinate to the personal realm* and not contrariwise, as the Lord indicated when He said that the Sabbath was made for man, and not man for the Sabbath. (§26, emphasis added)

Notice that in the italicized portion the disposition of society's affairs is subordinate to the personal realm. Protecting the personal realm is the most important factor in social life. Everything else is subordinate to it. This includes the many challenges facing the common good from an "increasingly universal complexion." Globalization notwithstanding, attempts by nations and world bodies to better tie one society to another fail the test of subsidiarity if they diminish the dignity of even one person. Thus subsidiarity is not only a principle for *how* to organize life; it is also a measure of how well or poorly the personal realm is protected.

We turn, finally, to the writings of Abraham Kuyper, who was not only a Protestant theologian within the Dutch Reformed community, but also served as the prime minister of the Netherlands from 1901 to 1905. Harking back to Calvin's view on the two kingdoms, Kuyper's reflections on subsidiarity resulted in the idea of "sphere sovereignty," concerning which he wrote in a book titled *Sovereignty in Its Own Sphere*.[5] Kuyper thought it to be a middle position between collectivist ideologies of Marxism (what he called "popular sovereignty") and the supremacy of the state ("state sovereignty"). Sphere sovereignty says that every part of life—work, family, education, arts and culture, and so on—are unique social spheres that possess their own unique sovereignty.[6] Moreover, every sphere is entirely dependent on God for its existence.

Abraham Kuyper (1837–1920)

✓ Graduated from the University of Leiden in 1863
✓ Pastored first a church in Beesd and then the main church in Utrecht
✓ Founded the newspaper *De Standaard* (ceased publication in 1944), from which he taught his fellow Dutch citizens about Calvinism and political theory
✓ Elected to Parliament in 1874 and eventually formed the Anti-Revolutionary Party
✓ Founded the Vrij Universiteit Amsterdam (The Free University of Amsterdam) in 1880
✓ Elected prime minister of the Netherlands from 1901 to 1905

God's creative insight brought everything into existence, including human reason, which created these very spheres. Thus the sovereignty of each sphere is little more than a recognition of God's hand in creating it for the benefit of humans. Thus government and its many institutional levels are not sovereign in any sphere other than their own, for which God allowed them to be created. Likewise, families are sovereign within themselves, in accordance with God's purpose for families, but have no authority outside themselves. The same is true for every sphere. What Kuyper did, in effect, was turn subsidiarity back to the individual person. If every sphere is sovereign, then every sphere of which an individual is a part demands of that individual the assumption of responsibility to do what is needed to ensure that the sphere's divine mandate, or its divinely ordained end, is carried out.

Illustrations of the Principle

As is by now evident, subsidiarity is partly a principle of limited government. Power should be devolved to the lowest level of social organization (e.g., from a federal to a state level, or from a state to a city level) whenever possible to solve a social problem. For example, if an enemy nation were to launch a nuclear missile at a major city, the lowest possible level that is most competent to solve this problem is usually a federal government's national defense system. This is because cities are neither competent in nuclear deterrence nor sufficiently resourced to stop such a problem. By contrast, a spike in homelessness within a given city is probably best solved by that city itself, or perhaps the state in which the city is located, rather than the federal government. This is because the city is more competent than the federal government to understand why the homelessness has occurred and to know what resources are available within the city to help those who are suffering.

Concerns regarding the health of the environment are another good illustration of the principle of subsidiarity. Consider the problem of a polluted river that winds its way through multiple cities or states. Whether the river is a source of drinking water or merely a place for recreation, the pollution is likely causing a problem for citizens in those cities or states, and thus every city or state that is affected has a vested interest in solving the problem. The question that immediately presents itself is which institution is best suited to solving the problem. For dealing with the source of the pollution, the city in which the polluter is located is the lowest-level institution. Assuming that it possesses the necessary laws to shut down the operations of the polluter, it has not only the capacity to act but also the positive duty to do so. If it does not have the necessary enforcement tools for stopping the pollution, then it is obliged to yield its autonomy to a higher-level institution, which may well involve a federal government agency. But what about the existing pollution present within the river itself, which crosses several jurisdictions? Ideally, the cities and states would form a task force of individuals and agencies with the competence to clean the entire river system. If they cannot do this, then there is a positive duty of a higher-level institution to step in to clean the river. The duty to act is driven by commitment to the common good. The river contributes to human flourishing in any of several ways; leaving the river polluted is not an option.

What if you extend this problem of a polluted river out to the widest degree of a polluted climate system, or an endangered climate? Today we know the world's climate has been adversely affected, in part, by human activities. To reduce further negative impact on the environment, it is incumbent on societies to rethink the type and the extent of human activities that may be permitted. This is a problem on a global scale, so the lowest-level institution that *can* and *ought to* solve the problem is likely a global one, such as the United Nations or other multination entities. Subsidiarity suggests that those global institutions are best suited to articulate what needs to be done to rebalance human impact on the climate. Yet, when it comes to exercising control over particular activities of particular humans that affect climate changes, subsidiarity obliges us to shift our concern back to much lower, more local institutions. Individual citizens should want, on their own, to change their behaviors to reduce their negative impact on the environment, but individual efforts alone will likely not be enough. Thus particular cities or particular states or countries are

Subsidiarity and the Public Pool

What's not to love about spending a hot summer's day enjoying the slides and diving boards and splashing in the water of a large, public pool? But if you bother to read the long list of rules at any public pool, you'll soon wonder if any part of the experience is worth it: Only one

person at a time on the slide. No catching your children (or younger siblings) when they dive off the diving board. No use of outside floatation devices. No outside food or beverages allowed. These rules are so much more restrictive than the rules at a neighbor's private pool.

What does this have to do with subsidiarity? Many of us choose to visit public pools because we do not own a private pool. At a private pool you can make any rules you want, and you have complete autonomy over what happens. At a public pool, you have to give up some of that autonomy. If you want to enjoy the resources of a higher social organization, such as a city government's public pool, you must be willing to follow its rules. And its rules will always be more restrictive than what you would set for yourself at a private pool. Yet for the sake of the common good, you will continue to advocate for the existence of a public pool; and for the right to continue to access it, you will agree to give up some autonomy so that everyone can enjoy the resource together. This is subsidiarity in action.

more competent and better positioned to reduce human behavior's negative impacts on the climate. Such institutions can impose controls on things such as housing density, driving patterns, energy sources, and farming practices. They can incentivize helpful behavior by individuals through mixed-use zoning in urban planning, carbon-capture programs, and tax deductions for efficiency improvements to cars, homes, or factories.

Another good illustration of subsidiarity is the health of individuals. Much like environmental health, meeting an individual's need for health and health care involves multiple levels within a social organization, and each level has both negative and positive duties. Individuals have a duty to manage their health as much as possible. They also have a responsibility to pay for their medical expenses as much as possible. Yet medical care and medical costs can quickly skyrocket beyond any one individual's ability to manage them. As a society, we have created intermediate institutions such as insurance companies and social safety-net programs like Medicaid and Medicare to spread the costs of expensive medical care across a large group of individuals. Sometimes the costs grow so large over such a long period of time for so many people that society has felt it necessary to spend money on research to find a cure for the disease rather than continuing to pay for management of it. This was the case with diseases like polio and smallpox in the early twentieth century, with AIDS in the late twentieth century, and with heart disease, diabetes, and several types of cancers in the twenty-first century. Citizens in the United States, for example, have agreed to create a National Institute of Health and to funnel to it about $18 billion per year to fund research into a variety of diseases. If cures are found, that is money well spent, considering the millions of dollars that would otherwise have to be spent per person to treat these diseases.

Consider the case of a young person who has developed Type 1 diabetes. The person has a manageable but chronic disease. In order to remain alive, certain medical tests and medicines are required every single day. Until a cure is discovered, this means that if the individual does not spend money on medical care every single day, death is certain. A further burden is the diabetic's daily obligation to calculate proper doses of insulin medication after weighing both food intake and physical activity before, during, and after the insulin injection. Subsidiarity enters the picture as one evaluates a host of questions in regard to this individual, such as who is responsible for ensuring that the diabetic has the necessary medicine, who is responsible for ensuring that it is taken, what is to be done for the diabetic who cannot afford the medicine, and how much oversight a doctor should have in managing the individual's disease. There are also larger institutional issues, such as research for a cure, funding for that research, prioritizing research for one disease over others, providing access points to required medications and medical equipment, and

Financial Realities of a Chronic, Nationwide Disease

According to the American Diabetes Association, the annual cost to treat patients with diabetes in the United States is $176 million (as of 2012, the last date for which data is available). The medical costs for diabetes care average $7,900 per person every year. That means a person with diabetes has to spend more than $21 on medical care and supplies every single day to stay alive. Imagine having these expenses without the support of an insurance plan. Fortunately, 62 percent of these costs are paid by American citizens through their taxes to support Medicare, Medicaid, and other government insurance programs. In fact, $1 out of every $3 Medicare pays is for diabetes-related care. Eighty-six million Americans are prediabetic, which means chances are good they will develop Type 2 diabetes, and this will increase costs further.

Source: American Diabetes Association, "Economic Costs of Diabetes in the U.S. in 2012." *Diabetes Care* 36 (2013): 1033–46.

putting the appropriate pressures on manufacturers of medicine and medical equipment to make those products affordable.

In this space one cannot exhaust the subsidiarity functions of every social institution in confronting each one of these questions. Considering that an estimated 1.5 million individuals in the United States have Type 1 diabetes, it is not reasonable to expect hospitals or doctors to spend time every day managing each person's medical situation. Ideally, as much responsibility as possible for disease management falls on the individual person. The role of the doctor should be limited to training the individual to manage the disease and serving as a resource going forward. However, what is the medical system to do for the person with diabetes who is unable to make proper calculations of medicine against food intake and activity levels? Or what is one to do for the person who, for a variety of reasons, cannot afford the needed medications and equipment? Such individuals will quickly become regular visitors to the emergency room of a local hospital, which is the most expensive type of care available but where at least the care can be given. The nondiabetic person might say these problems are not their concern, but they would be wrong. Medical insurance is structured in the United States (and most Western countries) in such a way that everyone actually contributes to paying for medical care. Everyone pays for the medical costs of others, either through higher insurance premiums or through taxes that pay for social safety-net programs.

Thus it is in the interest of every member of society to solve these problems, if for no other reason than to reduce one's own insurance premiums and taxes. Subsidiarity helps us to address the problem. If the lowest-level institution, the individual with diabetes, is not competent to manage the medical condition, that person must turn to higher-level institutions for a solution. For patients who cannot afford their medications, it behooves the wider society to set up a fund (managed by an insurance company or perhaps a local or a federal government—again, the most competent level will need to be decided) to pay for some or all of these costs. The amount of money required for daily disease management pales in comparison to the astoundingly high cost of emergency care, so society would already be saving money by simply giving the medications away rather than paying for that individual to visit the emergency room every day for those same medications. And once society gets involved at this level in managing someone's medical care, questions about the cost of the medicine and equipment from the manufacturer become a concern, and still different institutions within the society will want to get involved in finding a way for those costs to be lowered. The person with diabetes whose intellectual aptitude is insufficient to manage the disease presents still further social organization questions regarding inadequate education services, assistance for family involvement, and to what extent private enterprise or a government entity ought to get involved in designing new medical devices that conduct these calculations for patients in order to reduce some of their burdens in the first place.

Summary

As the other *how* principle in social ethics, along with solidarity, it is easy to see many ways in which the principle of subsidiarity may be implemented to improve social life. Subsidiarity reminds people of their responsibility (1) to take care of oneself and then (2) to care for others whose problems are too great for them to handle alone. Subsidiarity also enhances the appreciation for civic institutions and political structures. They make life better for everyone by solving problems that individuals cannot solve alone. Even the paying of taxes can start to look rather good if one sees that the resources are being spent on things that only that level of government can properly solve (e.g., federal taxes for national defense or local taxes for road maintenance). The downside of subsidiarity, if one may speak of it as a downside, is the need for each person to accept some loss of autonomy to enjoy the benefits of resources that only higher-level institutions can provide.

Main Points of the Chapter

» Subsidiarity holds that problems within a social organization ought to be solved at the lowest possible level of that social organization.

» Determining what that lowest level of social organization is requires an assessment of the negative and positive duties of each organization.

» An organization's negative duty is that it *should not* or *cannot* intervene in a problem if a lower-level institution can solve it.

» An organization's positive duty is that it *can* or *must* intervene in a problem if a lower-level institution cannot solve it.

» An individual who agrees to participate in the services provided by a higher-level institution accepts some loss of autonomy.

Part 3 Summary

Joining God in the work of restoring order out of chaos, which was the subject of part 1 of this book, requires not only an appreciation for how Christians have participated in this work in past centuries, which was the subject of part 2, but also a grasp of several principles to guide their work. Part 3 introduced readers to the principles of human dignity, common good, justice, solidarity, and subsidiarity. This diagram summarizes how these principles work together.

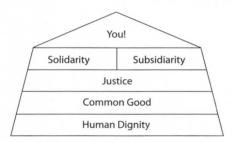

Everything in social ethics begins with a commitment to human dignity. It is because humans have dignity that social life exists. Society is for humans' benefit and not the other way around. Consequently, social life is to be organized with the good of every person in mind, the common good, not just the good of the majority or the good of those who can take care of themselves. Society does this by organizing its resources in such a way that every person has the opportunity to access the resources needed to flourish. When access to those resources breaks down, then that society is not treating its individuals fairly. Justice has broken down. The restoration of justice may be rectified by greater attention to solidarity, subsidiarity, or both.

These are the principles of Christian social ethics, but they remain only principles and do not translate into action unless you, the reader, accept the challenge of being part of the solution to social problems. In accepting that challenge, you follow in the footsteps of Christian men and women throughout the past twenty centuries. More important, you follow in the footsteps of Jesus, who invited his followers to redirect their attention to the needs of those on the margins. Giving preference to their needs highlights every one of the principles described above.

The principles reveal that Protestant or, more broadly, Christian social ethics is not an *either/or* system. It is not about *either* protecting private property *or* in giving all one's property away. It is not about *either* promoting free-market capitalism *or* promoting Marxism. It is not about *either* more social welfare programs *or* more individual responsibility. It is not about *either* more charity *or* more justice. It is not about *either* wealth *or* poverty. It is not about *either* helping society move back to God *or* embracing nonsectarian, rationalist-oriented ethics. Christian social ethics is always *both/and*. Christian social ethics wants *both* private property *and* an appreciation for the nonabsolute right to private property. Christian social ethics wants *both* free-market capitalism *and* regulations to curb its excesses. Christian social ethics wants *both* social welfare programs *and* more people taking responsibility for themselves and for their own actions. Take any issue in our political discourse today where opposite positions are being put forward, and if you are a well-trained Christian social ethicist, you will say you want something from both sides.

Notes

Introduction

1. One especially provocative book on this subject of redefining the notion of personhood is Daryl Wenneman's *Posthuman Personhood* (Lanham, MD: University Press of America, 2013), which argues for a new naming convention in ethical and artificial intelligence circles for the concept of person and that we should distinguish between humans both in terms of whether they are biological and in terms of whether they are moral. That is to say, it is possible for a nonbiological human (i.e., an artificially intelligent human) to be moral in the same way that it is possible for a biological human to be immoral. Consequently, according to Wenneman, the term "person" should be reserved for moral humans, biological or nonbiological.

2 See, e.g, J. Philip Wogaman, *Christian Ethics: A Historical Introduction*, 2nd ed. (Louisville: Westminster John Knox, 2011); Gary Dorrien, *Social Ethics in the Making: Interpreting an American Tradition* (Malden, MA: Wiley-Blackwell, 2011); Harry J. Huebner, *An Introduction to Christian Ethics: History, Movements, People* (Waco: Baylor University Press, 2012).

3. My presentation follows the English Old Testament rather than the Hebrew Bible.

Chapter 1 The Pentateuch

1. For more on the narrative unity of the Pentateuch, see John Barton, "Law and Narrative in the Pentateuch," *Communio Viatorum* 51 (2009): 126–40; Paul R. Hinlicky, "The Book of the Torah: The Narrative Integrity of the Pentateuch," *Pro Ecclesia* 2 (1993): 493–97; Thomas W. Mann, *The Book of the Torah: The Narrative Integrity of the Pentateuch* (Atlanta: John Knox, 1988); Jean-Pierre Sonnet, "The Fifth Book of the Pentateuch: Deuteronomy in Its Narrative Dynamic," *Journal of Ancient Judaism* 3 (2012): 197–234; John Sailhamer, *The Pentateuch as Narrative* (Grand Rapids: Zondervan, 1992).

2. Hesiod, *Theogony and Works and Days*, trans. M. L. West, Oxford World's Classics (Oxford: Oxford University Press, 1999). Several essays comparing and contrasting chaos concepts in ancient creation stories are in Jo Ann Scurlock and Richard H. Beal, eds., *Creation and Chaos: A Reconsideration of Herman Gunkel's Chaoskampf Hypothesis* (Winona Lake, IN: Eisenbrauns, 2013). See also Carolina López-Ruiz, "How to Start a Cosmogony: On the Poetics of Beginnings in Greece and the Near East," *Journal of Ancient Near Eastern Religions* 12 (2012): 30–48; Hermann Spieckermann, "Is God's Creation Good? From Hesiodus to Ben Sira," in *Beyond Eden: The Biblical Story of Paradise (Genesis 2–3) and Its Reception History*, ed. Konrad Schmid and Christoph Riedweg (Tübingen: Mohr Siebeck, 2008), 79–94; Charles Francis Whitley, "The Pattern of Creation in Genesis, Chapter 1," *Journal of Near Eastern Studies* 17 (1958): 32–40.

3. Scholars debate what city or place the Genesis reference to Abram's "Ur of the Chaldees" (Gen. 11: 31) refers. Cf. A. R. Millard, "Where Was Abraham's Ur? The Case for the Babylonian City," *Biblical Archaeology Review* 27, no. 3 (May 2001): 52; Shubert Spero, "Was Abram Born in Ur of the Chaldees?," *Jewish Bible Quarterly* 24 (1996): 156–59; Edwin M. Yamauchi, "Abraham and Archaeology: Anachronisms or Adaptations?," in *Perspectives on Our Father Abraham: Essays in Honor of Marvin R. Wilson*, ed. Steven A. Hunt (Grand Rapids: Eerdmans, 2010), 15–32.

4. For further discussion of interpretations on Abraham lying about Sarah (Gen. 12 and 20), see Dong-Gu Han, "The Crisis of a Patriarch's Wife (Gen 20:1–18): A Multicultural Interpretation of the Patriarchal Narrative," in *Mapping and Engaging the Bible in Asian Cultures: Congress of the Society of Asian Biblical Studies 2008 Seoul Conference*, ed. Yeong Mee Lee and Yoon Jong Yoo (Korea: Christian Literature Society of Korea, 2009), 73–87; Fredrik Carlson Holmgren, "Looking Back on Abraham's Encounter with a Canaanite King: A Reversal of Expectations (Genesis 20:1–18)," *Currents in Theology and Mission* 37 (2010): 366–77; David Smith, "How Not to Bless the Nations," *Perspectives* 20 (2005): 6–11; Vered Tohar, "Abraham and Sarah in Egypt (Genesis 12:10–20): Sexual Transgressions as Apologetic Interpretations in Post-biblical Jewish Sources," *Women In Judaism* 10 (2013), http://wjudaism.library.utoronto .ca/index.php/wjudaism/article/view/20896/17059.

5. "Now therefore, if you obey my voice and keep my covenant, you shall be my treasured possession out of all the peoples. Indeed, the whole earth is mine, but you shall be for me a priestly kingdom and a holy nation. These are the words that you shall speak to the Israelites" (Exod. 19:5–6). For more on the Mosaic Covenant and its role within the wider ethos of Scripture, see William D. Barrick, "The Mosaic Covenant," *The Master's Seminary Journal* 10 (1999): 213–32; Bryan D. Estelle, J. V. Fesko, and David VanDrunen, eds., *The Law Is Not of Faith: Essays on Works and Grace in the Mosaic Covenant* (Phillipsburg, NJ: P&R, 2009); Peter J. Gentry, "The Covenant at Sinai," *Southern Baptist Journal of Theology* 12 (2008): 38–63; Mark W. Karlberg, "Reformed Interpretation of the Mosaic Covenant," *Westminster Theological Journal* 43 (1980): 1–57; Cleon Rogers Jr., "The Covenant with Moses and Its Historical Setting," *Journal of the Evangelical Theological Society* 14 (1971): 141–55; Brooks Schramm, "Exodus 19 and Its Christian Appropriation," in *Jews, Christians, and the Theology of the Hebrew Scriptures*, ed. Alice Ogden Bellis and Joel S. Kaminsky (Atlanta: Society of Biblical Literature, 2000), 327–52; Ralph Allan Smith, "The Royal Priesthood in Exodus 19:6," in *Glory of Kings: A Festschrift in Honor of James B. Jordan*, ed. Peter J. Leithart and John Barach (Eugene, OR: Pickwick, 2011), 93–111; Gordon J. Wenham, "Legal Forms in the Book of the Covenant," *Tyndale Bulletin* 22 (1971): 95–102.

6. Cf. George W. Ramsey, "Is Name-Giving an Act of Domination in Genesis 2:23 and Elsewhere?," *Catholic Biblical Quarterly* 50 (1988): 24–35, esp. 34.

7. Terry Lehane, "Isaac's Wells and Israel's Return: Some Parallels," *Jewish Bible Quarterly* 22 (1994): 259–63; Victor H. Matthews, "The Wells of Gerar," *Biblical Archaeologist* 49 (1986): 118–26.

8. Much has been written by scholars on Zipporah, particularly her role in circumcising her and Moses's son. Among other sources, see Fred Blumenthal, "The Circumcision Performed by Zipporah," *Jewish Bible Quarterly* 35 (2007): 255–59; Peter F. Lockwood, "Zipporah in the Account of the Exodus: Literary and Theological Perspectives on Exodus 4:24–26," *Lutheran Theological Journal* 35 (2001): 116–27; Stephen Newman, "Why Moses Did Not Circumcise His Son," *Jewish Bible Quarterly* 44 (2016): 50–52; David P. Pettit, "When the Lord Seeks to Kill Moses: Reading Exodus 4.24–26 in Its Literary Context," *Journal for the Study of the Old Testament* 40 (2015): 163–77; Bernard Robinson, "Zipporah to the Rescue: A Contextual Study of Exodus 4:24–26," *Vetus Testamentum* 36 (1986): 447–61.

Similarly, much has been written about Jethro and his relationship to Moses. See Viktor Ber, "Moses and Jethro: Harmony and Conflict in the Interpretation of Exodus 18," *Communio Viatorum* 50 (2008): 147–70; Phillip Lerner, "Redefining *Hatĕlā'â*: An Assurance of Israel's Return to the Land in Jethro's Covenant," *Biblica* 87 (2006): 402–11; Adriane B. Leveen, "Inside Out:

Jethro, the Midianites and a Biblical Construction of the Outsider," *Journal for the Study of the Old Testament* 34 (2010): 395–417; Theodore Steinberg, "Jethro—Who Was He?," *Jewish Bible Quarterly* 26 (1998): 57–59.

9. Robert B. Coote, "Meaning of the Name Israel," *Harvard Theological Review* 65 (1972): 137–42.

10. God shows favor to a donkey by protecting it from certain danger in traveling farther down a road (Num. 22:15–35).

11. There is a wide array of interest in Hagar's story among scholars not only of Scripture but also of pastoral theology, patristics, Islamic history, and medieval studies, just to name a few. See, e.g., Hayyim Angel, "Sarah's Treatment of Hagar (Genesis 16): Morals, Messages, and Mesopotamia," *Jewish Bible Quarterly* 41 (2013): 211–18; Tony Maalouf, "The Inclusivity of God's Promises: A Biblical Perspective," *Cultural Encounters* 7 (2011): 27–35; Yvonne Sherwood, "Hagar and Ishmael: The Reception of Expulsion," *Interpretation* 68 (2014): 286–304; Nicolas Wyatt, "The Meaning of *El Roi* and the Mythological Dimension in Genesis 16," *Scandinavian Journal of the Old Testament* 8 (1994): 141–51.

Chapter 2 Historical, Poetical, and Wisdom Literature

1. Pss. 19:1–6; 29:3–9; 31:13–14; 50:1–2.

2. Pss. 9:7; 11:4; 18:7–15; 21:1; 22:28; 24:1; 29:10; 31:12; 44:4–7; 46:5–11; 47:1–9; 48:1–8; 66:4.

3. Pss. 13:5; 18:25–26; 23:1–6; 31:21; 36:5–7; 51:1; 57:3, 10; 62:12.

4. For literature on *chesed*, see James A. Montgomery, "Hebrew *Ḥesed* and Greek *Charis*," *Harvard Theological Review* 32 (1939): 97–102; Emanuel Rackman, "The Centrality of the Concept *Chesed*," in *Jacob Dolnitzky Memorial Volume: Studies in Jewish Law, Philosophy, Literature and Language*, ed. Morris Casriel Katz (Skokie, IL: Hebrew Theological College, 1982), 44–50; Robin L. Routledge, "*Ḥesed* as Obligation: A Re-Examination," *Tyndale Bulletin* 46 (1995): 179–96; Charles Francis Whitley, "The Semantic Range of *Chesed*," *Biblica* 62 (1981): 519–26.

5. Pss. 3:7–8; 13:5–6; 18:1–6; 22:19–25; 25:22; 34:17–20; 41:10.

6. For literature on lament psalms, see Gabriel Mendy, "The Theological Significance of the Psalm of Lament," *American Theological Inquiry* 8, no. 1 (August 1, 2015): 61–71; Andreas Schuele, "'Call on Me in the Day of Trouble . . .': From Oral Lament to Lament Psalms," in *Interface of Orality and Writing: Speaking, Seeing, Writing in the Shaping of New Genres*, ed. Annette Weissenrieder and Robert B. Coote (Tübingen: Mohr Siebeck, 2010), 322–34; Bruce K. Waltke, James M. Houston, and Erika Moore, *The Psalms as Christian Lament: A Historical Commentary* (Grand Rapids: Eerdmans, 2014).

7. Cf. Pss. 10:11–12; 12:5; 14:1; 36:1–2; 42:3; 70:3.

8. Pss. 5:3; 17:1; 26:1–2; 28:2; 30:8; 37:7; 58:10–11.

9. Pss. 11:1; 16:1; 17:7; 25:20; 30:1–3; 31:1–4; 32:7; 35:10; 40:13; 46:1; 54:4; 57:1–2. For literature on God as refuge, see David G. Firth, "Yahweh My Refuge: A Critical Analysis of Psalm 71," *Journal for the Study of the Old Testament* 32 (2008): 117–18; Gerald T. Sheppard, "'Blessed Are Those Who Take Refuge in Him': Biblical Criticism and Deconstruction," *Religion and Intellectual Life* 5 (1988): 57–66.

10. Pss. 5:8; 9:3–4; 14:4–7; 56:13; 60:3.

11. Pss. 9:4; 11:7; 17:2, 13–14; 18:17–20; 20:2, 6; 31:17–18; 33:5; 36:6; 50:4–7; 55:23. For literature on God and justice in the psalms, see Jacqueline E. Lapsley, "'Bring on Your Wrecking Ball': Psalm 73 and Public Witness," *Theology Today* 70 (2013): 62–68; J. Clinton McCann Jr., "Righteousness, Justice, and Peace: A Contemporary Theology of the Psalms," *Horizons in Biblical Theology* 23 (2001): 111–31; J. Clinton McCann Jr., "The Hope of the Poor: The Psalms in Worship and Our Search for Justice," in *Touching the Altar: The Old Testament for Christian Worship*, ed. Carol M. Bechtel (Grand Rapids: Eerdmans, 2008), 155–78.

12. Pss. 34:21; 35:22–26; 37:9–10, 13; 39:11; 56:7; 58:10.

13. Some psalms remind their readers of what they ought to do and what they ought to avoid doing in order to keep clear of God's wrath—e.g., Ps. 15 encourages slandering no one, honoring righteous people in the community, keeping one's word, and not loaning out money to others with interest; Ps. 34:13–14 instructs the reader to avoid lying and to seek peace with others; Ps. 37:8 warns against anger, wrath and, interestingly enough, fretting.

14. Pss. 33:18–19; 34:7, 15–17; 37:18–19, 23–31.

Chapter 3 Prophets

1. For the composition dates of the individual books of the prophets, consult survey textbooks on the Old Testament, which often include discussions of the date, authorship, and historical context for each of the books. See, e.g., Andrew Hill and John Walton, *Survey of the Old Testament* (Grand Rapids: Zondervan, 1991), part 4; Werner Schmidt, *Old Testament Introduction* (New York: De Gruyter, 1999), part 3.

2. The fall of the northern kingdom of Israel to the Assyrian Empire is related only briefly in the Old Testament (2 Kings 17:3–6), but the Assyrians left far more detailed records of the events. They had pictures carved into stone blocks (as reliefs) that depict their conquest of the northern kingdom, and particularly their siege of the city of Lachish in Judah, the southern kingdom. These reliefs may be seen today in the British Museum in London. See Ariel M. Bagg, "Palestine under Assyrian Rule: A New Look at the Assyrian Imperial Policy in the West," *Journal of the American Oriental Society* 133 (2013): 119–44; Mogens Trolle Larsen, *The Conquest of Assyria: Excavations in an Antique Land* (New York: Routledge, 1996); Simon Anglim et al., *Fighting Techniques of the Ancient World, 3000 BC–AD 500* (London: Amber Books, 2013).

3. For more on the conquest of Judah by Babylon and the later history of the Babylonian Empire, see Hans M. Barstad, "The City State of Jerusalem in the Neo-Babylonian Empire: Evidence from the Surrounding States," in *By the Irrigation Canals of Babylon: Approaches to the Study of Exile*, ed. John J. Ahn and Jill Middlemas (New York: T&T Clark, 2012), 34–48; William G. Dever, "Archaeology and the Fall of Judah," *Eretz-Israel* 29 (2009): 29–35; *Cambridge Ancient History*, vol. 3, part 2, *Assyrian and Babylonian Empires and Other States of the Near East: From 8th to 6th cents BC*, ed. John Boardman et al., 2nd ed. (Cambridge: Cambridge University Press, 1991); David S. Vanderhooft, *The Neo-Babylonian Empire and Babylon in the Latter Prophets* (Atlanta: Scholars Press, 1999); David B. Weisberg, "The Neo-Babylonian Empire," in *Royal Cities of the Biblical World*, ed. Joan Goodnick Westenholz (Jerusalem: Bible Lands Museum Jerusalem, 1996), 221–33.

4. For more on idolatry practices among Israel, especially its kings, see Leila L. Bronner, *The Stories of Elijah and Elisha as Polemics against Baal Worship*, Pretoria Oriental Series 6 (Leiden: Brill, 1968); Joel F. Drinkard, "Religious Practices Reflected in the Book of Hosea," *Review & Expositor* 90 (1993): 205–18; Avraham Gileadi, ed., *Israel's Apostasy and Restoration: Essays in Honor of Roland K. Harrison* (Grand Rapids: Baker, 1988), esp. the essay by Peter R. Gilchrist, "Israel's Apostasy: Catalyst of Assyrian World Conquest," 99–114; Jerry Hwang, "The Unholy Trio of Money, Sex, and Power in Israel's 8th-Century BCE prophets," *Jian Dao* 41 (2014): 183–207; Jacob Milgrom, "The Nature and Extent of Idolatry in Eighth-Seventh Century Judah," *Hebrew Union College Annual* 69 (1998): 1–13.

5. For more on Ezekiel's critique of idolatry, in addition to commentaries on Ezekiel, see Silviu Bunta, "Yhwh's Cultic Statue after 597/586 BCE: A Linguistic and Theological Reinterpretation of Ezekiel 28:12," *Catholic Biblical Quarterly* 69 (2007): 222–41; John N. Day, "Ezekiel and the Heart of Idolatry," *Bibliotheca Sacra* 164 (2007): 21–33; Tova Ganzel, "The Defilement and Desecration of the Temple in Ezekiel," *Biblica* 89 (2008): 369–79.

6. For more on Hosea's children and Gomer, in addition to commentaries on Hosea, see Yosef Green, "Hosea and Gomer Revisited," *Jewish Bible Quarterly* 31 (2003): 84–89; Herbert May, "An Interpretation of the Names of Hosea's Children" *Journal of Biblical Literature* 55 (1936): 285–91; Joshua Moon, "Honor and Shame in Hosea's Marriages," *Journal for the*

Study of the Old Testament 39 (2015): 335–51; Gerrie Snyman, "Social Reality and Religious Language in the Marriage Metaphor in Hosea 1–3," *Old Testament Essays* 6 (1993): 90–112.

7. For further information regarding Jeremiah's reference to God changing his mind, in addition to commentaries on Jeremiah, see Mark E. Biddle, "Contingency, God and the Babylonians: Jeremiah on the Complexity of Repentance," *Review & Expositor* 101 (2004): 247–66; Terence E. Fretheim, "The Repentance of God: A Study of Jeremiah 18:7–10," *Hebrew Annual Review* 11 (1987): 81–92; Anthony Gelston, "The Repentance of God," in *On Stone and Scroll: Essays in Honour of Graham Ivor Davies*, ed. James K. Aitken, Katharine J. Dell, and Brian A. Mastin (Berlin: De Gruyter, 2011), 453–62.

8. On the rhetorical structure of Amos 1–3 and the charges made by God against the nations, in addition to commentaries on Amos, see Kevin Hall, "Listen Up People! The Lion Has Roared; A Study of Amos 1–2," *Southwestern Journal of Theology* 38 (1995): 11–19; Jack R. Lundbom, "The Lion Has Roared: Rhetorical Structure in Amos 1:2–3:8," in *Milk and Honey: Essays on Ancient Israel and the Bible in Appreciation of the Judaic Studies Program at the University of California, San Diego*, ed. Sarah Malena and David Miano (Winona Lake, IN: Eisenbrauns, 2007), 65–75; Gene M. Tucker, "The Social Location of Amos: Amos 1:32:16," in *Thus Says the Lord: Essays on the Former and Latter Prophets in Honor of Robert R. Wilson*, ed. John J. Ahn and Stephen L. Cook (New York: T&T Clark, 2009), 273–84; Archibald L. H. M. van Wieringen, "The Prophecies against the Nations in Amos 1:2–3:15," *Estudios bíblicos* 71 (2013): 7–19.

9. On Jonah's reaction to God's benevolence toward the Assyrians, in addition to relevant commentaries, see Mercedes García Bachmann, "Conflicting Visions of Jonah—or Rather Diversity?," *Mission Studies* 23 (2006): 45–59; Robert French II, "Judgment, Anger, Benevolence, and Jonah: Exploring Human Responses to Divine Benevolence via the Framework of the Judeo-Christian Worldview," *Evangelical Journal* 33 (2015): 82–88; Colin J. Hemer, "Jonah: The Messenger Who Grumbled," *Currents in Theology and Mission* 3 (1976): 141–50; Robin Payne, "The Prophet Jonah: Reluctant Messenger and Intercessor," *Expository Times* 100 (1989): 131–34.

10. Seemingly countless works have been written on the "new covenant" proclamation in Jeremiah 31. See, e.g., Fẹmi Adeyẹmi, "What Is the New Covenant 'Law' in Jeremiah 31:33?," *Bibliotheca Sacra* 163 (2006): 312–21; J. Coleman Baker, "New Covenant, New Identity: A Social-Scientific Reading of Jeremiah 31:31–34," *The Bible & Critical Theory* 4 (2008): 1–11; Walter Kaiser Jr. "The Old Promise and the New Covenant: Jeremiah 31:31–34," *Journal of the Evangelical Theological Society* 15 (1972): 11–23; Harry D. Potter, "The New Covenant in Jeremiah 31:31–34," *Vetus Testamentum* 33 (1983): 347–57.

11. The concept of the messiah in the Old Testament is also a subject about which much has been written. See, e.g., Walter Kaiser Jr. *The Messiah in the Old Testament* (Grand Rapids: Zondervan, 1995); Stanley Porter, ed., *The Messiah in the Old and New Testaments* (Grand Rapids: Eerdmans, 2007); Roy A. Rosenberg, "The Slain Messiah in the Old Testament," *Zeitschrift für die alttestamentliche Wissenschaft* 99 (1987): 259–61.

Chapter 4 Jesus in the New Testament

1. The literature on this topic is vast, but a good place to begin is with Peter Doble, "Was the Birth of Jesus According to Scripture?," *Journal for the Study of the New Testament* 36 (2014): 38–39; cf. Leo Depuydt, "The Date of Death of Jesus of Nazareth," *Journal of the American Oriental Society* 122 (2002): 466–80; Daryn Graham, "Dating the Birth of Jesus Christ," *Reformed Theological Review* 73 (2014): 147–59; Massey Hamilton Shepherd, "Are Both the Synoptics and John Correct about the Date of Jesus' Death?," *Journal of Biblical Literature* 80 (1961): 123–32; Kurt M. Simmons, "The Origins of Christmas and the Date of Christ's Birth," *Journal of the Evangelical Theological Society* 58 (2015): 299–324.

2. For further information about Herod and the Herodian dynasty, see Peter Richardson, *Herod: King of the Jews and Friend of the Romans* (Minneapolis: Fortress, 1999).

3. For further information about the messiah concept in the first century, see Otto Betz, "Messianic Expectations in the Context of First-Century Judaism," in *Christology in Dialogue*, ed. Robert F. Berkey and Sarah A. Edwards (Cleveland: Pilgrim, 1993), 31–43; Richard A. Horsley and J. S. Hanson, *Bandits, Prophets, and Messiahs: Popular Movements in the Time of Jesus* (Minneapolis: Winston, 1985); Hermann Lichtenberger, "Messianic Expectations and Messianic Figures in the Second Temple Period," in *Qumran-Messianism*, ed. James H. Charlesworth et al. (Tübingen: Mohr Siebeck, 1998), 9–20.

4. Other Gospel texts were written in the centuries after Jesus's life, but they reveal more about the diversity of the Christian community in the second through fourth centuries than they do about the Jesus of the early first century. The *Gospel of Thomas* is perhaps one exception; it is a collection of sayings purportedly by Jesus—some of which are also found in the New Testament Gospels, and some of which are not. Early versions of this Gospel may even date to the middle of the first century, which would make it contemporaneous with some of the New Testament Gospels. The *Gospel of Thomas* is quoted as Scripture in a surviving letter by Clement, one of the earliest bishops of Rome, and it seems also to have been a source of information about Jesus for other early Christian writers. It fell into disuse in later centuries, but scholars today consider it a potential source of information about Jesus's life.

5. Cf. Eric Eve, *Behind the Gospels: Understanding the Oral Tradition* (Minneapolis: Fortress, 2014).

6. For further information regarding Mary's song, also known as the Magnificat, in addition to relevant commentaries, see Kenneth E. Bailey, "The Song of Mary: Vision of a New Exodus (Luke 1:46–55)," *Theological Review* 2 (1979): 29–35; Ruth Ann Foster, "Mary's Hymn of Praise in Luke 1:46–55: Reflections on Liturgy and Spiritual Formation," *Review & Expositor* 100 (2003): 451–63; Bruce Grigsby, "Compositional Hypotheses for the Lucan 'Magnificat': Tensions for the Evangelical," *Evangelical Quarterly* 56 (1984): 159–72; Valdir R. Steuernagel, "Doing Theology with an Eye on Mary," *Evangelical Review of Theology* 27 (2003): 100–112.

7. One of the more famous early Christian treatises on this topic is Athanasius of Alexandria's *On the Incarnation* (New York: Macmillan, 1981), which teaches the idea that what God did not assume, God did not save. By assuming human flesh, God saved humanity and therefore expressed the dignity of, and his solidarity with, the human race. Cf. Frederick D. Aquino, "The Incarnation: The Dignity and Honor of Human Personhood," *Restoration Quarterly* 42 (2000): 39–46; James P. Scullion, "Creation-Incarnation: God's Affirmation of Human Worth," in *Made in God's Image: The Catholic Vision of Human Dignity* (New York: Paulist Press, 1999), 7–28.

8. For more on the social situation of tax collectors in the first century, see Hyam Maccoby, "How Unclean Were Tax-Collectors?," *Biblical Theology Bulletin* 31 (2001): 60–63; A. M. Okorie, "The Characterization of the Tax Collectors in the Gospel of Luke," *Currents in Theology and Mission* 22 (1995): 27–32; William Walker Jr., "Jesus and the Tax Collectors," *Journal of Biblical Literature* 97 (1978): 221–38; Vitor Westhelle, "Exposing Zacchaeus," *Christian Century* 123 (2006): 27–31.

9. For more on the economic situation of those in the fishing industry of first-century Galilee, see Gary M. Burge, "Fishers of Fish: The Maritime Life of Galilee's North Shore, Jesus' Headquarters," *Christian History* 17, no. 3 (1998): 36–37; K. C. Hanson, "The Galilean Fishing Economy and the Jesus Tradition," *Biblical Theology Bulletin* 27 (1997): 99–111; Sharon Lea Mattila, "Revisiting Jesus' Capernaum: A Village of Only Subsistence-Level Fishers and Farmers?," in *Galilean Economy in the Time of Jesus* (Atlanta: Society of Biblical Literature, 2013), 75–138; Mendel Nun, "Cast Your Net upon the Waters: Fish and Fishermen in Jesus' Time," *Biblical Archaeology Review* 19 (November 1993): 46–56, 70.

10. The more ancient manuscripts of the Gospel of John do not include this story, and other manuscripts of the New Testament that include this story do not locate the story in the same place of this Gospel. Some manuscripts even insert the story into Luke's Gospel. Thus biblical scholars do not tend to think that this story was original to the Gospel of John. Having said

that, the textual problems that point away from concluding that it was original to John's Gospel have no bearing on deciding whether the story is true.

11. Cf., e.g., George Aichele, "Reading Jesus Writing," *Biblical Interpretation* 12 (2004): 353–68; Jennifer Wright Knust and Tommy Wasserman, "Earth Accuses Earth: Tracing What Jesus Wrote on the Ground," *Harvard Theological Review* 103 (2010): 407–46; Edmond Power, "Writing on the Ground: (Joh. 8, 6. 8)," *Biblica* 2 (1921): 54–57; Hershel Shanks, "Why Did Jesus Write on the Ground?," *Bible Review* 14, no. 6 (1998): 2; Harvey A. Stob, "Perplexing Texts: [John 8:6]," *Reformed Journal* 29 (1979): 7–8.

12. For more on these three groups, see Anthony J. Saldarini, *Pharisees, Scribes, and Sadducees in Palestinian Society: A Sociological Approach* (Grand Rapids: Eerdmans, 2001); Julius Wellhausen, *The Pharisees and the Sadducees: An Examination of Internal Jewish History*, trans. Mark E. Biddle (Macon, GA: Mercer University Press, 2001).

Chapter 5 The Early Decades of Christianity

1. For more on the early history of Christianity, see Justo González, *The Story of Christianity*, vol. 1, *The Early Church to the Dawn of the Reformation*, 2nd ed. (New York: HarperOne, 2010), esp. chaps. 11, 15, and 25.

2. For more on the composition of early Christian communities, see Jan N. Bremmer, "Pauper or Patroness: The Widow in the Early Christian Church," in *Between Poverty and the Pyre: Moments in the History of Widowhood* (New York: Routledge, 1995), 31–57; Jonathan A. Draper, "Children and Slaves in the Community of the Didache and the Two Ways Tradition," in *The Didache: A Missing Piece of the Puzzle in Early Christianity*, ed. Jonathan A. Draper and Clayton N. Jefford (Atlanta: Society of Biblical Literature, 2015), 85–121; Dimitra Koukoura, "Women in the Early Christian Church," in *Orthodox Women Speak: Discerning the "Signs of the Times,"* ed. Kyriaki Karidoyanes FitzGerald (Geneva: WCC Publications, 1999), 69–74; D. J. Kyrtatas, *The Social Structure of the Early Christian Communities* (London; Verso, 1987); D. B. Martin, "Ancient Slavery, Class, and Early Christianity," *Fides et Historia* 23 (1991): 105–13; Charles Pietri, "Christians and Slaves in the Early Days of the Church (2nd–3rd Centuries)," in *Dignity of the Despised of the Earth*, ed. Jacques Pohier and Dietmar Mieth (New York: Seabury, 1979), 31–39.

3. For more on the use of *apokatastasis* language in early Christianity, see James Parker III, *The Concept of Apokatastasis in Acts: A Study in Primitive Christian Theology* (Austin: Schola, 1978); Ilaria Ramelli, *The Christian Doctrine of Apokatastasis: A Critical Assessment from the New Testament to Eriugena*, Supplements to Vigiliae Christianae 120 (Leiden: Brill, 2013).

4. For further reflection on Peter's encounter with Cornelius, see appropriate commentaries on Acts 10 and vanThanh Nguyen, *Peter and Cornelius: A Story of Conversion and Mission* (Eugene, OR: Pickwick, 2012); Mark A. Plunkett, "Ethnocentricity and Salvation History in the Cornelius Episode (Acts 10:1–11:18)," *Society of Biblical Literature Seminar Papers* 24 (1985): 465–79; J. B. Tyson, "Guess Who's Coming to Dinner: Peter and Cornelius in Acts 10:1–11:18," *Forum* 3 (2000): 179–96.

5. For more on this conflict, in addition to commentaries on Galatians and 2 Peter, see Michael R. Cosby, "When Apostolic Egos Collide: Paul, Peter and Barnabas in Galatians 2," *Conversations with the Biblical World* 35 (2015): 1–21; Michael Goulder, *St. Paul versus St. Peter: A Tale of Two Missions* (Louisville: Westminster John Knox, 1994); Margaret M. Mitchell, "Peter's 'Hypocrisy' and Paul's: Two 'Hypocrites' at the Foundation of Earliest Christianity," *New Testament Studies* 58 (2012): 213–34.

6. The Jerusalem Council is the subject of much scholarly interest. Some recent literature on the subject includes Cornelis Bennema, "The Ethnic Conflict in Early Christianity: An Appraisal of Bauckham's Proposal on the Antioch Crisis and the Jerusalem Council," *Journal of the Evangelical Theological Society* 56 (2013): 753–63; Arthur Just Jr., "The Apostolic Councils of Galatians and Acts: How First-Century Christians Walked Together," *Concordia Theological*

Quarterly 74 (2010): 261–88; Veselin Kesich, "Apostolic Council at Jerusalem," *St. Vladimir's Seminary Quarterly* 6 (1962): 108–17; Daniel Leyrer, "Acts 15:20: What Was Prohibited by the Jerusalem Council?," *Wisconsin Lutheran Quarterly* 108 (2011): 47–49; John Meier, "Biblical Reflection: The Jerusalem Council—Gal 2:1–10; Acts 15:1–29," *Mid-Stream* 35 (1996): 465–70; Hyung Dae Park, "Drawing Ethical Principles from the Process of the Jerusalem Council: A New Approach to Acts 15:4–29," *Tyndale Bulletin* 61 (2010): 271–91; J. Lyle Story, "Luke's Instructive Dynamics for Resolving Conflicts: The Jerusalem Council," *Journal of Biblical and Pneumatological Research* 3 (2011): 99–118; Timothy Wiarda, "The Jerusalem Council and the Theological Task," *Journal of the Evangelical Theological Society* 46 (2003): 233–48.

7. For further study of Paul and his view of Judaism, see the literature, pro and con, on what has been called "the new perspective" on Paul, including James D. G. Dunn, *The New Perspective on Paul*, 2nd ed. (Grand Rapids: Eerdmans, 2008); Kent L. Yinger, *The New Perspective on Paul: An Introduction* (Eugene, OR: Cascade, 2011); Magnus Zetterholm, *Approaches to Paul: A Student's Guide to Recent Scholarship* (Minneapolis: Fortress, 2009).

8. For more on the term *koinōnia* in the New Testament, see John Campbell, "ΚΟΙΝΩΝΙΑ and Its Cognates in the New Testament," *Journal of Biblical Literature* 51 (1932): 352–80; Jeffrey J. Kloha, "Koinonia and Life Together in the New Testament," *Concordia Journal* 38 (2012): 23–32; George Panikulam, *Koinōnia in the New Testament* (Rome: Biblical Institute Press, 1979); Barbara R. Rossing, "Models of Koinonia in the New Testament and Early Church," *LWF Documentation* 42 (1997): 65–80.

9. For accounts of the fate of some of the early Christians, see Eusebius, *Ecclesiastical History* 2. The apocryphal *Acts of Peter* also records the story of Peter being crucified upside down.

10. Unfortunately for readers of this volume, most of the literature on this controversy has been written in German. Nevertheless, literature supporting the position that the early Christians were not proto-communists includes Étienne Chastel, *Études historiques sur l'influence de la charité durant les premiers siècles chrétiens, et considérations sur son rôle dans les sociétés modernes* (Paris: Capelle, 1853), ET: *The Charity of the Primitive Churches: Historical Studies upon the Influence of Christian Charity during the First Centuries of Our Era, with Some Considerations Touching Its Bearings upon Modern Society*, trans. George-Auguste Matile (Philadelphia: Lippincott, 1857); Edmond Le Blant, "La richesse et las christianisme à l'âge des persécutions," *Revue archéologique*, 2nd series, 39 (1880): 220–30; Gerhard Uhlhorn, *Die christliche Liebestätigkeit*, vol. 1, *In der alten Kirche* (Stuttgart: Gundert, 1882); Shailer Matthews, *The Social Teachings of Jesus: An Essay in Christian Sociology* (New York: Macmillan, 1897).

Literature suggesting that the early Christians did have proto-communist leanings includes W. Haller, "Die Eigentum im Glauben und Leben der nachapostolischen Kirche," *Theologische Studien und Kritiken* 64 (1891): 478–563; Lujo Brentano, "Die wirtschaftlichen Lehren des christlichen Altertums," in *Sitzungsberichte der philosophische-philologischen und der historischen Klasse der kgl. [königliche] Akademie der Wissenschaften* (Munich: 1902), 141–93; Karl Kautszy, *Der Ursprung des Christentums, eine historische Untersuchung* (Stuttgart: J. H. W. Dietz Nachf., 1908), of which there were many later editions; Gérard Walter, *Les origines du communisme, judaïques, chrétiennes, grecques, latines* (Paris: Payot, 1931).

Chapter 6 Late Antiquity

1. For more on the development of the New Testament canon, see survey texts such as Michael Kruger, *Canon Revisited: Establishing the Origins and Authority of the New Testament Books* (Wheaton: Crossway, 2012); Bruce M. Metzger, *The Canon of the New Testament: Its Origin, Development, and Significance* (Oxford: Clarendon, 1997); Arthur Patzia, *The Making of the New Testament: Origin, Collection, Text and Canon* (Downers Grove, IL: IVP Academic, 2011).

2. Early Christian leaders considered the many texts of a spiritual nature circulating within the Christian community as falling into one of several categories: books to be read in church, books useful for personal devotion, and books that are spurious or dubious. For an example

of these types of divisions, see the Muratorian Canon and Eusebius of Caesarea, *Ecclesiastical History* 3.25.

3. For more on the development of the church's hierarchy in Late Antiquity and its role in administering the church's affairs during that time, see Christopher A. Beeley, *Leading God's People: Wisdom from the Early Church for Today* (Grand Rapids: Eerdmans, 2012); Claudia Rapp, *Holy Bishops in Late Antiquity: The Nature of Christian Leadership in an Age of Transition* (Berkeley: University of California Press, 2005); Francis Sullivan, *From Apostles to Bishops: The Development of the Episcopacy in the Early Church* (New York: Paulist Press, 2001).

4. For a good survey of the development of early Christian doctrine, see Khaled Anatolios, *Retrieving Nicaea: The Development and Meaning of Trinitarian Doctrine* (Grand Rapids: Baker Academic, 2011); cf. Lewis Ayres, *Nicaea and Its Legacy: An Approach to Fourth Century Trinitarian Theology* (Oxford: Oxford University Press, 2006); J. N. D. Kelly, *Early Christian Doctrines*, 5th ed. (New York: Continuum, 1977).

5. Justin Martyr, *Apology* 1.67; ET in *Justin Martyr: The First and Second Apologies*, trans. Leslie William Barnard (Mahwah, NJ: Paulist Press, 1997), 71–72; critical text in *Apologie pour les Chrétiens*, ed. and trans. Charles Munier, Paradosis: Études de littérature et de théologie anciennes 39 (Fribourg, Switzerland: Éditions Universitaires, 1995), 122.

6. Tertullian, *Apology* 39; ET in *Tertullian: Apologetical Works . . .*, trans. Emily Joseph Daly, FC 10 (Washington, DC: Catholic University of America Press, 1950), 98–99; critical text in Tertullian, *Opera*, part 1, *Opera catholica: Adversus Marcionem*, ed. Eligius Dekkers, Janus G. P. Borleffs, and R. Willems, Corpus Christianorum: Series Latina 1 (Turnhout: Brepols, 1954), 151.

7. On the life and writings of John Chrysostom, see Pauline Allen and Wendy Mayer, *John Chrysostom*, The Early Church Fathers (London: Routledge, 1999); Wendy Mayer, *The Homilies of St. John Chrysostom: Provenance; Reshaping the Foundations* (Rome: Pontificio Istituto orientale, 2005).

8. John Chrysostom, *Homilies on Matthew* 66.3 [on Matt. 20:29–30]; ET in *Homilies on the Gospel of Matthew*, trans. George Prevost, rev. M. B. Riddle, NPNF[1] (repr., Grand Rapids: Eerdmans, 1979), 10:407; primary text in PG 58:629.

9. Some studies of poverty in Late Antique Roman society include Evelyne Patlagean, *Pauvreté économique et pauvreté sociale à Byzance: 4e–7e siècles* (Paris: Mouton, 1977); Peter Brown, *Poverty and Leadership in the Later Roman Empire* (Hanover, NH: Brandeis University Press, 2002); Steven J. Friesen, "Injustice or God's Will? Early Christian Explanations of Poverty," in *Wealth and Poverty in Early Church and Society*, ed. Susan Holman (Grand Rapids: Baker Academic, 2008), 17–36.

10. On the life and writings of Basil of Caesarea, see Stephen Hildebrand, *Basil of Caesarea*, Foundations of Theological Exegesis and Christian Spirituality (Grand Rapids: Baker Academic, 2014); Andrew Radde-Gallwitz, *Basil of Caesarea: A Guide to His Life and Doctrine*, Cascade Companions (Eugene, OR: Wipf & Stock, 2012).

11. Basil of Caesarea, *Homilies* 8; in PG 31:321; ET by Susan Holman, *The Hungry Are Dying: Beggars and Bishops in Roman Cappadocia*, Oxford Studies in Historical Theology (Oxford: Oxford University Press, 2001), 190. I have substituted "murderous" for Holman's "a homicide" at this point in her translation. This is not only a better rendering of the Greek *androphonos*, but it also makes better sense in English.

12. See Gregory of Nazianzus, *Orations* 14; in PG 35:857–910; ET by Martha Vinson, *Saint Gregory of Nazianzus: Select Orations*, FC 107 (Washington, DC: Catholic University of America Press, 2004), 39–71.

13. A translation of his relevant sermons is in Holman, *The Hungry Are Dying*.

14. For more on Basil's project, see Peter Brown, *Poverty and Leadership in the Later Roman Empire* (Boston: University Press of New England, 2001), 33–44, esp. 41–42, providing a fresh evaluation of Basil's own actions in light of a possible redating of the construction of the *Basileia* (from 368 to 370); Brian Daley, "Building a New City: The Cappadocian Fathers and

the Rhetoric of Philanthropy," *Journal of Early Christian Studies* 7 (1999): 431–61. Basil defends his *Basileia* and its benefit to the state in his *Ep.* 94; in *Saint Basile: Lettres*, 3 vols., ed. Yves Courtonne (Paris: Belles Lettres, 1957–66), 1:204–7).

15. Literature on the social welfare institutions built by Christians is largely available in non-English sources. E.g., a fairly extensive list of *diakonia* and institutions for poor relief in Constantinople in Late Antiquity has been compiled by Konstantina Mentzou-Meimari, "Eparkhiaka evagé idrymata mekhri tou telous tés eikonomakhias," *Byzantina* 11 (1982): 243–308. For oratories and their association with hospitals and *xenodocheia*, see Thomas Sternberg, *Orientalium more secutus* (Münster: Aschendorff, 1991), 174–77; E. Monaco, "Ricerche sotto la diaconia di S. Teodoro," *RendPontAcc* [*Rendiconti della Pontificia Accademia romana di Archeologia*] 45 (1972–73): 223–41.

16. The significance of Christian schooling was heightened when Julian became emperor (361–363). He sought to ban Christians from teaching students, which created problems for Christians around the eastern part of the Roman Empire.

17. Clement of Alexandria, *Quis dives salvetur* 11; ET, *Salvation of the Rich*, in ANF (Grand Rapids: Eerdmans, 1994), 2:594; critical text in *Clement of Alexandria: Quis dives salvetur*, ed. J. Armitage Robinson, Texts and Studies: Contributions to Biblical and Patristic Literature 5.2 (Cambridge: Cambridge University Press, 1897; repr., Eugene, OR: Wipf & Stock, 2004), 5.

18. Andreas Kessler, *Reichtumskritik und Pelagianismus: Die pelagianische Diatribe "De divitiis": Situierung, Lesetext, Übersetzung, Kommentar, Paradosis*, vol. 43 (Freiburg, Switzerland: Universitätsverlag, 1999); ET by B. R. Rees, *The Letters of Pelagius and His Followers* (Suffolk, UK: Boydell, 1991), 171–211. Cf. Elizabeth Clark, *Reading Renunciation: Asceticism and Scripture in Early Christianity* (Princeton: Princeton University Press, 1999), 94–99; Carlo Scaglioni, "'Guia a voi ricchi!': Pelagio e gli scritti pelangiani," in *Per foramen acus: Il cristianesimo antico di fronte alla pericope evangelica del "giovane ricco,"* Studia Patristica Mediolanensia 14 (Milan: Vita e Pensiero, 1986), 361–98.

Chapter 7 Middle Ages

1. Students interested in a survey of the history of the Middle Ages are directed to Susan Bauer, *The History of the Medieval World: From the Conversion of Constantine to the First Crusade* (New York: Norton, 2010); Morris Bishop, *The Middle Ages*, Mariner Books ed., American Heritage Library (Boston: Houghton Mifflin, 2001); Jeffrey Singman, *The Middle Ages: Everyday Life in Medieval Europe* (New York: Sterling, 2013).

2. Population studies of the Middle Ages are often restricted to examinations of small data sets, usually data for one region during one particular period of time. This is due to the lack of reliable data about population across large regions or across large time spans. For more on this type of work, see Irene Barbiera and Dalla-Zuanna Gianpiero, "Population Dynamics in Italy in the Middle Ages: New Insights from Archaeological Findings," *Population and Development Review* 35, no. 2 (2009): 367–89; Vern Bullough and Campbell Cameron, "Female Longevity and Diet in the Middle Ages," *Speculum* 55 (1980): 317–25; G. Duby, "The Agrarian Life of the Middle Ages," *Economic History Review*, n.s., 21 (1968): 159–65; K. F. Helleiner, "Population Movement and Agrarian Depression in the Later Middle Ages," *Canadian Journal of Economics and Political Science* / *Revue canadienne d'économique et de science politique* 15 (1949): 368–77; M. A. Jonker, "Estimation of Life Expectancy in the Middle Ages," *Journal of the Royal Statistical Society*, series A (Statistics in Society) 166 (2003): 105–17.

3. For more on the changes taking place within Christianity during this period, see Marios Costambeys et al., *The Carolingian World*, Cambridge Medieval Texts (Cambridge: Cambridge University Press, 2011); cf. studies of key personalities and key texts, such as Eleanor Duckett, *Carolingian Portraits: A Study in the Ninth Century* (Ann Arbor: University of Michigan Press, 1989); Paul Dutton, *Carolingian Civilization: A Reader*, 2nd ed., Readings in Medieval Civilizations and Cultures (Toronto: University of Toronto Press, 2004).

4. For more on the history of medieval universities, see Charles Haskins, *The Rise of Universities* (Ithaca, NY: Cornell University Press, 1957); Hunt Janin, *The University in Medieval Life, 1179–1499* (Jefferson, NC: McFarland, 2008). The texts and images of the original charters of several medieval universities appear via Joseph Hermans and Marc Nelissen, *Charters of Foundation and Early Documents of the Universities of the Coimbra Group* (Groningen: Coimbra Group, 1994).

5. For more on the development of medieval medicine, including the role of Christianity, see Darrel Amundsen and Gary Ferngren, "Medicine and Religion: Early Christianity through the Middle Ages," in *Health/Medicine and the Faith Traditions: An Inquiry into Religion and Medicine*, ed. Martin E. Marty and Kenneth L. Vaux (Philadelphia: Fortress, 1982), 93–131; Peter Biller and Joseph Ziegler, eds., *Religion and Medicine in the Middle Ages* (Woodbridge, UK: York Medieval Press, 2001); Vern L. Bullough, "Status and Medieval Medicine," *Journal of Health and Human Behavior* 2 (1961): 204–10; Faith Wallis, *Medieval Medicine: A Reader*, Readings in Medieval Civilizations and Cultures (Toronto: University of Toronto Press, 2010).

6. For a good survey of this topic, see John A. F. Thomson, *The Western Church in the Middle Ages* (London: Arnold, 1998).

7. For the relevant documents associated with church–state relations during the Middle Ages, see Brian Tierney, *The Crisis of Church and State, 1050–1300* (Toronto: University of Toronto Press, 1988).

8. For more on Thomas Aquinas's views on justice, see Thomas Aquinas, *Political Writings*, trans. and ed. R. W. Dyson (Cambridge: Cambridge University Press, 2002); cf. Steven Edwards, *Interior Acts: Teleology, Justice, and Friendship in the Religious Ethics of Thomas Aquinas* (Lanham, MD: University Press of America, 1986); Jeremiah Newman, *Foundations of Justice: A Historico-Critical Study in Thomism* (Cork, Ireland: Cork University Press, 1954); Daniel Porzecanski, "Friendship and the Circumstances of Justice according to Aquinas," *Review of Politics* 66 (2004): 35–54; Matthew Rigney, "Justice in the Teaching of St. Thomas," *Life of the Spirit* 15, no. 170/171 (1960): 93–100.

9. For further study of the concept of natural law and its legal tradition, see Jesse Covington, Bryan McGraw, and Micah Watson, eds., *Natural Law and Evangelical Political Thought* (Lanham, MD: Lexington Books, 2013); Jonathan A. Jacobs, ed., *Reason, Religion, and Natural Law: From Plato to Spinoza* (Oxford: Oxford University Press, 2012); Steven Jensen, *Knowing the Natural Law: From Precepts and Inclinations to Deriving Oughts* (Washington, DC: Catholic University of America Press, 2015).

10. For more on the history of the mendicant religious orders during the Middle Ages, see Herbert Grundmann, *Religious Movements in the Middle Ages: The Historical Links between Heresy, the Mendicant Orders, and the Women's Religious Movement in the Twelfth and Thirteenth Century; With the Historical Foundations of German Mysticism*, trans. Steven Rowan (Notre Dame, IN: University of Notre Dame Press, 1995); Clifford Lawrence, *The Friars: The Impact of the Mendicant Orders on Medieval Society* (London: Tauris, 2013); Karen Melvin, *Building Colonial Cities of God: Mendicant Orders and Urban Culture in New Spain* (Stanford, CA: Stanford University Press, 2012); Donald Prudlo, ed., *The Origin, Development, and Refinement of Medieval Religious Mendicancies* (Leiden: Brill, 2011).

11. For more on Teresa of Avila, see her autobiography, available in several English versions, including Teresa of Avila, *The Book of Her Life*, trans. Kieran Kavanaugh and Otilio Rodriguez (Indianapolis: Hackett, 1995). For a study of her life and writings, see Barbara Mujica, *Teresa de Avila: Lettered Woman* (Nashville: Vanderbilt University Press, 2009); Rowan Williams, *Teresa of Avila* (London: Continuum, 2003).

12. For more on the development of Teresa's discalced (barefoot) Carmelite communities, see Teresa's own Constitutions that she wrote for each new community, as in *The Collected Works of Teresa of Avila*, vol. 3, trans. Kieran Kavanaugh and Otilio Rodriguez (Washington, DC: Institute for Carmelite Studies, 1985). See also Alison Weber, "Spiritual Administration:

Gender and Discernment in the Carmelite Reform," *Sixteenth Century Journal* 31 (2000): 123–46.

Chapter 8 Reformations Era

1. For surveys of the Reformations around Europe during the sixteenth century, see Hans Hillerbrand, *The Protestant Reformation* (New York: Perennial, 2009); Carter Lindberg, *The European Reformations* (Oxford: Blackwell, 1996), Diarmaid MacCulloch, *The Reformation* (New York: Penguin, 2005).

2. For more on the Council of Trent, see its published decrees, as in H. J. Schroeder, *The Canons and Decrees of the Council of Trent* (Charlotte, NC: Tan Books, 2009). Cf. John W. O'Malley, *Trent: What Happened at the Council* (New York: Belknap, 2013).

3. For more on the early history of the Jesuits, see Thomas Worcester, *The Cambridge Companion to the Jesuits* (Cambridge: Cambridge University Press, 2008), esp. chaps. 1–3, 4, and 9.

4. Lindberg, *European Reformations*, 41–42.

5. The "Avignon papacy" usually refers to a period of time (1309–77) during which those duly elected to the office of pope, or bishop of Rome, managed the affairs of the Catholic Church from Avignon rather than from Rome. This decision had much to do with a desire on the part of the Avignon popes to maintain political ties with the powerful French kings rather than with the divergent political factions in Italy. In 1377 then-pope Gregory XI decided the time was right to return the office back to Rome. He died the following year. The election of the new pope in 1378, Urban VI, proved to have been unwise, and soon the church elected a replacement pope. Eventually a third individual also claimed the title of pope. This situation, in which at least three individuals claimed to be rightfully elected pope, led to the reestablishment of the papal court at Avignon in 1378–1417 for at least one of those three claimants. It is the second period of an Avignon papacy to which Lindberg refers in his assessment of the state of the Catholic Church. However, the Catholic Church does not consider those who reestablished the papal court at Avignon during 1378–1417 to have been duly elected and so regards them as antipopes.

6. For more on the Avignon papacy and the Council of Constance, see Joelle Rollo-Koster and Thomas Izbicki, eds., *A Companion to the Great Western Schism (1378–1417)*, Brill's Companions to the Christian Tradition 17 (Leiden: Brill, 2009); Phillip Stump, *The Reforms of the Council of Constance, 1414–1418* (Leiden: Brill, 1994).

7. For more on the medieval guilds and their place in society, see Steven Epstein, *An Economic and Social History of Later Medieval Europe, 1000–1500* (Cambridge: Cambridge University Press, 2009); Steven Epstein, *Wage Labor and Guilds in Medieval Europe* (Chapel Hill: University of North Carolina Press, 1991); Alfred Kieser, "Organizational, Institutional, and Societal Evolution: Medieval Craft Guilds and the Genesis of Formal Organizations," *Administrative Science Quarterly* 34 (1989): 540–64. There are also more specialized works about particular guilds, such as Laura Crombie, *Archery and Crossbow Guilds in Medieval Flanders, 1300–1500* (New York: Boydell, 2016).

8. Further information about the plague may be found in Joseph Byrne, *Encyclopedia of the Black Death* (Santa Barbara, CA: ABC-CLIO, 2012).

9. Scholarly and popular biographies of Luther and books on his theologies of grace and justification are not lacking. See Scott Hendrix, *Martin Luther: Visionary Reformer* (New Haven: Yale University Press, 2015); Michael Mullett, *Martin Luther*, Routledge Historical Biographies (New York: Routledge, 2015); Denis R. Janz, *The Westminster Handbook to Martin Luther* (Louisville: Westminster John Knox, 2010).

10. Peter Lombard's *Sentences*, 4 vols., trans. Giulio Silano, Medieval Sources in Translation (Toronto: Pontifical Institute for Medieval Studies, 2007, 2008, 2008, 2010), was composed by this bishop of Paris in the twelfth century. It was one of the earliest textbooks employed for the study of theology at the medieval-era universities.

11. Martin Luther, *The Christian in Society*, LW 44 (Philadelphia: Fortress, 1966), 129.

12. LW 44:130.

13. Both of these letters appear in LW 49.

14. LW 44:137.

15. Martin Luther, *Secular Authority: To What Extent It Should Be Obeyed*, in *Works of Martin Luther* (Philadelphia: Holman, 1930), 3:237. Cf. Harro Höpfil, ed., *Luther and Calvin on Secular Authority*, Cambridge Texts in the History of Political Thought (Cambridge: Cambridge University Press, 1991), 12.

16. As with Luther, biographies of John Calvin abound. See, e.g., William Bouwsma, *John Calvin: A Sixteenth-Century Portrait* (New York: Oxford University Press, 1988); Donald McKim, *The Cambridge Companion to John Calvin* (Cambridge: Cambridge University Press, 2004); Thomas Parker, *John Calvin: A Biography* (Philadelphia: Westminster, 1975).

17. John Calvin, *Institutes of the Christian Religion*, Library of Christian Classics 20–21 (Philadelphia: Westminster, 1960), 2:1486.

18. This and the preceding quotes from §3 are from ibid., 1488.

19. Ibid., 1518.

20. Ibid.

21. For further study of Calvin's notion of the two kingdoms, see Harro Höpfl, *The Christian Polity of John Calvin* (Cambridge: Cambridge University Press, 1982).

22. On the Genevan Consistory, see Robert Kingdon, "Calvin and the Establishment of Consistory Discipline in Geneva: The Institution and the Men Who Directed It," *Nederlands Archief voor Kerkgeschiedenes / Dutch Review of Church History* 70 (1990): 158–72. Kingdon has also edited the records of the Consistory (Consistoire de Genève, *Registres du Consistoire de Genève au temps de Calvin* [Grand Rapids: Eerdmans, 1996–2015]) and has translated a portion of those records. See Robert Kingdon, Isabella Watt, and Thomas Lambert, eds., *The Registers of the Consistory of Geneva at the Time of Calvin*, vol. 1, *1542–1544* (Grand Rapids: Eerdmans, 2002). See also Jeffrey Watt, "Women and the Consistory in Calvin's Geneva," *Sixteenth Century Journal* 24 (1993): 429–39.

23. On the Council of 60 and its role in Geneva's pastoral care, see Scott Manetsch, *Calvin's Company of Pastors: Pastoral Care and the Emerging Reformed Church, 1536–1609*, Oxford Studies in Historical Theology (New York: Oxford University Press, 2013).

24. A helpful resource for understanding these matters is D. G. Hart, *Calvinism: A History* (New Haven: Yale University Press, 2013).

25. For the text of these confessions in one volume, see Joel Beeke and Sinclair Ferguson, eds., *Reformed Confessions Harmonized* (Grand Rapids: Baker, 1999), esp. 198–99, 230–34.

26. For a biographical study of Ulrich Zwingli, see Jaques Courvoisier, *Zwingli: A Reformed Theologian* (Richmond: John Knox, 1963); George Potter, *Ulrich Zwingli* (Cambridge: Cambridge University Press, 1976); W. Peter Stephens, *Zwingli: An Introduction to His Thought* (Oxford: Clarendon, 1992).

27. See John H. Yoder, ed., *The Schleitheim Confession* (Scottdale, PA: Herald Press, 1977). Cf. Leland Harder, "Zwingli's Reaction to the Schleitheim Confession of Faith of the Anabaptists," *Sixteenth Century Journal* 11 (1980): 51–66.

28. For the text of the Schleitheim Confession, see, e.g., Denis R. Janz, *A Reformation Reader: Primary Texts with Introductions*, 2nd ed. (Minneapolis: Fortress, 2008), 208–11, here 208.

29. Ibid., 209.

30. Ibid., 210.

31. Ibid., 211.

32. See *The Trial and Martyrdom of Michael Sattler* (1527), the *Trial and Martyrdom of Elizabeth Dirks* (1549), and Janneken Muntsdorp's *Letter to Her Daughter* (1573), each in Janz, *Reformation Reader*, 212–14 and 228–36.

33. Samuel Torvend, *Luther and the Hungry Poor: Gathered Fragments* (Minneapolis: Fortress, 2008), esp. 40–42, 55, 77–79, 105–11.

34. John Calvin, *Sermons on Deuteronomy*, trans. Arthur Golding, Sixteenth-Seventeenth Century Facsimile Editions (Edinburgh: Banner of Truth, 1987), a reprint of the only ET ever made, in 1583. Text is accessible online at several locations.

35. LW 45.

36. For the "Letter on Usury," see, e.g., Janz, *Reformation Reader*, 262–65; and online.

Chapter 9 Post-Reformations Era

1. The right of rulers to establish a religion in their region had earlier been decided by the Peace of Augsburg (1555). From it emerged the principle *cuius regio, eius religio* (whose realm, his religion).

2. Thomas Hobbes, *Leviathan*, ed. C. B. Macpherson (London: Penguin, 1985); John Locke, *Two Treatises of Government and a Letter concerning Toleration* (New Haven: Yale University Press, 2003). For more on the documentary evidence connecting Locke's influence (among others) to America's "founding fathers," see John E. Semonche, *Religion and Constitutional Government in the United States: A Historical Overview with Sources* (Carrboro, NC: Signal Books, 1986).

3. This separation of the church from the state had been hard won by earlier Baptists and Radical Reformers. As far back as 1612, Baptist leader John Smyth had written, "The magistrate is not by virtue of his office to meddle with religion, or matters of conscience," and Thomas Helwys had written that the king had "nothing to do" with the church. Then, two years later, a member of Helwys's congregation, Leonard Busher, wrote *Religious Peace; or, a Plea for Liberty of Conscience*. Frustrated by the increasing pressure on nonconformist groups to more fully align with the Church of England, Busher wrote in his text, "No King nor Bishops can, or is able to command faith, *That is the gift of God, who worketh in vs both the wil & the deed of his owne good pleasure*, set him not a day therefore, in which, if his creature heare not and beleeue not, you will imprison and burne him" (emphasis original); Leonard Bucher, *Religious Peace* (London: John Bachilor, 1646), 2. See the full text of this work: http://quod.lib.umich .edu/e/eebo/A17345.0001.001. Cf. J. de Hoop Scheffer, *History of the Free Churchmen Called the Brownists, Pilgrim Fathers and Baptists in the Dutch Republic, 1581–1701*, ed. William Elliot Griffis (Ithaca, NY: Andrus & Church, 1922), 176–77.

4. US House of Representatives, "June 8, 1789," in *Annals of Congress. 1st Congress. 1st Session* (Philadelphia: US Congress, 1789), 451.

5. James Madison, "To F. L. Schaeffer (Letter dated December 3, 1821)," in *Letters and Other Writings of James Madison, in Four Volumes: Published by Order of Congress* (Philadelphia: Lippincott, 1865), 3:242–43.

6. Thomas Jefferson, "Letter to the Danbury Baptist Association (January 1, 1802)," in "Jefferson's Letter to the Danbury Baptists: The Draft and Recently Discovered Text," *Library of Congress Information Bulletin* 57, no. 6 (June 1998). Online: http://www.loc.gov/loc/lcib/9806 /danpost.html.

7. René Descartes, *Discourse on Method and Meditations in Philosophy* (New York: Hackett, 1999).

8. Giorgio de Santillana, *The Crime of Galileo* (Chicago: University of Chicago Press, 1967), 312.

9. For more on the Second Great Awakening, see John H. Armstrong, ed., "The Second Great Awakening," *Reformation and Revival* 6 (1997): 9–182, with articles about leading figures and events that shaped the Second Great Awakening. Cf. Barry Hankins, *The Second Great Awakening and the Transcendentalists* (Westport, CT: Greenwood, 2004).

10. Reinhold Niebuhr, "The Quality of Our Lives," *Christian Century*, May 11, 1960, 568.

11. Karl Barth, *The Knowledge of God and the Service of God according to the Teaching of the Reformation: Recalling the Scottish Confession of 1560* (London: Hodder & Stoughton,

1938); Emil Brunner, *The Divine Imperative: A Study in Christian Ethics* (Philadelphia: Westminster, 1932; repr., 1947); Reinhold Niebuhr, *Moral Man and Immoral Society: A Study in Ethics and Politics*, Library of Theological Ethics (Philadelphia: Westminster, 1932; 2nd ed., Louisville: Westminster John Knox, 2013).

12. This fourfold division comes from Henry Parker, *A Discourse concerning Puritans*, 2nd ed. (London: Printed for Robert Bostock, 1641), 13, as cited by Christopher Hill, *Society and Puritanism in Pre-Revolutionary England* (New York: Schocken Books, 1964), 20.

13. Hill, *Society and Puritanism*, 124–44.

14. Thomas Hooker, *A Survey of the Summe of Church-Discipline* (London: Printed by A. M. for John Bellamy, 1648), 188, as cited in Stephen Foster, *Their Solitary Way: The Puritan Social Ethic in the First Century of Settlement in New England* (New Haven: Yale University Press, 1971), 16.

15. Foster, *Their Solitary Way*, 67–68.

16. Ibid., 23n25.

17. Ibid., 90.

18. Ibid., 99–103. In critique of this aspect of the social covenant, Foster remarks that it "provided one more justification for inequality among men" (102).

19. Ibid., 132.

20. F. L. Cross and E. A. Livingston, eds., "John Wesley," in *The Oxford Dictionary of the Christian Church* (Oxford: Oxford University Press, 1997), 1727–28.

21. At that time the phrase "sweating system" referred to the practice of companies exploiting their laborers by giving them raw materials and then expecting the laborers to produce the final goods in their own homes. Worse still, the companies only paid the laborers for the number of units ultimately produced rather than for the hours spent in production. Congress conducted an investigation into such practices and condemned them in a report in 1893 (House Report No. 2309, dated Feb. 8, 1893), but the practices continued.

22. Text of the law appears in Samuel Parker, *A Textbook in the History of Modern Elementary Education* (Chicago: Ginn & Co., 1912), 60.

23. Manfred Marquardt, *John Wesley's Social Ethics: Praxis and Principles* (Nashville: Abingdon, 1992), 54.

24. For more on the history of Sunday schools in America, see Anne Boylan, *Sunday School: The Formation of an American Institution, 1790–1880* (New Haven: Yale University Press, 1988); Edwin Rice, *The Sunday School Movement, 1780–1917, and the American Sunday-School Union, 1817–1917* (New York: Arno, 1971); Jack Seymour, *From Sunday School to Church School: Continuities in Protestant Church Education in the United States, 1860–1929* (Lanham, MD: University Press of America, 1982).

25. Horace Mann's own writings on the subject are in *Horace Mann on the Crisis in Education*, ed. Louis Filler (Lanham, MD: University Press of America, 1983); cf. Robert Downs, *Horace Mann: Champion of Public Schools* (New York: Twayne, 1974).

26. Cf. William Ringenberg, *The Christian College: A History of Protestant Higher Education in America*, 2nd ed. (Grand Rapids: Baker Academic, 2006).

27. Marquardt, *John Wesley's Social Ethics*, 68.

28. Jacob H. Dorn, "The Social Gospel and Socialism: A Comparison of the Thought of Francis Greenwood Peabody, Washington Gladden, and Walter Rauschenbusch," *Church History* 62 (1993): 82–100, here 84.

29. Francis Peabody, *Jesus Christ and the Social Question: An Examination of the Teaching of Jesus in Its Relation to Some of the Problems of Modern Social Life* (New York: Macmillan, 1900), 5–20. Cf. Dorn, "Social Gospel and Socialism," 85–86.

30. See Martin Luther King Jr., "Pilgrimage to Nonviolence," *Christian Century*, April 13, 1960, 439–41, esp. 440; also online: https://kinginstitute.stanford.edu/king-papers/documents/pilgrimage-nonviolence.

31. E.g., David P. Gushee and Glen Stassen, *Kingdom Ethics: Following Jesus in Contemporary Context*, 2nd ed. (Grand Rapids: Eerdmans, 2016); Glen Stassen, *A Thicker Jesus: Incarnational Discipleship in a Secular Age* (Louisville: Westminster John Knox, 2013).

While not a particular proponent of social gospel theology, Ron Sider's work *Rich Christians in an Age of Hunger*, rev. ed. (Nashville: Nelson, 2005), nevertheless addresses significant issues in structural and social sins around economic justice. His work certainly highlights the types of concerns that animated the earlier social gospel proponents. Also, the work of social ethicist and Mennonite scholar John Howard Yoder is worth mentioning, particularly his extensive writings on pacifism and social justice, including his best-known work, *The Politics of Jesus*, 2nd ed. (Grand Rapids: Eerdmans, 1994). However, in recent years many details have emerged regarding his exploitation of and inappropriate contacts with women during his years of ministry and teaching (see, e.g., David Cramer, Jenny Howell, Paul Martens, and Jonathan Tran, "Theology and Misconduct: The Case of John Howard Yoder," *Christian Century*, August 20, 2014, 20–23). I mention him briefly here because of his influence but also want to avoid promoting his work any further due to his actions.

Chapter 10 Contemporary Catholic Social Ethics

1. The text of the Joint Declaration on the Doctrine of Justification (1999) is online: http://www.vatican.va/roman_curia/pontifical_councils/chrstuni/documents/rc_pc_chrstuni _doc_31101999_cath-luth-joint-declaration_en.html.

2. For more on antimodernism campaigns in the Catholic Church's history, see Darrell Jodock, *Catholicism Contending with Moderning: Roman Catholicism and Anti-Modernism in Historical Context* (Cambridge: Cambridge University Press, 2000); Marvin O'Connell, *Critics on Trial: An Introduction to the Catholic Modernist Crisis* (Washington, DC: Catholic University of America Press, 1995); Don O'Leary, *Roman Catholicism and Modern Science: A History* (New York: Continuum, 2006).

3. For further information on Vatican Council I, see Roger Aubert, *Vatican I*, Histoire des conciles oecuméniques 12 (Paris: Éditions de l'Orante, 1964); Kristin Colberg, *Vatican I and Vatican II: Councils in the Living Tradition* (Collegeville, MN: Liturgical Press, 2016); Richard Costigan, *The Consensus of the Church and Papal Infallibility: A Study in the Background of Vatican I* (Washington, DC: Catholic University of America Press, 2005).

4. Most of the academic literature on John XXIII's call for aggiornamento is in languages other than English. However, see Jonathan Robinson, *Faith and Reform: A Reinterpretation of Aggiornamento* (New York: Fordham University Press, 1969); Karim Schelkens et al., eds., *Aggiornamento? Catholicism from Gregory XVI to Benedict XVI* (Leiden: Brill, 2013). On John XXIII, see Thomas Cahill, *Pope John XXIII*, Penguin Lives Series (New York: Viking, 2002); Massimo Faggioli, *John XXIII: The Medicine of Mercy* (Collegeville, MN: Liturgical Press, 2014).

5. There is an overwhelming amount of literature on Vatican II, as it continues to be a subject of debate within the Catholic Church. The texts of the council are available in Austin Flannery, ed., *Vatican Council II*, vol. 1, *The Conciliar and Post Conciliar Documents*, rev. ed. (Northport, NY: Costello, 1975). See also the resources produced by the Center for the Study of Vatican II, at the Catholic University of Leuven, Belgium. Such works include Lieven Boeve, Mathijs Lamberigts, and Terrence Merrigan, eds., *The Contested Legacy of Vatican II: Lessons and Prospects* (Leuven: Peeters, 2015).

6. For more on the decline in religious vocations within the Catholic Church, see Laurie Felknor, ed., *The Crisis in Religious Vocations: An Inside View* (New York: Paulist Press, 1989); Rodney Stark and Roger Finke, "Catholic Religious Vocations: Decline and Revival," *Review of Religious Research* 42, no. 2 (2000): 125–45.

7. For a listing of documents that comprise Catholic social teaching, see David J. O'Brien and Thomas A. Shannon, *Catholic Social Thought: The Documentary Heritage* (Maryknoll,

NY: Orbis Books, 1992); Kenneth Himes, ed., *Modern Catholic Social Teaching: Commentaries and Interpretations* (Washington, DC: Georgetown University Press, 2005). For Catholic social teaching that predates the late nineteenth century, see Michael Schuck, *That They Be One: The Social Teaching of the Papal Encyclicals, 1740–1989* (Washington, DC: Georgetown University Press, 1991).

8. *Quadragesimo anno* §§91–98. Cf. the commentary on *Quadragesimo anno* in Oswald von Nell-Breuning, *Reorganization of Social Economy: The Social Encyclical Developed and Explained*, trans. Bernard W. Dempsey (New York: Bruce, 1936); J. Kelly, "The Influence of Aquinas' Natural Law Theory on the Principle of Corporatism in the Thought of Leo XIII and Pius XI," in *Things Old and New: Catholic Social Teaching Revisited*, ed. Francis McHugh et al. (Lanham, MD: University Press of America, 1993).

9. This phrase has been employed in a great breadth of topics by Catholics (and also Protestants). See, e.g., T. Howland Sanks, ed., *Reading the Signs of the Times: Resources for Social and Cultural Analysis* (Mahwah, NJ: Paulist Press, 1993); Stephen Torraco, "From 'Social Justice' to 'Reading the Signs of the Times': The Hermeneutical Crisis of Catholic Social Teaching," in *Faith Seeking Understanding: Learning and the Catholic Tradition* (Manchester, NH: Saint Anselm College Press, 1991), 247–60.

10. US Conference of Catholic Bishops, "Economic Justice for All" (1986).

11. US Conference of Catholic Bishops, "The Challenge of Peace" (1983).

12. These are called the CELAM documents. The abbreviation stands for Consejo Episcopal Latinoamericano, the bishops' conference in Latin America. Included within this collection are documents written during meetings in Medellín (1968) and Puebla (1979); the latter promoted the idea of a "preferential option for the poor."

13. Gustavo Gutiérrez, *A Theology of Liberation: History, Politics, and Salvation* (Maryknoll, NY: Orbis Books, 1973; rev. ed., 1988).

14. See, e.g., the story of Óscar Romero in *Romero's Legacy: The Call to Peace and Justice*, ed. Pilar Closeky and John Hogan (Lanham, MD: Rowman & Littlefield, 2007).

15. The documentary evidence for this has been collected in Alfred Hennelly, ed., *Liberation Theology: A Documentary History* (Maryknoll, NY: Orbis Books, 1990).

16. The phrase "domestic church" seems to have originated with John Chrysostom, *Sermons on Genesis* 6.2 and 7.1. See John Chrysostom, *Sermons sur la Genèse*, ed. Laurence Brottier, SC 433 (Paris: Éditions du Cerf, 1998), 296, 302. It was picked up in two documents from Vatican II, *Lumen gentium* (1964) and *Apostolicam actuositatem* (1965), then later in *Evangelii nuntiandi* §71 (1975), and again in *Familiaris consortio* (1981). For further study of the history of the use of the phrase "domestic church," including its recovery and usage in Catholic teaching, see Florence Caffrey Bourg, *Where Two or Three Are Gathered: Christian Families as Domestic Churches* (Notre Dame, IN: University of Notre Dame Press, 2003).

Chapter 11 Human Dignity

1. Mette Lebech, "What Is Human Dignity?," *Maynooth Philosophical Papers* (2006): 59–69, here 59.

2. Cf. Matt. 22:36–40 and John 13:35.

3. For more on the connection between agency and human dignity, see R. Jerome Boone, "Created for Shalom: Human Agency and Responsibility in the World," in *Spirit Renews the Face of the Earth: Pentecostal Forays in Science and Theology of Creation*, ed. Amos Yong (Eugene, OR: Pickwick, 2009), 17–29; Richard Bosley, "Being Human: The Problem of Agency," *Religious Studies and Theology* 23 (2004): 143–50; Alisa Carse, "Vulnerability, Agency, and Human Flourishing," in *Health and Human Flourishing: Religion, Medicine, and Moral Anthropology* (Washington, DC: Georgetown University Press, 2006), 33–52; Thomas Pfau, *Minding the Modern: Human Agency, Intellectual Traditions, and Responsible Knowledge* (Notre Dame,

IN: University of Notre Dame Press, 2013); R. Kendall Soulen and Linda Whitehead, eds., *God and Human Dignity* (Grand Rapids: Eerdmans, 2006).

4. Literature on the connection between human dignity and human rights is vast. See, e.g., Michael Novak, "Human Dignity, Human Rights," *First Things* 97 (1999): 39–42; cf. Alfons Brüning, "Different Humans and Different Rights? On Human Dignity from Western and Eastern Orthodox Perspectives," *Studies in Interreligious Dialogue* 23 (2013): 150–75; Johannes Fischer, "Human Dignity and Human Rights," *Zeitschrift für evangelische Ethik* 58 (2014): 40–50; Glenn Hughes, "The Concept of Dignity in the Universal Declaration of Human Rights," *Journal of Religious Ethics* 39 (2011): 1–24; Troels Nørager, "Theistic or Secular Grounding of Human Rights? Human Dignity according to Nicholas Wolterstorff and George Kateb," *Studia Theologica* 68 (2014): 100–121; Bharat Ranganathan, "Should Inherent Human Dignity Be Considered Intrinsically Heuristic?," *Journal of Religious Ethics* 42 (2014): 770–75; Jordan Wessling, "A Dilemma for Wolterstorff's Theistic Grounding of Human Dignity and Rights," *International Journal for Philosophy of Religion* 76 (2014): 277–95.

5. J. Witte, *The Reformation of Rights: Law, Religion, and Human Rights in Early Modern Calvinism* (Cambridge: Cambridge University Press, 2007), 57–58.

6. For more on the connections between human dignity and the *imago Dei* in the Christian tradition, see Thomas Howard, ed., *Imago Dei: Human Dignity in Ecumenical Perspective* (Washington, DC: Catholic University of America Press, 2014); Joan O'Donovan, "Human Dignity and Human Justice: Thinking with Calvin about the *Imago Dei*," *Tyndale Bulletin* 66 (2015): 121–36; Riccardo Saccenti, "The 'Imago Dei' in Scholastic Theology (XIIth–XIIIth Centuries)," in *The Image of God: Foundations and Objections within the Discourse on Human Dignity; Proceedings of the Colloquium Bologna and Rossena (July 2009) in Honour of Pier Cesare Bori*, ed. Alberto Melloni and Riccardo Saccenti (Berlin: Lit, 2010), 295–313; Claudia Welz, ed., *Ethics of Invisibility: Imago Dei, Memory, and Human Dignity in Jewish and Christian Thought* (Tübingen: Mohr Siebeck, 2015); John Kilner, ed., *Why People Matter: Christian Engagement with Rival Views of Human Significance* (Grand Rapids: Baker Academic, 2017).

7. The capacity of animals to reason is the subject of controversy in academic and popular literature and animates discussion about the rights of animals in terms of their use for medical testing and our consumption of them for food. David Hume (1711–76) famously investigated the subject in "Of the Reason of Animals," in *An Enquiry concerning Human Understanding* (London: Printed for A. Millar, 1748, online: http://www.davidhume.org/texts/ehu.html). For more on this subject, see Gary Matthews, "Augustine and Descartes on the Souls of Animals," in *From Soul to Self*, ed. M. James C. Crabbe (London: Routledge, 1999), 89–107; David Werther, "Animal Reason and the Imago Dei," *Religious Studies* 24 (1988): 325–35; Basil Wrighton, *Reason, Religion and the Animals* (Washington, DC: Catholic Study Circle for Animal Welfare, 1987).

8. For more on sin and its impact on the *imago Dei*, see Paul Allen, "Sin and Natural Theology: An Augustinian Framework beyond Barth," *Neue Zeitschrift für systematische Theologie und Religionsphilosophie* 57 (2015): 14–31; Nathaniel Sutanto, "Herman Bavinck on the Image of God and Original Sin," *International Journal of Systematic Theology* 18 (2016): 174–90; Heather Thomson, "Fallen Image and Redeemed Dust: Being Human in God's Creation," *St Mark's Review* 212 (2010): 65–74; Nicolaas Vorster, "Calvin on the Created Structure of Human Nature: The Influence of His Anthropology on His Theology," *Journal of Theology for Southern Africa* 151 (2015): 162–81; Daniel Weiss, "Direct Divine Sanction, the Prohibition of Bloodshed, and the Individual as Image of God in Classical Rabbinic Literature," *Journal of the Society of Christian Ethics* 32 (2012): 23–38.

9. For Augustine, *De Trinitate*, see Saint Augustine, *The Trinity*, trans. Edmund Hill, Works of Saint Augustine (New York: New City Press, 1991); for *De libero arbitrio*, see Augustine, *On the Free Choice of the Will, On Grace and Free Choice, and Other Writings*, trans. Peter King (Cambridge: Cambridge University Press, 2010).

10. Thomas Aquinas, *ST*, vol. 16, page 1.

11. John Calvin, *Institutes* 1.15.7.

12. See Thomas V. Berg and Edward J. Furton, eds., *Human Embryo Adoption: Biotechnology, Marriage, and the Right to Life* (Thornwood, NY: Westchester Institute for Ethics and the Human Person, 2006); Sandra Johnson et al., eds., *Health Law and Bioethics: Cases in Context* (New York: Aspen, 2009); John F. Kilner, Paige C. Cunningham, and W. David Hager, eds., *The Reproduction Revolution: A Christian Appraisal of Sexuality, Reproductive Technologies, and the Family* (Grand Rapids: Eerdmans, 2000).

Chapter 12 Common Good

1. It will prove helpful to some readers to have an acquaintance with the language resources lying behind the phrase "common good," since there are a range of terms from which this idea emerged. In the Western intellectual tradition, one can look back to the Greek or Roman philosophers. In Greek, the most natural expression would be *koinon agathon*, but, surprisingly, it is quite uncommon. Similarly, the phrase *koinon sympheron* (common advantage), which lends itself to a materialistic notion, is nearly as rare. Somewhat more common is Aristotle's *koinon lysiteloun* (common profit), but most common is *koinon ōpheleia*, or the crasis *koinōphelēs* (common profit or benefit), which are found in the Greek fathers of the Christian church. This construction lends itself to a variety of contexts for the fathers, to include the Christian as well as the political community. Anything that contributes to health or stability in those communities may be deemed for *koinōphelēs*. On the Latin side, Cicero used two expressions: *salus populi* (health of the people) and *utilitatis communione* (community of interests). These expressions lend themselves to intangible, rather than materialistic, ideas of what is the common good. Not dissimilarly, Augustine used the expression *bonum commune* when talking about what is the type of life offered to citizens in the city of God, as opposed to the inhumanity and discontent found in the earthly city, and it is this expression that we find in the writings of most Western intellectuals of the Middle Ages and later periods.

2. Theodoret of Cyrus, *Comm. on Romans* 12.4–5 (PG 82:188). See also Gregory of Nyssa, *De vita s. Ephraem* (PG 46:841); Gregory of Nyssa, *On Virginity* 2 (GNO 8.1:255); Origen, *Contra Celsum* 7.59–60; Ps.-Chrysostom, *In parabolam de filio prodigo* 1 (PG 59:515); John Chrysostom, *Homilies on Matthew* 78.3 (7.775A; PG 58:714; ET in NPNF[1] 10:472).

3. Basil, *Homilies* 6.5, ET by M. F. Toal, *Sunday Sermons of the Great Fathers* (London: Henry Regnery, 1967), 3:329, slightly altered.

4. Cf. Roman Garrison, *Redemptive Almsgiving in Early Christianity*, Library of New Testament Studies (New York: Bloomsbury Academic, 2015).

5. Cf. John Chrysostom, *Homilies on Matthew* 77.5, urging everyone to share what they have and then focusing principally on why the wealthy must distribute their goods. See also John Chrysostom, *Peccata fratrum non evulganda* [*Against Publicly Exposing the Sins of the Brethren*] 1 (PG 51:355); John Chrysostom, *Homilies on 1 Corinthians* 10.4; John Chrysostom, *Homilies on John* 15.3.

6. Gregory of Nazianzus, *Oration* 4.75 (PG 35:600); ET in C. W. King, *Julian the Emperor, Containing Gregory Nazianzen's Two Invectives and Libanius' Monody* (London: George Bell & Sons, 1888), 44, with a change only of King's "peculators" to "embezzlers." Similarly, we read a lengthy diatribe about the effect of oppressive taxation on the good of communities (particularly on the artisans, tradespeople, and the poor within the communities), in Salvian of Marseille's mid-fifth-century text *De gubernatore Dei* 5; see *Oeuvres*, vol. 2, *Du gouvernement de Dieu*, ed. Georges Lagarrigue, SC 220 (Paris: Cerf, 1975), 310–58; ET, *The Writings of Salvian the Presbyter*, trans. Jeremiah F. O'Sullivan, FC 3 (Washington, DC: Catholic University of America Press, 1947), 127–50.

7. Augustine, *City of God* 14.28; ET in *Augustine: City of God, Christian Doctrine*, trans. Marcus Dods, NPNF[1] 2:282–83; see also Robert A. Markus, "*De civitate Dei*: Pride and the Common Good," in *Collectanea Augustiniana: Augustine: "Second Founder of the Faith,"* ed.

Joseph C. Schnaubelt and Frederick Van Fleteren (Frankfurt: Peter Lang, 1990), 245–59, esp. 253–54. See also Basil of Caesarea, *Homilies* 12.2 (aka *Homilia in principium Proverbiorum*; PG 31:389), which praises the biblical king Solomon for his goodness, a goodness that manifests itself in his looking out for the common good rather than his own private good.

8. Irenaeus, *Against Heresies* 5.24 (*ANF* 1:552).

9. Cf. Clement of Alexandria, *Stromateis* 1.27 (*ANF* 2:339); John Chrysostom, *Homilies on the Acts of the Apostles* 5.4 (PG 60:55).

10. Jean Porter, "The Common Good in Thomas Aquinas," in *In Search of the Common Good*, ed. Dennis P. McCann and Patrick D. Miller (New York: T&T Clark, 2005), 94–120, here 96. Porter documents several differences between Augustine and the twelfth-century context out of which Aquinas emerged and exposes some reasons why Aquinas writes of the common good in natural-law terms as opposed to the theological terms used by Augustine.

11. Thomas Aquinas, *ST* 13:133–35.

12. Cf. Yong Won Son, "The Common Good in the Theology of John Calvin," PhD diss., University of Edinburgh, 2012.

13. LW 31:371.

14. LW 45:92.

15. Cf. Wanda Diefelt, "Seeking the Common Good: Lutheran Contributions to Global Citizenship," *Intersections* 29 (2009): 22–27.

16. Cf. Jeremy Bentham, *Introduction to the Principles of Morals and Legislation* (London: T. Payne & Son, 1789), which introduced the concept of utility as happiness for the greatest number of people; John Stuart Mill, *Utilitarianism* (London: Longman, Green, Reader & Dyer, 1867).

Chapter 13 Justice

1. D. W. Boonstra, "The Idea of Justice in Christian Perspective," *Calvin Theological Journal* 14 (1979): 271; Daniel Maguire, "The Primacy of Justice in Moral Theology," *Horizons* 10 (1983): 72–85; J. Philip Wogaman, "Toward a Christian Definition of Justice," *Transformation* 7 (1990): 18–23. Cf. Wayne P. Pomerleau, "Western Theories of Justice," in *Internet Encyclopedia of Philosophy*, www.iep.utm.edu/justwest/.

2. Here I am indebted to Mary Elsbernd and Reimund Bieringer, *When Love Is Not Enough: A Theo-Ethic of Justice* (Collegeville, MN: Liturgical Press, 2002), chap. 5. Cf. Karen Lebacqz, *Six Theories of Justice: Perspectives from Theological and Philosophical Ethics* (Minneapolis: Augsburg, 1986).

3. Linell Cady, "Hermeneutics and Tradition: The Role of the Past in Jurisprudence and Theology," *Harvard Theological Review* 79 (1986): 439–63; Ronald Dworkin, "'Natural Law' Revisited," *University of Florida Law Review* 34 (1982): 165–88.

4. Reinhold Niebuhr, *Love and Justice: Selections from the Shorter Writings of Reinhold Niebuhr*, ed. D. B. Robertson (Philadelphia: Westminster, 1957); Merle Longwood, "Niebuhr and a Theory of Justice," *Dialog* 14 (1975): 253–62; Jenny Wright, "Justice between Fairness and Love? Christian Ethics in Dialogue with Rawls and Niebuhr," *International Journal of Public Theology* 6 (2012): 306–28.

5. John Rawls, *A Theory of Justice* (Cambridge, MA: Harvard University Press, 1971). Cf. Henry Clark, "Justice as Fairness and Christian Ethics," *Soundings* 56 (1973): 359–69. See also the debate between Harlan Beckley and Gregory Jones: Harlan Beckley, "A Christian Affirmation of Rawls's Idea of Justice as Fairness, Part 1," *Journal of Religious Ethics* 13 (1985): 210–42, and "Part 2," *Journal of Religious Ethics* 14 (1986): 229–46; L. Gregory Jones, "Should Christians affirm Rawls' Justice as Fairness: A Response to Professor Beckley," *Journal of Religious Ethics* 16 (1988): 251–71.

6. Edward Gardner, "Justice, Virtue, and Law," *Journal of Law and Religion* 2 (1984): 393–412; David Herbert, "Virtue Ethics, Justice and Religion in Multicultural Societies," in

Virtue Ethics and Sociology: Issues of Modernity and Religion (Hampshire, UK: Palgrave, 2001), 51–67; Alasdair MacIntyre, *After Virtue: A Study in Moral Theology* (Notre Dame, IN: University of Notre Dame Press, 1984); Alasdair MacIntyre, *Whose Justice? Which Rationality?* (Notre Dame, IN: University of Notre Dame Press, 1988); Charles Taylor, "Justice after Virtue," in *After MacIntyre: Critical Perspectives on the Work of Alasdair MacIntyre*, ed. John Horton and Susan Mendus (Cambridge, UK: Polity, 1994).

7. This theory is built on the "normativity of the future" hermeneutical model for reading Scripture devised by Reimund Bieringer and Mary Elsbernd, with Susan M. Garthwaite et al., *Normativity of the Future: Reading Biblical and Other Authoritative Texts in an Eschatological Perspective*, Annua Nuntia Lovaniensia 61 (Leuven: Peeters, 2009). The model's application to justice is argued in Elsbernd and Bieringer, *When Love Is Not Enough*, chap. 6.

8. Elsbernd and Bieringer, *When Love Is Not Enough*, 150.

9. H. G. Liddell and R. Scott, *Greek-English Lexicon with a Revised Supplement* (Oxford: Clarendon, 1996), 429, s.v. *dikaiosynē*.

10. For more on justice in the Bible, see Matthew Coomber, *Bible and Justice: Ancient Texts, Modern Challenges* (London: Oakville, 2011); John Donahue, *Seek Justice That You May Live: Reflections and Resources on the Bible and Social Justice* (New York: Paulist Press, 2014); J. B. Payne, "Justice," in *New Bible Dictionary* (repr., Downers Grove, IL: InterVarsity, 1991), 644–46; Nicholas Wolterstorff, "Why Care about Justice?," *Reformed Journal* (1986): 9–14.

11. Augustine, *Concerning the Morals of the Catholic Church*, trans. Richard Stothert, NPNF[1] (repr., Peabody, MA: Hendrickson, 1995), 4:48.

12. Augustine, *City of God* 2–3; trans. Marcus Dods, in NPNF[2] (repr., Peabody, MA: Hendrickson, 1995), 2:23–63.

13. Augustine, *The Teacher, The Free Choice of the Will, Grace and Free Will*, trans. Robert Russell, FC 59 (Washington, DC: Catholic University of America Press, 2004), 80–83.

14. For more on the concept of justice in Thomas Aquinas, see Matthias Lutz-Bachmann, "The Discovery of a Normative Theory of Justice in Medieval Philosophy: On the Reception and Further Development of Aristotle's Theory of Justice by St. Thomas Aquinas," *Medieval Philosophy and Theology* 9 (2000): 1–14; Jean Porter, "The Virtue of Justice (IIa IIae, qq. 58–122)," in *Ethics of Aquinas* (Washington, DC: Georgetown University Press, 2002), 272–86. For justice in Luther, see Ferdinand Cranz, *An Essay on the Development of Luther's Thought on Justice, Law, and Society* (Mifflintown, PA: Sigler, 1998); Heinz Bluhm, "Idea of Justice in Luther's First Publication," *Concordia Theological Monthly* 37 (1966): 565–72; A. W. G. Raath, "The Justness of Love: The Essence and Status of Justice in Luther's Theology," *Studia Historiae Ecclesiasticae* 32 (2006): 335–54. For Calvin and the Reformed tradition, see Carol Johnston, "Essential Connections: Spirituality and Justice in a Reformed Perspective," *Church & Society* 83 (1992): 33–41; Michael Turner, "The Place of Desert in Theological Conceptions of Distributive Justice: Insights from Calvin and Rawls," *Journal of The Society of Christian Ethics* 31 (2011): 131–49; Calvin Van Reken, "The Church's Role in Social Justice," *Calvin Theological Journal* 34 (1999): 198–202; Peter Vander Meulen, "The Church and Social Justice," *Calvin Theological Journal* 34 (1999): 202–6.

15. Thomas Hobbes, *Leviathan*, trans. J. C. A. Gaskin, Oxford World's Classics (Oxford: Oxford University Press, 1998).

16. David Hume, *Enquiries concerning Human Understanding and concerning the Principles of Morals*, trans. L. A. Selby-Bigge and P. H. Nidditch, 3rd ed. (Oxford: Oxford University Press, 1975), 21.

17. Immanuel Kant, *Fundamental Principles of the Metaphysics of Morals*, trans. Mary Gregory and Jens Timmerman, Cambridge Texts in the History of Philosophy (Cambridge: Cambridge University Press, 2012), 58.

Chapter 14 Solidarity

1. Fuller treatment of this definition for solidarity may be found in Marie Bilgrien, "Solidarity as a Virtue and the Common Good," in *Foundation Theology 2000: Faculty Essays for Ministry Professionals* (Bristol, IN: Wyndham Hall Press, 2000), 1–18; Danny Collum, "Roots of the Common Good," *Sojourners Magazine* 41 (2012): 48, "Solidarity may be all but dead in our politics, but . . . [it] still lives around the edges of our culture"; John Fitzgerald, "Law's Virtues: Fostering Autonomy and Solidarity in American Society," *Journal of Law and Religion* 30 (2015): 339–42; Elizabeth Hinson-Hasty, "Solidarity and Social Gospel: Historical and Contemporary Perspectives," *American Journal of Theology and Philosophy* 37 (2016): 137–50; Douglas Sturm, "Resisting Individualism, Advocating Solidarity," in *Resist! Christian Dissent for the 21st Century* (Maryknoll, NY: Orbis Books, 2008), 137–58.

2. John Paul II, *Sollicitudo rei socialis* (Rome: Libreria Editrice Vaticana, 1987).

3. There is an interesting evaluation of the notion of "limited solidarity" as a realistic approach to the common good in David Hollenbach, *The Common Good and Christian Ethics* (Cambridge: Cambridge University Press, 2002), esp. 173–211.

4. For more on the role sin plays in constructive reflection on solidarity as a social ethic, see Ada María Isasi-Díaz, "To Be Fully Alive Is to Work for the Common Good: Spirituality, Justice, and Solidarity Are Combined in This Struggle," *Church & Society* 89 (1998): 11–18; John Langan, "Solidarity, Sin, Common Good, and Responsibility for Change in Contemporary Society," in *The Making of an Economic Vision: John Paul II's "On Social Concern"* (Lanham, MD: University Press of America, 1991), 275–85; Clint Le Bruyns, "Religion and the Economy? On Public Responsibility through Prophetic Intelligence, Theology and Solidarity," *Journal of Theology for Southern Africa* 42 (2012): 80–97; John Sheveland, "Restoring Intimacy: Christian-Buddhist Resources toward Solidarity," *Studies in Interreligious Dialogue* 24 (2014): 152–70.

5. Racial deed covenants in housing sale contracts were ubiquitous in America well into the mid-twentieth century. The University of Washington has compiled a list of over 400 such covenants in the Seattle metropolitan area alone: http://depts.washington.edu/civilr/covenants _database.htm. Further analysis of this issue appears in Jeffrey Gonda, *Unjust Deeds: The Restrictive Covenant Cases and the Making of the Civil Rights Movement* (Chapel Hill: University of North Carolina Press, 2015); Clement Vose, *Caucasians Only: The Supreme Court, the NAACP, and the Restrictive Covenant Cases* (Berkeley: University of California Press, 1959); Charles Abrams, "Homes for Aryans Only: The Restrictive Covenant Spreads Legal Racism in America," *Commentary* 3 (1947): 421–27.

6. For more on the connections between the concepts of solidarity and "option for the poor," see Stephen Pope, ed., *Hope and Solidarity: Jon Sobrino's Challenge to Christian Theology* (Maryknoll, NY: Orbis Books, 2008).

7. Cf., e.g., *Epistle to Diognetus* 10.1–6; Shepherd of Hermas, *Visions* 3.9; Clement of Alexandria, *Miscellanies* 3.6–8 and *Paedogogus* 2.12; Cyril of Alexandria, *Paschal Homilies* 11.5; Basil of Caesarea, *Homilies* 7 ("Against the Rich") and *Homilies* 8 ("In the Time of Famine and Drought") §8; Gregory of Nazianzus, *Orations* 14.25; John Chrysostom, *Homilies on 1 Timothy* 12.4 and *Homilies on Matthew* 77.3; Theodoret of Cyrus, *Discourses on Providence* 6.25–27.

8. Further reflection on this question appears in Michael Novak, *The Catholic Ethic and the Spirit of Capitalism* (New York: Free Press, 1993), 147–52; Manfred Spieker, "The Universal Destination of Goods: The Ethics of Property in the Theory of a Christian Society," *Journal of Markets and Morality* 8 (2005): 333–54

9. For the legal tradition that emerged, see the twelfth-century foundational text in Gratian, *Decretum* 47: *Decretum Magistri Gratiani*, in *Corpus Iuris Canonici*, ed. Emil Friedberg, vol. 1 (Leipzig: Bernhard Tauchnitz, 1879). Thomas Aquinas discusses the same question at *ST* II-II, q. 66, art. 7.

10. Cf., e.g., Ambrose of Milan, *On Naboth* 53; John Chrysostom, *Homilies on Lazarus* 2.5; Gregory the Great, *Rule for Pastors* 3.21.

11. For more on the Old Testament covenants and their relationship to the gentile nations, see Martin Goodman et al., eds., *Abraham, the Nations, and the Hagarites: Jewish, Christian, and Islamic Perspectives on Kinship with Abraham* (Leiden: Brill, 2010). Cf. Walter Kaiser, "Davidic Promise and the Inclusion of the Gentiles (Amos 9:9–15 and Acts 15:13–18): A Test Passage for Theological Systems," *Journal of the Evangelical Theological Society* 20 (1977): 97–111; Lothar Ruppert, "The Foreigner and Association with Foreigners in the Old and New Testaments," *Covenant Quarterly* 55 (1997): 151–63.

12. Cf. Dieter Hessel, "Solidarity Ethics: A Public Focus for the Church," *Review of Religious Research* 20 (1979): 251–63; Robert Hovda, "Reconciliation/Solidarity: A Hard Saying," *Worship* 62 (1988): 442–48; Jacobus Kok, "Mission and Ethics in 1 Corinthians: Reconciliation, Corporate Solidarity and Other-Regard as Missionary Strategy in Paul," *HTS Teologiese Studies / Theological Studies* 68, no. 1 (2012): 220–31, http://www.hts.org.za/index.php/HTS /article/view/1222/2417.

13. Christians were involved in movements of solidarity in places like Poland during the Communist era and among workers organizing themselves into unions during the nineteenth and early twentieth centuries. Perhaps without using the term, Christians nevertheless pursued aims consonant with solidarity. David Elliot, "The Christian as *Homo Viator*: A Resource in Aquinas for Overcoming 'Worldly Sin and Sorrow,'" *Journal of the Society of Christian Ethics* 34 (2014): 101–21, argues that Thomas Aquinas employed worldliness as something of an antonym for solidarity in suggesting that it degrades humans' capacity to properly love the poor.

14. For two provocative works that incorporate solidarity language into their challenge to rethink our relationship with animals and the wider environment, see Charles Camosy, *For Love of Animals: Christian Ethics, Consistent Action* (New York: Franciscan Media, 2013); Grace Kao, "Creaturely Solidarity: Rethinking Human–Nonhuman Relations," *Journal of Religious Ethics* 42 (2014): 742–68.

Chapter 15 Subsidiarity

1. Fuller treatment of this definition for subsidiarity may be found in Jonathan Chaplin, "Subsidiarity as a Political Norm," in *Political Theory and Christian Vision: Essays in Memory of Bernard Zylstra* (Lanham, MD: University Press of America, 1994), 81–100; Peter Huizing, "Subsidiarity," in *Synod 1985: An Evaluation* (Edinburgh: T&T Clark, 1986), 118–23; Bruno Manno, "Subsidiarity and Pluralism: A Social Philosophical Perspective," in *Toward Vatican III: The Work That Needs to Be Done* (New York: Seabury, 1978), 319–33; Franz Mueller, "The Principle of Subsidiarity in the Christian Tradition," *American Catholic Sociological Review* 4 (1943): 144–57; Johan Verstraeten, "Solidarity and Subsidiarity," in *Principles of Catholic Social Teaching* (Milwaukee: Marquette University Press, 1998), 133–47.

2. Analysis of Thomas Aquinas's use of these terms may be found in Nicholas Aroney, "Subsidiarity, Federalism and the Best Constitution: Thomas Aquinas on City, Province and Empire," *Law and Philosophy* 26 (2007): 161–228, here 174. Cf. Björn Weiler, "The 'Negotium Terrae Sanctae' in the Political Discourse of Latin Christendom, 1215–1311," *International History Review* 25 (2003): 1–36.

3. Frederick Carney, *The Politics of Johannes Althusius* (London: Eyre & Spottiswoode, 1965), 12.

4. For further information about the role of subsidiarity in political theory, see Gregory Beabout, "The Principle of Subsidiarity and Freedom in the Family, Church, Market, and Government," *Journal of Markets & Morality* 1 (1998): 130–41; Simona Beretta, "Wealth Creation and Distribution in the Global Economy: Human Labor, Development and Subsidiarity," *Communio* 27 (2000): 474–89; Joseph Burke, "Distributive Justice and Subsidiarity: The Firm and the State in the Social Order," *Journal of Markets & Morality* 13 (2010): 297–317; Gregorio Guitián, "John XXIII and the Encyclical *Pacem in terris*: The Relationship between Common Good and Subsidiarity," *Scripta Theologica* 46 (2014): 381–99; Joshua Hochschild, "The Principle

of Subsidiarity and the Agrarian Ideal," in *Faith, Morality, and Civil Society* (Lanham, MD: Lexington, 2003), 37–64; John Paul Szura, "Economic Rights and the Principle of Subsidiarity," in *Economic Justice: CTU's Pastoral Commentary on the Bishops' Letter on the Economy* (Washington, DC: Pastoral Press, 1988), 65–72; Robert Vischer, "Solidarity, Subsidiarity, and the Consumerist Impetus of American Law," in *Recovering Self-Evident Truths: Catholic Perspectives on American Law* (Washington, DC: Catholic University of America Press, 2007), 85–103.

5. Abraham Kuyper, *Souvereiniteit in eigen kring: Rede ter inwijding van de vrije Universiteit den 20sten October 1880 gehouden in het koor der nieuwe kerk te Amsterdam* (Amsterdam: J. H. Kruyt, 1880). Cf. Kent van Til, "Subsidiarity and Sphere Sovereignty: A Match Made in . . . ?," *Theological Studies* 69 (2008): 610–36.

6. For more on the concept of sphere sovereignty, see Jonathan Chaplin, "Subsidiarity and Sphere Sovereignty: Catholic and Reformed Conceptions of the Role of the State," in *Things Old and New: Catholic Social Teaching Revisited* (Lanham, MD: University Press of America, 1993), 175–202; David McIlroy, "Subsidiarity and Sphere Sovereignty: Christian Reflections on the Size, Shape and Scope of Government," *Journal of Church and State* 45 (2003): 739–63; Van Til, "Subsidiarity and Sphere-Sovereignty."

Scripture Index

Subject Index

Thomas of Aquinas 84, 89–91, 94, 163, 176–77, 188, 197, 208
Torah. *See* law: Mosaic
Troelstch, Ernst 133
truth 13, 28, 45, 59, 105, 115, 118–19, 139–40, 145–46, 150, 177
tyranny 187

unemployment 203
United Nations 159, 205, 212

Vatican II 140–41, 144
violence 109–10, 202, 234
vocation 125, 236

Weber, Max 125
Wesley, John 122, 124–25, 235
Wycliffe, John 100

Zwingli, Ulrich 97–98, 108–9